PROVERBS

The Hodder Bible Commentary

Edited by Lee Gatiss

PROVERBS

KIRSTEN BIRKETT

The Hodder Bible Commentary
Series Editor: Lee Gatiss

First published in Great Britain in 2025 by Hodder & Stoughton
An Hachette UK company

1

A CIP catalogue record for this title is available from the British Library

Hardback ISBN 978 1 399 81935 0
ebook ISBN 978 1 529 30201 1

Typeset in Bembo Std and Utopia by Palimpsest Book Production Ltd, Falkirk, Stirlingshire

Printed and bound in Great Britain by Clays Ltd, Elcograf S.p.A.

Hodder & Stoughton policy is to use papers that are natural, renewable and recyclable products and made from wood grown in sustainable forests. The logging and manufacturing processes are expected to conform to the environmental regulations of the country of origin.

Hodder & Stoughton Ltd
Carmelite House
50 Victoria Embankment
London EC4Y 0DZ

The authorised representative in the EEA is Hachette Ireland, 8 Castlecourt Centre, Castleknock Road, Castleknock, Dublin 15, D15 XTP3, Republic of Ireland (email: info@hbgi.ie)

www.hodderfaith.com
www.hodderbiblecommentary.com

Contents

PART TWO: PROVERBS 10–24

PART THREE: PROVERBS 25–9

PART FOUR: PROVERBS 30–31

For Susannah

Series Preface

The unfolding of your words gives light.
(Psalm 119:130)

The Hodder Bible Commentary aims to proclaim afresh in our generation the unchanging and unerring word of God, for the glory of God and the good of his people. This fifty-volume commentary on the whole Bible seeks to provide the contemporary church with fresh and readable expositions of Scripture which are doctrinally sensitive and globally aware, accessible for all adult readers but particularly useful to those who preach, teach and lead Bible studies in churches and small groups.

Building on the success of Hodder's NIV Proclamation Bible, we have assembled as contributors a remarkable team of men and women from around the world. Alongside a diverse panel of trusted Consultant Editors, they have a tremendous variety of denominational backgrounds and ministries. Each has great experience in unfolding the gospel of Jesus Christ and all are united in our aim of faithfully expounding the Bible in a way that takes account of the original text, biblical theology, the history of interpretation and the needs of the contemporary global church.

These volumes are serious expositions – not overly technical, scholarly works of reference but not simply sermons either. As well as carefully unpacking what the Bible says, they are sensitive to how it has been used in doctrinal discussions over the centuries and in our own day, though not dominated by such concerns at the expense of the text's own agenda. They also try to speak not only into a white, middle-class, Western context (for example), as some might, but to be aware of ways in which other cultures hear and need to hear what the Spirit is saying to the churches.

As you tuck into his word, with the help of this book, may the glorious Father 'give you the Spirit of wisdom and revelation, so that you may know him better' (Ephesians 1:17).

Lee Gatiss, Series Editor

Series Preface

Consultant Editors

The Series Editor would like to thank the following Consultant Editors for their contributions to the Hodder Bible Commentary:

Shady Anis (*Egypt*)
Kirsten Birkett (*UK*)
Felipe Chamy (*Chile*)
Ben Cooper (*UK*)
Mervyn Eloff (*South Africa*)
Keri Folmar (*Dubai*)
Kerry Gatiss (*UK*)
Kara Hartley (*Australia*)
Julian Hardyman (*Madagascar*)
Stephen Fagbemi (*Nigeria*)
Rosanne Jones (*Japan*)
Henry Jansma (*USA*)
Samuel Lago (*USA*)
Andis Miezitis (*Latvia*)
Adrian Reynolds (*UK*)
Peter Ryan (*Australia*)
Sookgoo Shin (*South Korea*)
Myrto Theocharous (*Greece*)

Be very careful, then, how you live – not as unwise but as wise, making the most of every opportunity, because the days are evil.

(Ephesians 5:15–16)

Acknowledgements

Thanks to the friendly staff of Cornerstone café in Denton Holme, Carlisle, where I spent many hours working on this book. It was a warm and bright place to be.

Thanks to Chris Ansberry who graciously let me see a pre-publication manuscript of his excellent commentary, to Eric Ortlund for his Hebrew expertise and to Andrew Towner for his encouragement and generous loan of commentaries.

Introduction

The book of Proverbs was written as a guidebook for life (1:2–6). Yet it seems far from being used that way today, even by Christians who consider it part of inspired Scripture. Why is this? Why is a book that is introduced as 'for giving prudence to those who are simple, knowledge and discretion to the young' (1:4) not the first thing we give to new Christians or the foundation of youth-group studies, and why is it not considered essential to Christian reading?

There are probably many reasons. To many people today the book of Proverbs can seem trivial; the English notion of a 'proverb' suggests some trite folk wisdom, true enough but not all that important. It is easy to assume that the book of Proverbs is mostly on this level, especially since many of its sayings are in a similar epigrammatic form. Some of its sayings are even considered just plain wrong, especially when it seems to promise automatic success if you do the right thing – that sounds dangerously close to a prosperity gospel.

The mention that this is the wisdom of Solomon also gives us pause. Yes, he was famed for his wisdom to start with – but fell into sin, and idolatry. Surely, *he* is not the example to follow! Why would we want anything from him?

Proverbs is also challenging because it is so contrary to modern western life. It is absolutist about morals, and teaches that wisdom and the best kind of knowledge are primarily about morality, not information. The wisdom of Proverbs is very strong on sexual morality and chastity, which are uncomfortable topics in the West today and becoming increasingly so in other parts of the world influenced by western culture. Proverbs is unapologetic about the need for correction and rebuke as part of teaching, especially of young people, and it similarly values age and the elderly – again, both attitudes that are increasingly unpopular in the West. Proverbs is positive about women but is addressed to men and from the male point of view, which sits uncomfortably with modern feminism. Most of all, Proverbs seems out of step with modern culture when it says that the pinnacle of human wisdom is to trust God, not yourself. Any part of the world that has been affected by Enlightenment thinking puts this exactly the other way around. Wisdom, in our Enlightened modern world, is considered to be about autonomous secular reason and absolute freedom of expression of the self. Proverbs could hardly be more different.

Yet it is not as if western assumptions about wisdom, and what count as wise choices in life, have proved themselves so wonderful. Hillary Clinton bewails the collapse of community, of volunteering, of family, and the rise in loneliness and isolation.[1] But what is to be expected from a philosophy that promotes individual fulfilment, career and achievement? The very western self-focus that she embodies and champions isolates individuals and sets them against each other.

Another reason why perhaps the book of Proverbs is not as valued as it ought to be is that it is hard to read. Those of us who read it in an English translation will probably miss many of its literary features, the effect of its poetical units and the careful construction of its terse sayings. In English, most of Proverbs can seem like a diverse set of sayings, randomly grouped together. The book, however, is more carefully constructed than that, and it is hoped that this short commentary can aid in understanding its structure.

1. *Proverbs and Wisdom literature*

Part of understanding how to read Proverbs requires understanding the kind of writing that it is. Proverbs has been considered part of the biblical category known as Wisdom literature.[2] The books of

1 Hillary Rodham Clinton, 'The weaponization of loneliness', *The Atlantic*, 7 August 2023.

2 This is undergoing a change – see Will Kynes, *An Obituary for 'Wisdom Literature': The Birth, Death, and Intertextual Reintegration of a Biblical Corpus* (Oxford: Oxford University Press, 2019).

Ecclesiastes, Job and certain psalms are also often considered to be Wisdom literature. We need to understand what people mean by that category.

The category is not something identified by Scripture itself, and you will not find it as a division of Jewish Bibles. Why, then, do we identify Wisdom literature as a separate category at all? Is it just something imposed on Scripture?

Not entirely. Even though Wisdom literature is not specifically mentioned in the Bible, similar literature existed in the ancient Near East long before Proverbs. There was, in many ancient Near-Eastern cultures, literature that taught about how life works and therefore how we should live. Proverbs bears many similarities to this literature of other countries, which is often cast in the form of a father teaching a son, using a combination of lectures or short sayings, teaching a range of social and personal ethical norms that show how to live well.[3]

Sumerians in the late third and early second millennium BC wrote riddles, collections of proverbs and reflective essays, some dealing with the problem of suffering in a way reminiscent of Job. The *Instructions of Shuruppak*, Proverbs-like literature (2200 BC or earlier), were known in Old Babylonian and later Babylonian versions. This text contains sayings in a form similar to Proverbs: 'A loving heart maintains a family; a hateful heart destroys a family (lines 202–3); 'You should not speak arrogantly to your mother; that causes hatred for you (lines 255–60).[4] *Ludlul Bel Nemeqi*, known as the 'Babylonian Job', is a variation of a tale going back to the second millennium at

3 See Michael V. Fox, 'Ancient Near Eastern Wisdom Literature (Didactic)', *Religion Compass* 5.1 (2011): 1–11, and 'Two decades of research in Egyptian wisdom literature', *Zeitschrift für ägyptische Sprache und Altertumskunde* 107.1 (1980): 120–35. See also Samuel L. Adams, 'Wisdom literature in Egypt', in Samuel L. Adams and Matthew Goff (eds.), *The Wiley Blackwell Companion to Wisdom Literature* (Hoboken: John Wiley & Sons, 2020); Richard J. Clifford (ed.), *Wisdom Literature in Mesopotamia and Israel* (Atlanta: Society of Biblical Literature, 2007); Richard J. Clifford, *Proverbs: A Commentary* (Louisville: Westminster John Knox, 1999), 7–19; Duane A. Garrett, *Proverbs, Ecclesiastes, Song of Songs* (Nashville: Broadman, 1993), 434–41.

4 'The instructions of Shuruppag: translation', The Electronic Text Corpus of Sumerian Literature, University of Oxford, https://etcsl.orinst.ox.ac.uk/section5/tr561.htm.

least; Babylonian literature also included Counsels of Wisdom and a Babylonian version of *Instructions of Shuruppak*. Later came *Words of Ahikar*, known primarily in a fifth-century Aramaic version, with an Assyrian setting dating from the seventh century BC. It contains wisdom in a similar form and sometimes similar content to Proverbs: 'Withhold not thy son from the rod, else thou wilt not be able to save [him from wickedness].' 'A word is a bird: once released no man can recapture it.'[5] There are also quotations from fables and parables in letters from Old Babylonian times. Ebla, an early Syrian kingdom, in the late third millennium BC already had parables, riddles and fables associated with wisdom writings. There is evidence of early written wisdom in the *el Amarna* letters of the fourteenth century BC, where Canaanite overlords quote proverbial sayings in letters to Pharaohs; and we also have the thirteenth-century Ugarit *Instructions of Sube-Awelim* in Akkadian and Hittite.

Similar streams of wisdom writings are found in Egypt. Written between 2700 and 2400 BC, the *Instruction of Imhotep*, the *Instruction of Ptah-hotep*, the *Instruction of Kegemni*, and the *Instruction of Hardidief* are compilations of wise sayings. The tradition continues in the *Instruction of Ani* and *Instruction of Amenemopet*, probably from the eleventh or tenth century BC. Social protest is seen in *The Eloquent Peasant*, theology in *Divine Attributes of Pharoah* and meditation in *In Praise of Learned Scribes*.

The pessimistic wisdom that characterises Ecclesiastes is also well attested in the ancient world, with the Egyptian *The Man Who was Tired of Life* from around 2300–2100 BC, *Song of the Harper* from approximately 2100 BC, the Babylonian Counsels of a pessimist, uncertain date, and *Dialogue of Pessimism* from approximately 1300 BC. The Mesopotamian *Epic of Gilgamesh* contains some similar sentiments.

The *Instruction of Amenemopet* is of particular interest, since Proverbs 22:17–23:11 is a close enough parallel that it is considered to be a Hebrew translation of the Egyptian, or at least dependent upon it.

---

5 H. L. Ginsberg's translation, in James B. Pritchard (ed.), *The Ancient Near East: An Anthology of Texts and Pictures* (Princeton: Princeton University Press, 2010), 379–80. Pritchard (*Proverbs*, 7–19) has English translations of several of these ancient texts as does Clifford; also, most can be found online.

There is, then, a recognisable body of Wisdom literature that the book of Proverbs fits into, although the biblical literature has notable differences, particularly in its dependence upon God. This is the wisdom of *Israel*, and so reflects a very different world view from other ancient Near-Eastern cultures.

Wisdom and creation

Wisdom literature is also distinct because it seems to draw much of its teaching from creation (rather than, say, revealed law). Wisdom theology has sometimes therefore been seen as a type of natural theology. For some, this is a negative. The Bible, however, has a robust doctrine of creation, so this would not make Wisdom literature any less theological.[6] This is legitimate within Old Testament faith, for Yahweh who encountered Israel is also creator, and so it would not be surprising that to some extent people can learn wisdom simply from observing the order that is there in the world. This is why there could be a category of Wisdom literature in the ancient world that overlapped with the biblical teaching. Proverbs teaches strong connections between wisdom as a concept and the creation of the world (Proverbs 8:22–31). Wisdom is part of the world's structure. It is there to be found.[7]

There are, however, provisos. To become accomplished in wisdom, Proverbs teaches, you will need the right attitude to God and a right humility, be prepared to listen to him and the teachers he appoints over you, and especially be willing to accept rebuke. The book of Proverbs, after all, is written instruction inspired by God. We learn wisdom from it, from this revelation, not just by going about our own natural studies.

This leads us to another characteristic of wisdom. Wisdom is something that can be learned, but especially can be taught, and is taught through wise sayings. The structure and wording of the saying

6 See Graeme Goldsworthy, *The Tree of Life: Reading Proverbs Today* (Sydney: AIO, 2000), 30.

7 David VanDrunen, 'Wisdom and the Natural Moral Order: The Contribution of Proverbs to a Christian Theology of Natural Law', *Journal of the Society of Christian Ethics* 33.1 (2013): 153–68.

is itself part of the instruction.[8] Studying these sayings, with a right fear of the Lord, is how we learn true wisdom. Best of all, we know as Christians that proper fear of the Lord, and the true secrets of wisdom, come from having the mind of Christ (1 Corinthians 2:16). That is how we attain the best knowledge of how to live, the right character to have, rightly formed desires and the right way to love others. In Christ, the wisdom we learn from Proverbs is brought to fulfilment.[9]

2. Reading Proverbs

The book of Proverbs, like all Scripture, is directly relevant to everyone. It is inspired by God and profitable 'for teaching, rebuking, correcting and training in righteousness' (2 Timothy 3:16–17). The New Testament writers considered it directly relevant to the church (see 1 Peter 5:5 and Proverbs 3:34; 1 Peter 2:17 and Proverbs 24:21; Romans 12:20 and Proverbs 25:21–2; Hebrews 12:5–6 and Proverbs 3:11–12).

When we come to the book of Proverbs, we have sayings about the world and about how we should live within it, but it can be difficult for the modern biblical reader to know how to approach these sayings. They are not law; they are not commands to follow. Indeed, some of the sayings are directly mutually contradictory. They give advice and general principles and need to be read together, in context; no one saying should be assumed to stand alone, without the qualifications offered by other sayings around it. To take them as single pieces of dogma is to misunderstand them. The world is not a machine, even a moral machine, in which effect follows cause invariably. There are generalities to be found; but there will be exceptions. Proverbs reflects this. The reader is left to consider whether

8 See Andrew Errington, *Every Good Path: Wisdom and Practical Reason in Christian Ethics and the Book of Proverbs* (New York: T&T Clark, 2020), chapter 3.

9 For a discussion on the relationship between wisdom in creation and wisdom as character, see 'Introduction' in William P. Brown, *Wisdom's Wonder: Character, Creation, and Crisis in the Bible's Wisdom Literature* (Cambridge: Eerdmans Publishing Company, 2014), 1–27.

individual sayings might have several levels of meaning, depending upon the context in which they are applied and given the way that other parts of the book of Proverbs qualify them.

Also, the world is God's world, and he freely upholds it as he wills. He is a God of order, and we can trust him; he made this world for us to inhabit, so we can expect it to continue with as much order as is necessary for us to live, practically. Yet he does what he does, and the many psalms asking God 'Why?' reflect the reality that sometimes we will not know God's reasons. We are fallen, and so is the world; moreover, we are limited. We are the creatures, he the creator. There are many things we will not know and will not be able to work out on our own, no matter how much power and ability and even true knowledge our image-bearing persons are capable of.

Nonetheless, there is a body of wisdom that is reliable enough to be passed down, and this is what the sages who wrote the Wisdom literature did. We are to learn from elders who have had a lifetime of learning to understand the world in the fear of the Lord, who have studied the Scriptures as the blessed person of Psalm 1 does, and sought to apply them to the world as they find it. We are to learn from parents and teachers, to listen to them and heed their advice. Proverbs records much of that advice, and the fact that it is so similar in parts to other sage advice from ancient cultures testifies to human ability to perceive and learn wisdom.[10]

The point of wisdom is a good life. It is for the making of wise decisions which lead to flourishing instead of death. The same choice lies before the man of Psalm 1. He can choose the

10 Other cultures have rich traditions of proverbs giving life advice, such as the *Thirukural* in India. For this and other examples see Paul Swarup, 'Proverbs', in Brian Wintle (ed.), *South Asia Bible Commentary* (Rajasthan: Open Door; Carlisle: Langham; Grand Rapids: Zondervan, 2015), 769–808, especially 770–71. For examples of Wisdom literature from Africa, see Tewoldemedhin Habtu, 'Proverbs', in Tokunboh Adeyemo (ed.), *Africa Bible Commentary* (Nairobi: World Alive; Carlisle: Langham; Grand Rapids: Zondervan, 2006), 773–812, especially 783, 796, 807. Early modern commentators in Europe were keen to compare God's wisdom with that of secular writers (such as from Greek and Roman literature), not always negatively. See David C. Fink (ed.), *Reformation Commentary on Scripture: Proverbs, Ecclesiastes, Song of Songs* (Downers Grove: IVP Academic, 2023), l.

flourishing life, the best life, by not walking with the wicked or standing with sinners or sitting with scoffers.[11] His flourishing, like a tree beside streams of water, comes from delighting in the law of the Lord, from knowing it and meditating upon it. Put like that, the choice seems obvious. Who would choose death over not just life, but the best life? But we live in a fallen and confusing world, and choices are not always so easy. Some paths look very attractive at first, and not at all as though they will lead to chaos and death. The point of the wise words of Proverbs is to provide us with the chance to know wisdom and so be able to make decisions as they are presented to us.

Therefore, wisdom in the Bible is overwhelmingly ethical. Our world doesn't necessarily think this. To have a flourishing life, people may look to wisdom that is psychological – how do our brains work best? What are the habits of daily care that will make us healthy and long-lived? What are the conditions of society or culture that best promote human wellbeing? Should I live a minimalist life with few material belongings? Should I move to a yurt in a sustainable community? Wisdom might be considered in regard to personal safety or financial security; weighing up risks and knowing when and where to invest. But while Proverbs touches on such themes, the main point of wisdom is to act morally towards God and other people. Righteousness is wisdom; and personal ease, financial security and me-time may well have to be sacrificed for it – and that would still be a flourishing life.

The intent of Proverbs 'is to train a person, to form character, to show what life is really like and how best to cope with it',[12] Roland Murphy says. That is what we want. Christianity is a journey towards maturity, and towards wisdom as we grasp the mind of Christ which we have been gifted. We are granted wisdom when we ask for it (James 1:5), but it is also something that requires work, learning and practice.

11 See Andrew Shead, *Walk His Way: Following Christ through the Book of Psalms* (London: IVP, 2023).
12 Roland E. Murphy, *The Tree of Life: An Exploration of Biblical Wisdom Literature* (Grand Rapids: Eerdmans, 1990), 15.

The Hebrew of Proverbs is frequently deliberately enigmatic.[13] There is so much more that could be said about every proverb, and indeed they are meant to be pondered, with time taken over them. Space does not permit me to spend the time reflecting on each verse that it deserves. I hope this book can nonetheless lead you through Proverbs as a connected whole, so you can see the context in which to understand this important teaching. Our English translations often try to soften the Hebrew text, to make it more understandable and applicable. That is not necessarily a bad thing – Bibles are meant to be readable. However, part of the gaining of wisdom through Proverbs comes through wrestling with the compactness and even apparent contradictions of the text. This commentary is written on the assumption that the sages who wrote these sayings were not careless (and God is never so). The very terse, epigrammatic and sometimes confusing form of the proverbs is designed to make us think – about the words and about the world they describe. We should not expect shortcuts.

Church Bible study groups, however, often want shortcuts. It can be unsettling to wrestle with text that doesn't always seem to sit nicely within neat doctrinal boxes. Yet the very wrestling – the discussion and disagreement and working together to understand what this part of God's word is teaching us about him, about ourselves and about the world he has created – is part of growing in wisdom. So do not be afraid of it, and do not seek to avoid it. God's word is good, and we can trust it.

Proverbs, especially in its later sections, can seem like a collection of isolated sayings. It is, however, more cohesive than that. It is a compilation of several authors and groups, but it has been put together deliberately. We can read even the tersest of bold sayings within the context of other sayings around it, in which themes emerge. New poems are often introduced by wisdom commendations. Endings are

---

13 This is not a technical commentary; for that see Paul Overland, *Proverbs* (London: Apollos, 2022); Bruce K. Waltke, *The Book of Proverbs (Volume I): Chapters 1–15* (Grand Rapids: Eerdmans, 2004); Bruce K. Waltke, *The Book of Proverbs (Volume II): Chapters 15–31* (Grand Rapids: Eerdmans, 2005); Christopher B. Ansberry, *Proverbs: A Discourse Analysis of the Hebrew Bible*, Zondervan Exegetical Commentary on the Old Testament (Grand Rapids: Zondervan Academic, 2024).

typically marked by some kind of summary. There are themes: look for them. Do not assume that this is just a jumble of disparate sayings. They have themes, and the thoughts often progress to a conclusion.

To understand Proverbs, we must, above all, *think* about it. This book should not be a quick read. The text is there for us to ponder, discuss and grow in understanding of it. We should be meditating on its sayings, writing them down, turning them around in our lives. Expect the study of Proverbs to be intriguing, absorbing and, finally, enlightening. The sayings are often riddles, comparing two things. Why are these two things put together? What is the point that is being made? And why is it within this particular collection of sayings? The literary form is closely analogous to poetry, and poetry is often like this (or at least, the best poetry is). The text is often dense and carefully constructed, with vivid imagery.[14] It forces us to think, and that is good for us. That is how wisdom grows.

Principles, not law

We do not, then, read Proverbs as law. Neither do we try to rewrite it. We know that righteousness is imputed through Christ's saving death; that does not mean we need to rewrite all mentions of 'the righteous' and give them a Christian gloss. We need to read Proverbs for what it is: sage advice, deliberately expressed sometimes in enigmatic ways, to make us reflect. It will give us general principles about how the world works and how the God-fearer should seek to live within it. Each saying might be thought of as encapsulated truth, but no one proverb is meant to say everything on a topic. They are meant to be read together. Any one proverb is not meant to cover every situation; it makes a strong and true point, to be read in conjunction with the others.

Ultimately, the secrets of wisdom are hidden in Christ, and so no book about wisdom will make sense without mention of Christ. The author of Ecclesiastes testifies to the bewilderment of the wise person trying to make sense of the world purely on its own terms (Ecclesiastes 1:1–11). We now know what the world was created

14 See Murphy, *The Tree of Life*, 5–13.

for – why it is here, what our place is within it and where it is heading. Knowing that framework, we are able to appreciate fully the wisdom that is contained within it. Scripture gives us the ability to comprehend and apprehend the wise principles upon which the world was created – not as ends in themselves, but as wisdom for how to live, now, in the light of the knowledge of God and his gracious provision.

3. Wisdom, order, morality and reward

Most often, the reasons for following the teaching here are given in practical terms. This way of living works. It should not be surprising that it works, for God stands behind this teaching (23:10–11). Wisdom depends on the fact that the world is ordered, and living in accordance with that order is likely to bring good outcomes. 'Wisdom for the Israelite sage may be defined as the observation of order in the natural, social, and divine realms,' Paul Overland observes, 'so as to discern by rational choice the path most effectively leading to an optimally flourishing life.'[15] Anyone can observe this order. Part of observing the world, however, is realising that not everyone *will* do so, even when rejecting it very clearly does not work.

This becomes most obvious when we consider the ethical world taught by Proverbs. In our world today, the mantras of sexual permissiveness, individualism and seeking personal fulfilment have led to epidemics of loneliness and mental illness along with the rise of harmful conspiracy theories and existential fear. Rejecting God's morality does not work, but this failed philosophy is still promoted through increasingly forceful means. It is appropriate, then, that the text frequently reminds us that taking the wrong path is not just unwise and often destructive in this life, but the destruction it may lead to is God's judgment. The teaching here is based on the wise patterns built into creation, but behind them is the God who is personally offended by unfaithful, dishonest and intemperate behaviour. That is why an attitude that wishes

15 Overland, *Proverbs*, 20. See also Errington, *Every Good Path*.

to know and obey him is essential to starting out on the path of wisdom.

As noted above, the surprising thing about wisdom as it is taught here is how much of it is directly moral. It was a modern western conceit until recently that wisdom, meaning knowledge and clear thinking – the sort of thing taught by academic philosophy and the sciences, for instance – stood independent of morality. That has been overturned more recently as attitudes to identity politics overcome proficiency or academic seniority in being acceptable intellectuals. The more recent attitude picks up on morality sometimes in a misguided or unbalanced manner, but the basic view is right: wisdom cannot be attained through the intellect alone. Right morality is essential to being a wise person. Wickedness, as Proverbs constantly tells us, is foolish. Indeed, as we will see, the balance in the end is that wisdom is chiefly moral, and that even when this morality leads to temporary suffering in this fallen world, it is still far more worth having than any riches. The world works, but it is marred in its working, and while we have advice for good habits for temporal success, a great deal of wisdom is coping with the fact that we also suffer evil. Wisdom means sticking to what is truly valuable, trusting that in the end the Lord will reward those who delight in the same things he delights in.

But when will God give this reward? There is no comprehensive view of the afterlife here, or of when such reward will take place; but simply knowing that it is the Lord who rewards makes following his way always the best (Proverbs 5:23). Proverbs teaches that the wicked will be punished and the righteous rewarded (Proverbs 10:2; 11:5–6, 23, 27). Righteousness is frequently promised the reward of life (*hayyim*). This is sometimes obviously referring to this bodily life (Proverbs 3:2; 4:10; 9:11; 14:30; 27:27; 31:12). Often, however, the reference is more general; it is something more than just bodily life, including other things such as prosperity, abundance and so on (Proverbs 3:21–2; 4:13; 8:35; 16:15; 21:21; 22:4). The tree of life goes further, to suggest eternal life (Proverbs 3:18; 11:30; 13:12; 15:4; see also Genesis 2:9; 3:24; Revelation 22:14).[16] The righteous have

16 See Daniel J. Treier, *Proverbs and Ecclesiastes* (Grand Rapids: Brazos Press, 2011), 27.

no death (Proverbs 12:28); while the book does not actually teach a bodily resurrection, Proverbs 15:24 talks of coming up from the grave, which is consonant with other biblical teaching.[17]

What about earthly rewards? It can seem that Proverbs teaches a rather bland doctrine of earthly reward for good behaviour (e.g., Proverbs 3:9–10). However, it also shows quite clearly that the righteous might not be rewarded in this life (Proverbs 16:8, 18–19). In particular, there are a number of 'better than' sayings that specifically teach that the wiser way might involve loss (Proverbs 12:9; 15:16–17; 16:8, 19; 17:1; 19:1; 28:6). In short, the teaching of Proverbs is entirely consistent with New Testament teaching on riches: namely that earthly wealth is a good thing, to be received with thanksgiving and used in generosity for the benefit of others (especially others of the Lord's people), but its value is only relative, not nearly as good as the much greater value of godliness.[18] 1 Timothy 6:5–6 tells us that it is false teachers who say that godliness is a means to financial gain; we know, however, that 'godliness with contentment is great gain'. Christ, like Solomon and the other sages, teaches that we might profitably endure or even choose suffering for righteousness in this world, given our hope of future glory (Proverbs 3:34; 10:16; Matthew 5:3–12).

Still, it can seem sometimes that Proverbs promises more than life delivers. I have heard various evangelical ways of toning down the teaching of Proverbs: 'It's advice, not promises,' is a favourite. It is true that Proverbs does speak in generalities, but some of the claims are fairly specific (Proverbs 3:2, 4, 6, 8, 10). So what is the resolution?

The problem only really arises if we think that all the proverbs of Proverbs stand alone. If, however, we read it as a body of work, with each teaching to be taken in the context of the others, the problem largely disappears. Because the proverbs are often epigrammatic, we often overlook the fact that as a whole there is a balance.

17 'We should not fear that God (who is always present with us) will fail to accomplish his promise. And this is so chiefly in regard to our spiritual health, and the eternal prosperity to which we must aspire, for we must not content ourselves with days and years of peace in this temporal life, or with earthly prosperity.' Michael Cop (Swiss Protestant Reformer, 1501–1566), *On the Proverbs of Solomon*, cited in Fink, *Reformation Commentary*, 31.

18 See the discussion in Treier, *Proverbs and Ecclesiastes*, 87–90.

Moreover, this is teaching to be considered and pondered. It is up to us to understand where particular sayings apply and where they are qualified by other parts of Proverbs, and when we should be looking for the promised reward in God's eternity rather than immediately.

Proverbs teaches a future beyond death. It also teaches justice. Justice will be done; we can trust God in this regard, just as we are taught to trust him (Proverbs 3:5–6a).

So what wise people do now is crucial. We see this dominantly in how Proverbs teaches us to speak wisely, how to deal with wealth wisely and how to act wisely in regard to sexual behaviour. 'The tongue has the power of life and death' (18:21), shaping beliefs that determine eternal destiny. Good speech is a tree of life (11:30) and a fountain of life (13:14). The tongue has the power to heal and destroy (6:12–15; 10:14; 11:9; 12:18; 16:24) – words can actually be far more powerful than sticks and stones. The tongue also can reward or damage oneself (10:10; 12:14; 18:6–7). Wise speech is gentle, not harsh (15:1), is restrained (10:19; 17:27, 28), is thoughtful (15:28; 18:13) and honest (8:7; 12:17, 19, 22). It does not gossip (11:12–13) and does not boast (27:1–2). How do we learn to speak well? It comes from the heart (16:23) and from listening to teaching (22:17–19).

In regard to wealth, New Testament readers already know how crucial it is to act rightly around money. Proverbs parallels this teaching. The father warns his son against easy money (1:10–19). The wealthy will tend to look for security in belongings, rather than to the Lord (10:15; 18:10–11). Money's value is limited (3:13–18). Having enough money is a blessing (30:7–9); the poor lack social capital as well as financial (14:20–21; 18:23; 22:7). Rather than greed, however, the best approach to money is to give God the firstfruits (3:9–10), be generous (11:23–8), work hard (10:4–5), be content (21:17) and patient (13:11), and be prudent in planning (24:27). Primarily, wealth comes from character, not method.

To be wise in Proverbs is also to be sexually moral. This is overwhelmingly important for both men and women, even though it is primarily the gullible young male who is addressed. Young women – and older people of either sex – can be gullible and subject to seduction too. Most of the proverbs are about *people*, and can (and should) be learned by both men and women. Proverbs assumes marriage, as is natural for an Old Testament context, but a lot of what is said about wise spousedom applies to any relationship and to all single people (27:6, 9). The qualities of diligence, honesty, faithfulness in relationships and in business apply to both men and women who will have friends, homes and ways of earning.

The unchaste woman, the symbol of sexual immorality for any person, is a symbol of unfaithfulness and rejection of God (2:16–19). She stands for sex without commitment. She is what western society idolises, and is where other societies are going as western liberal morality is imposed upon the majority world's cultures (in an imperialistic colonisation that is just as destructive and arrogant as any of the nineteenth century). The immoral, unchaste character has rejected God by being unfaithful to her husband (2:17) and will be rejected by God (5:21–3; 7:23–7). It is telling that Solomon himself lost his wisdom, his place and his kingdom because of the very danger the teaching in his name warns about here (see 1 Kings 11:1–6, 9–11).

In western society today, sexual relationships are so confused it seems aeons away from the world of Proverbs at the same time as being the direct focus of its needed teaching. Sex is worshipped as absolutely essential to health, wellbeing and mental and spiritual fulfilment, while also being treated as insignificant, casual, unimportant, hardly worth noticing. Sex with anyone who catches one's fancy, however fleeting, is regularly portrayed in popular entertainment as normal, inconsequential and unremarkable. Choice and consent are the only boundaries, two things so easily impaired by peer pressure, social atmosphere and ignorance, not to mention alcohol or drugs.

Yet at the same time, people will still (blessedly) absolutely see the need for laws about who you can't have sex with: children, the powerless, those rendered vulnerable by a power imbalance in a work or therapeutic relationship, for instance. The #MeToo movement has highlighted the absolute need for such restrictions. Rules about who you can have sex with matter, and the more they are eroded in the name of a questionable free choice, the more the vulnerable will suffer from the confusion.

The Bible's morality – sex only in lifelong, monogamous marriage between one man and one woman – is almost wholesale rejected by the liberal West, and under attack in most of the rest of the world.

Its protections, however, are lifegiving and absolutely necessary. The instructions on conducting oneself in love and faithfulness within marriage are also an essential part of the teaching.

Unfaithfulness in sexual relationships – the reality of temptation, the appearance of delight and freedom outside commitment – and the disastrous results are also a fitting metaphor for the dangers of rejecting God. It is no accident that marriage is a metaphor for God's relationship with his people, in both Testaments. God offers his commitment to us and demands it from us, for our good; yet we with twisted eyes see life without him as delightful and pleasing. We are wrong to do so, and will suffer, in frustration of life and in ultimate judgment.

4. Biblical anthropology in Proverbs

Wisdom is built into creation, and humanity is in many respects the pinnacle of God's creative work. In Genesis 1 the consistent pattern of the account suddenly changes after God has made the animals. He now wants to make a new kind of being, one more like himself (Genesis 1:26–8). This new being will have a special relationship with him and with the rest of creation. The new being, man and woman, will be in his image.

What is the 'image of God'? The phrase only occurs three times in Genesis. Genesis 1:26–8 distinguishes humankind, as male and female, from the other creatures. It is what entitles the humans to their dominion. We are set up on earth as representative rulers, to have dominion over the earth as God's representatives. We are meant to take the creative initiative to do things. But this is not autonomous rule. We are to rule the earth under God's authority. Genesis 5:1 repeats the idea of image when we read of Adam's line: we are told again that God created humans as male and female, 'in the likeness of God'. Again, humans are set apart as distinctive. Finally, in Genesis 9:6, being in the image of God is given as a reason for the prohibition of taking human life.

So humans are different, valuable, and are to function as rulers. For this, we need wisdom.

New Testament anthropology develops further the idea of the person. The primary distinction is that between the inner and outer nature (which are similar to, but do not exactly correlate to, mind and body). The inner person is hidden from others but known by God. It is referred to in terms of soul, spirit or heart. The soul is the conscious person (Luke 12:19) The heart can refer to the mind, emotions, tendencies and will (Romans 1:21; 1 Corinthians 7:37). The heart has intentions which are then carried out in the body; it directs a person's life. Spirit and heart are closely connected, but the heart is also an aspect of the soul, the conscious self.

'Heart' is therefore a good metaphor for understanding what is central to humans, and where their wisdom chiefly lies (see Proverbs 15:7–17:3). It provides a fuller idea than just 'rationality' as a way of understanding what a person in the image of God is like. The heart is more than just the mind, although it includes thoughts and the mind. It contains orientation and desire as well as pure thought. A right heart is the thing that would make us rule well, for our rule is ethical as well as rational. The heart is what makes it possible that we are able not just to understand God's order, but also to delight in it and set our wills in accord with it.[19]

This brings us back to wisdom. We are more than our intellect or rationality. We have characters that are meant to be shaped in accordance with Christ; our hearts are meant to learn wisdom (2:1–10; 3:1, 3).[20] We were created, in God's image, with moral capacity; we are to obey his law, and part of learning his ways is to learn the teachings of wisdom.

Wisdom, the fall and redemption

So humans are to rule creation, wisely, under God. We have a picture

19 '[W]isdom is by nature cognitive *and* emotional *and* aesthetic.' Michael V. Fox, 'The Epistemology of the Book of Proverbs', *Journal of Biblical Literature* 126.4 (2007): 669–84, p. 684.

20 'Therefore, when we hear the Proverbs of Solomon, let us not expect that he will lead us only to perform the works of the law outwardly, but that he primarily intends to conform our character to the fear and reverence of God.' Cop, *On the Proverbs of Solomon*, in Fink, *Reformation Commentary*, 7.

of what this might look like in Genesis 2, when the man names the animals: it is an example of his rule that he imposes a type of organisation and schemata on creation, with some authority. Man and woman are in harmony with each other, with God and with the rest of the created order.

But not for long. Rejecting God's authority and acting in a supremely unwise manner, the man and woman claim autonomy and the right to know on their own terms. Eve thought the fruit would be good for wisdom (Genesis 3:6), but she was utterly wrong. Now there is a broken relationship with God, each other and the rest of creation. The earth itself is cursed because of humanity's sin. It produces thorns and thistles. The whole of creation, in some sense, is put out of joint because of human rebellion. Wisdom is obscured.

Adam and Eve are thrown out of the garden and prevented from eating of the tree of life and so living for ever. Outside the garden, created order is disordered. It is not the chaos of Genesis 1:2, but it is frustrated. Work will be toil. Childbirth will come with pain. Death and its decay are now part of reality. Creation will never reach its intended goal; it can only hope for redemption. Creation has futility imposed upon it (Romans 8:20); it cannot achieve its purpose, and there is a sense in which its order is also frustrated. Order is still there: there are still seasons and rain and sunshine, but they do not work as well as they might. Crops are planted and harvested, but the rain might not fall at the time for the best yield. Disease might eat the crop. Wisdom, therefore, becomes much harder to attain; the world that should reveal it has become distorted.[21]

What we can say is that God's good order survives, but he allows a level of chaotic enmity to it. But God continues to care providentially for creation and humans. This is especially as he works out his salvation purposes. After all, the creation was always ultimately for Jesus (Colossians 1:16), and he is the wisdom of God (1 Corinthians 1:24). Jesus's incarnation, death and resurrection is the most important thing ever to happen in creation, and all creation headed towards that and is now heading to the final fulfilment when all things are brought under Christ's one headship (Ephesians 1). Jesus is the goal

21 See Goldsworthy, *The Tree of Life*, 20.

and fulfilment of creation, which will be seen in the new heavens and earth, the renewed creation which will far transcend the original created order. The frustration owing to sin will be removed, and much more. True wisdom will be possible, and obvious. We will no longer need Proverbs – or any other Scripture – to teach it to us.

We live in an orderly and ordered world. And it is the world we were made to live in. We are capable of the kind of concentrated observation that learns how things work; and although it takes a great amount of effort, we are capable of learning a lot about the world and how best to live in it. We can learn about people and how they best function, and even that which seems to us immediately worthwhile often is not. Psychological research will tell us that for flourishing we should not concentrate on accumulation of material goods or endless increase in monetary wealth. Rather, what is good for people is to have healthy relationships, to do good for others, to be altruistic, to be grateful. That is precisely what the wisdom teaching in Proverbs recommends, and we should not be surprised about that. As the parallels with other ancient Wisdom literature show, those who truly pay attention to what makes for a good life will be able to learn this kind of wisdom.

However, there are limits. There is a moral order in creation, but it has been distorted by the fall, and so have we. Viewed through sinful eyes, the order that is there is difficult to read. Ecclesiastes demonstrates that. Good people work hard all their lives and see their wealth stolen by others. Industry and diligence might reap a profit, or it might be undercut by natural disaster, crashing stock markets or corrupt governments. The young and healthy contract awful diseases and die. For many, crime pays. And what can we really learn from the animals? We are told to consider the ant's diligence and imitate it, but what of the ant's communal life where workers are worked to death and never able to breed? We might learn courage from a lion – do we also learn that groups of women should keep just one or two males handy for breeding, as lionesses do? Is culling the weak a good thing to do since it keeps the population healthy? Is survival of the fittest really what happens in nature, and what are we to learn from it?

There is an order, but we need revelation to show us what it is. That is why Proverbs insists on dependence upon the Lord. Proverbs is revelation; its teaching of wisdom is given. Its authors were already well versed in the law and God's teaching, so they could see where it was reflected in creation. Those without such revelation will frequently go wrong.

Image renewed

Jesus is the true image of God, and believers have their image restored when they are in him. The gospel is the power of God for salvation (Romans 1:16). Believers are predestined 'to be conformed to the image of his Son' (Romans 8:29). They have a 'new self, which is being renewed in knowledge in the image of its Creator' (Colossians 3:10). This new self is 'created to be like God' (Ephesians 4:24). Even though the 'image of God' may have been tarnished by the fall, it is being restored in Christ. Being 'in Christ' is to be found in the image of God, for Christ 'is the image of the invisible God' (Colossians 1:15; see also 2 Corinthians 4:4).

When we are renewed in Christ, we have right relationship with God. Also our minds are renewed, and we are part of a new creation. New creation people are able to do the will of God, and form a community that is able to love. This is not the same with the rest of creation. That is still in bondage to decay, subject to futility and frustration (Romans 8:20). Those in Christ, however, share in his very mind (1 Corinthians 2:16) and so have a new ability to know God's wisdom.

This idea, that the renewal of the image brings about a new community of love and a new ability to keep God's word, tells us more about image as well as about wisdom. It is about right relationships as well as right thought. Keeping God's good order in creation, learning wisdom from creation, is to do with treating people rightly as well as understanding nature rightly. The capacity to reason is certainly necessary to understand the mind of God and his order in creation, but that is not all. Right personal relationships with God and other humans require more than rationality; indeed, they will be horribly distorted if we limit ourselves to rationality. They require love and obedience, affections and emotions, will and desire, as well as rationality. We are in the image of God as the whole person, outer and inner, soul, spirit, heart and body.

5. *What is the wise person?*

We read Proverbs because we want to be wise. Proverbs teaches us that there are specific shades of anti-wisdom, which we can see in the words used to describe the kind of person we are not to be.

Don't be naïve or simple (*peti*). This is the person who lacks training, and so is gullible and easily misled. This person, however, is capable of being trained to be good and wise (1:4; 8:5; 21:11; see also 1:22; 9:4). Both wisdom and folly call to the naïve, the simple, in chapter 9, and Proverbs teaches how to listen to the right call. Being untrained, they are also characterised as young (1:4; 7:7), those who have not yet received their education. Because of this, they are lacking sense (7:7; 9:4, 16), not prudent (14:15, 18) and easily misled (7:7, 21–2). However, there is hope: because these young, untrained people are uncommitted, they can be led rightly (9:1–6) – or astray (9:13–18). But they are not fools – not yet. They need to repent of their ignorance, and until they do they will be grouped with the fools and mockers (1:22, 32; 8:5). They tend to believe anything (14:15) and wander into danger (22:3), so they need to leave their peers and learn (8:5; 9:4, 6) in order to live (9:6).

Worse than being naïve is to be a fool (*'ewil*) – someone who knows better but disregards right teaching and does not pay attention. This person is irreligious (14:9), is a burden (27:3) and annoys others (12:16; 17:25; 26:4). They are self-proud and do not listen (12:15). The youth who has gone this far may be rescued by discipline (22:15), but may be incurably foolish (27:22). Such foolishness is deadly (10:21).

Also, don't be stupid, a worse kind of fool (*kesil*). This is someone who hates wisdom; someone who has intelligence, but nonetheless rejects wise counsel. These people are overconfident (18:2; 26:12; 28:26) and reject learning (12:23; 15:2). They bring trouble (18:6, 7) and are reckless (14:16; 29:11). Worse still, they love wrongdoing (10:23). They waste money (17:16). Everyone can see their foolishness (13:16); they are dangerous (17:12). They are like the dog returning to its vomit (26:11).

These two, the foolish and stupid, are worse than the gullible, for they are certain they are right. They are the opposite of the wise. Being perverted in character, they act irrationally; they reject wisdom and delight in mocking the morality that will benefit the community. In effect, the two are the same. They both despise discipline and correction (15:5, 20), are without wisdom (10:14, 21; 14:33), are wrong in speech (10:8; 12:23; 15:2; 19:1; 27:3) and are insolent and stubborn (12:15; 15:14; 17:10; 18:2; 24:7; 26:5, 11; 28:26). They are hopelessly foolish (14:24; 17:10, 16; 23:9; 26:11; 27:22) and can't manage their lives (11:29; 21:20); they are without honour (3:35; 29:9).

Another person not to be is the mocker, the scoffer (*letz*) – the person who mocks wisdom and influences others to do so (see also Psalm 1:1; Isaiah 29:20). This may be the worst kind of person to be, because such people are determined to reject correction (Proverbs 9:7–8; 15:12). Their basic problem is pride (21:24), and such arrogance prevents wisdom (14:6). They create conflict and destroy community (22:10; 29:8). In fact, they are an abomination (24:9).

Then, there are the wicked (*resha'im*) – the deliberately bad, the guilty. Wickedness is the opposite of righteousness. These people are characterised by evil thoughts, words and deeds. Wickedness reveals a person's inner turmoil (Isaiah 57:20); it does not come out of peace and joy. In Proverbs these people are impious. They are greedy (10:3; 21:10), violent (10:6) and try to trap others (12:6; 24:15); they are deceitful (12:5) and cruel (12:10). They speak evil (10:32; 11:11; 15:28; 19:28). So the Lord hates them (15:9, 29). He rejects their sacrifices (15:8; 21:27). He does not approve of those who protect them (17:15; 18:5; 24:24).

Also, don't be a sluggard (*'atzel, remiyyah*), the person who is described in a more roundabout way in 18:9 and 21:17. These people are unreliable and irritating (10:26). They bring shame to their parents (10:5) and destroy their inheritance (19:15; 24:31). Laziness is portrayed as a moral issue, not just a personality trait, leading to loss of freedom (12:24), poverty (10:4; 20:13; 24:34) and destruction (6:6–11; 18:9; 21:25–6; 24:30–34). These people give nothing to the community. Unlike the poor who are victims of circumstance (13:23), their poverty is their own fault. The only thing they have plenty of is poverty (28:19).

Wise people (*chakham*), on the other hand, are able to become wise because they are teachable and seek knowledge (18:15), and then store it up (10:14). They listen to instruction (8:33; 13:1). They accept commands (10:8) and love reproof (9:8) – an usual trait indeed! Wise people walk with the wise (13:20) and try to increase their wisdom (1:5). They also spread their knowledge (15:7) and so are a fountain of life to the community (13:14); they bring joy to their parents (15:20; 23:24) and healing to others (12:18). They teach wise words (1:6; 22:17). They have control over their emotions (29:11).

Wise people are prudent (*'arum*: 14:8), so ignore insults (12:16), look where they're going (14:15) and so see and avoid danger (22:3). These people act knowledgeably (13:16; see also 14:18) but without vaunting their knowledge (12:23).

Wise people also have discretion (*mezimma*: 2:11; 3:21; 5:2; 8:12), which protects them (2:11; 5:2). Being wise means knowing when to be silent (11:12; 17:28), and knowing the difference between good and evil (2:9, 20) – this is a profound inversion of original sin. Insightful people seek and find knowledge (15:14; 18:15), accept rebuke (19:25) and have wisdom in their hearts (14:33).

Wise people also have a practical understanding of the world (*tevuna*: 11:12; 15:21; 20:5). They are pragmatic and work for practical good in society. They have self-control (17:27), patience (14:29), and understand others (20:5). Fools and tyrants don't like this quality, or lack it (18:2; 28:16).

Overall, wise people do what is right (*tzedeq*) and just (*mishpat*) and fair (*mesharim*) (1:3). The righteous help the community even to their own disadvantage; the wicked do the opposite.

Being wise, then, is being righteous, and that is more than just doing right things. It is a pattern of life and a disposition of character. It is who you are and what your whole life reveals. This is because wisdom is in the heart, acquired through the mind via wise words (2:1–11). Wise people are consistent and trustworthy, in heart, actions and words. They depend on the Lord (3:5) who guarantees true profit and security (2:11; 10:2, 3). Wisdom is no trivial quality. It is life and death (11:19; 21:12).

Because wisdom is so much a matter of character and inner being, it requires having a right mind or heart *(lev)*, which is mentioned in ninety-five verses and is associated with knowing or perceiving.[22] To be without it, to be lacking *lev*, is to be senseless, lacking right thoughts, and morally so.[23] Those who lack this sense are the gullible (7:7; 9:4, 16) and the unchaste (6:32); one who despises neighbour (11:12) and chases fantasy (12:11), enjoys folly (15:21) and is a sluggard (24:30). Lacking *lev* is to be the opposite of righteous (10:21) and wise (10:13). In fact, all fools lack *lev*.

As well as a right mind, we should have right desires – wisdom is not just knowing but desiring good. Appetite (*nefesh*) is in fifty-four verses. Proverbs gives us a picture of what wise people love, as well as what they do.[24]

6. Structure of Proverbs

We are given seven headings throughout the book of Proverbs, which tell us their authors. Most of the proverbs are attributed to Solomon (1:1; 10:1; 25:1). We also have sayings of the wise (22:17; 24:23) and two other authors: Agur son of Jakeh (30:1) and King Lemuel (31:1).

Part one: Initial training

Chapters 1–9

We see in chapters 1–9 the sage speaking to the pupil, beginning this student's training in wisdom. The style is quite straightforward, like a lecture, as is fitting for beginners. They need to be persuaded why wisdom is a good thing to seek, and given initial instruction

22 See Michael V. Fox, 'Ethics and wisdom in the book of Proverbs', *Hebrew Studies* 48 (2007): 75–88.

23 Unlike the English phrase 'lacking heart', or being heartless, which primarily means lacking emotion or compassion. Hebrew does not see the heart as the seat of emotion as English does. Ludwig Koehler, Walter Baumgartner and Johann J. Stamm, *The Hebrew and Aramaic Lexicon of the Old Testament* (HALOT), trans. and ed. under the supervision of Mervyn E. J. Richardson, 4 vols (Leiden: Brill, 1994–99), 513–16.

24 See Derek Kidner, *Proverbs: An Introduction and Commentary* (Leicester: Inter-Varsity Press, 1964, 37–8.

in moral character and behaviour – wisdom in values and wisdom in conduct, of mind and body. Right relationships and especially right sexual behaviour are essential foundations for the wise and flourishing life.

If humankind ever needed instruction in that, it is now. These are the basics. We need to get them right before we can progress in wisdom. Any 'progressive' view that fails in sexual morality and faithfulness cannot even get started; it will entirely fail to progress.

Part two: The Proverbs of Solomon

Chapters 10–24

The book starts with getting the basics right: chastity and faithfulness within marriage. Without ever leaving this theme behind, the teacher now moves on to what will be another major challenge in life: the right attitude to money and wealth. How do we gain wealth, and what should we do with it? Are there things more worth having than money? What are their pros and cons? This will lead to other important life topics: the value of a well-informed mind, relationships, friendship and noble character. This is more-advanced training, which begins to teach how to teach others. The sayings are less obvious and require more work to unpack. It assumes that the pupil has become convinced of the value of wisdom and so does not need so much persuasion to pursue it, although wisdom continues to be praised, especially at the start of new teaching sections. As more topics are covered, the pupil is setting about becoming a sage him or herself.

Part three: Royal wisdom

Chapters 25–9

Kings and courtiers are addressed here. Leadership will involve dealing with others' dishonesty as life will not be straightforward in a fallen world. As a leader, how do you help your people prosper?

Part four: Agur and Lemuel

Chapters 30–31

Contentment, not greed, and administering justice will be necessary for the king or leader. We end by seeing that the topics we started with will always need wisdom: right relationships and care with money. The right attitudes here will be necessary for the successful life and the flourishing community. Themes from earlier in the book are picked up and emphasised. This is for everyone, setting out the foundational principles for the wise life. All can benefit from this, within and outside Israel.

Within these four main sections I have largely followed Overland's section divisions. We will often see the pattern that praise of wisdom starts a section, and a description of the wise person as opposed to the foolish person sums up a section. However, the book could be divided in a number of different ways, and the strict divisions are often not as important as understanding the themes as they develop. Frequently, a new unit is marked out by a verse in praise of wisdom or of the wise; these verses appear to punctuate the text, marking that a new topic or at least a new emphasis is about to be started.

There is certainly debate about how to divide the sections. In the end, it matters more that we pay attention to the text. There is certainly development of themes; elementary and broad-brushstroke in chapters 1–9, moving on to more detailed and advanced training; some specific to certain roles, such as the royal court.

PART ONE

PROVERBS 1–9

I

Initial Training

Chapters 1–9 present the contrast between two rival paths: wisdom (righteousness) as against foolishness (evil). This sets up the basic contrast that will be followed in the rest of the book. Both men and women will appear, preaching messages of anti-wisdom. The two major temptations of humankind – greed for illicit money and greed for illicit sex – are exemplified by wicked/foolish men and women respectively, but of course both sexes are capable of both sins. These sins lead to death; this is no low-stakes contest. To both are contrasted true wisdom, personified by the woman who was with God at creation, who will lead her followers to flourishing life according to the principles that were built into creation itself.[1] These principles will be shown to be practical in bringing peace and enough material wealth for living; but more than that, wisdom will show that living ethically, even despite possible poor outcomes or in the face of opposition, brings a flourishing beyond earthly wealth because it is what pleases God.

The lectures, and wisdom's call, are addressed to the young. It can be sad to move beyond youth; most of us mourn it. However, it is also a good thing to grow up. Our western culture worships youth and the youthful viewpoint; indeed, it is very afraid of upsetting the young. I read of a senior academic who found his work on a conservative topic rejected by his publisher on the grounds that if they published a book of that kind, they would have difficulty keeping their young editors. Why, he asked, does a major publishing house let its editorial policy be dictated by its most inexperienced staff?

1 'Lady Wisdom' and 'Dame Folly' can seem rather old-fashioned and potentially patronising, so I have avoided these titles.

Nonetheless, there are a lot of advantages to being young. Younger minds tend to be at the peak of their flexibility and creativity; many Nobel Prize winners, especially in physics, did their winning work before the age of thirty. There is a huge amount of youthful energy that can be invested in the slog of groundwork to establish a reputation, a career or a groundbreaking discovery. Youth is in itself very attractive.

It is not, however, usually very *wise*. That is because humans are not innately wise. It seems to be something we forfeited in the fall (Genesis 3), when we took that devastatingly unwise step of thinking ourselves better equipped to make decisions than God is. That, of course, is the essence of youthful energy – to think that we *know*, indeed know *best*, and should simply be left alone to get on with what we want to do. That might be true in terms of cleverness and ability to do astonishing things, but it is not the essence of wisdom, which is about prudence, discretion and right judgment, not just cleverness. It takes experience, making mistakes and correcting them, humility and learning from others, to grow in wisdom; it requires, above all else, the willingness to listen and be corrected, especially to and by God. That is not a quality the young generally have in abundance. It is something they need to learn.

This is what wisdom calls for, in her poetic exhortations, and the father urges his son to learn. In this introductory section of the book, we are still in the phase of being persuaded to understand the value of and to accept wisdom; the young apprentice sage is receiving heavy persuasion to accept wisdom over other apparently attractive but deceptive paths.

The introductory section ends with chapter 9. Again, Wisdom will address the foolish, in contrast to the woman Folly who is also calling loudly. To whom will we listen? This is the decision that must be made before proceeding. It is no good going into further teaching if the fundamental commitment to wisdom is not made now. The father has been teaching his family, as the mother has evidently been doing as well (1:8; 6:20), while Wisdom has been out in public, spreading this message more generally. There are two paths before us. Which shall we choose?

2

Getting Started

PROVERBS 1:1–9

Chapters 1–9 are not a collection of aphorisms, as later parts of Proverbs will be, but a series of poems in praise of wisdom. They are meant to motivate readers, whether beginners or already versed in wisdom, to study the rest of the book.

1. What the book is for • Proverbs 1:1–7

Proverbs 1:1–7 forms an introduction and gives the context to the first nine chapters of Proverbs, and also to the book as a whole. We see in 1:1–7 what this teaching is for: it develops character. This, truly, is spiritual formation, and at the heart of it is moral virtue, as emphasised by the structure of this introduction.

Purpose and theme

1 The proverbs of Solomon son of David, king of Israel:

2 for gaining wisdom and
instruction;
for understanding words of
insight;
3 for receiving instruction in
prudent behaviour,
doing what is right and just
and fair;
4 for giving prudence to those
who are simple,[a]
knowledge and discretion to
the young –
5 let the wise listen and add to
their learning,
and let the discerning get
guidance –
6 for understanding proverbs
and parables,
the sayings and riddles of the
wise.[b]

7 The fear of the LORD is
the beginning of
knowledge,

but fools[c] despise wisdom and
instruction.

a 4 The Hebrew word rendered simple in Proverbs denotes a person who is gullible, without moral direction and inclined to evil.

b 6 Or *understanding a proverb, namely, a parable, / and the sayings of the wise, their riddles*

c 7 The Hebrew words rendered *fool* in Proverbs, and often elsewhere in the Old Testament, denote a person who is morally deficient.

These are proverbs, wise sayings (1:1). The book is announced as taking a particular literary form, teaching through a certain kind of poetic structure (although covering more types of literature than the modern English proverb, which only refers to a pithy aphoristic saying). From the start, then, we are alerted to the fact that the way the teaching is expressed is important. The book is also announced as collected wisdom, from Solomon, a royal source known for his wisdom (1 Kings 4:29–34, even if later in life he failed to follow his own teaching). Other authors are attributed throughout the book, and whether Solomon personally wrote these or they follow a Solomonic tradition does not change their importance.

The purpose of these proverbs, the parallelism of the second verse tells us, is to gain wisdom and instruction, which means (or happens through) understanding words of insight (1:2). There are two elements here: gaining, that is becoming aware of something; and the thing to be gained, which is wisdom, which requires instruction (*musar* is a 'chastening lesson', a lesson that corrects, with moral overtones). It requires understanding, but not just intellectual knowledge; it is moral knowledge to do with character and the inner person. It requires humility and determination on the part of the learner; we do not want hearers who hear without understanding (Isaiah 6:9). The things to be understood are *words* of insight – the wisdom here is learned through the normal means of communicating in words, not through immediate apprehension or simply following an example.[1]

The listener must receive this teaching, and the teaching will be about the way to have a good life, in a whole range of areas. It is for fairness, rightness, justice. Here we see the purpose of wisdom sayings

1 It was probably learned through writing: 'in ancient Israel most children were literate' (Waltke, *The Book of Proverbs*, I.176); see Deuteronomy 6:9; 11:20; Judges 8:14.

and who they are for. They give knowledge of how to achieve good ends (1:3), and they give prudence – the skill or quality that enables one to see and plan those good ends. 'Discretion' is a similar internal quality, something requiring intellectual acumen, but also moral discernment.

The people who need to hear this teaching are those who are simple: the young, anyone who is not a mature adult – the naïve young person who lacks training (1:4)[2] – and also those who already have some wisdom (1:5) to grow further. Both immature and mature can benefit from, and need, this training.

The proverbs here will also teach the skill of understanding proverbs (1:2b, 6a). The form of the teaching is part of the teaching. So pay attention! The difficulty of understanding some of this teaching is all part of the process.

The most important reason and foundation for wisdom is in 1:7. Don't be the fool, the person with the opportunity to gain wisdom who instead rejects it. Instead, understand that wisdom is worth having, and this is how to begin: with the fear of the Lord.

Fear of the Lord

Fear of the Lord is not dread, but deep respect and awe; knowing who God is and responding appropriately.[3] This is the chief, main thing, the first principle.[4] This right fear of God is key to Proverbs, framing the introduction (1:7, 9:10) and ending the whole book (31:30). Without it – without understanding that God is God and

2 'Collecting these proverbs is of great advantage in admonishing and teaching the young and uncultivated, and in bending them to diligence by forming their character, both with respect to God and with respect to people.' Philipp Melancthon, *Exposition of the Proverbs of Solomon*, in Fink, *Reformation Commentary*, 11. It is notable that Melancthon produced more commentary on Proverbs than any other biblical book other than Romans and Colossians (Fink, *Reformation Commentary*, xlix).

3 Although Martin Luther (1483–1546) emphasises the fear of punishment: 'This is the highest wisdom: to go about our tasks in full awareness of God's wrath. In this way we are made ready, like the earth for the plow, to receive the divine seed, the fruit of which is eternal life.' Martin Luther, *Commentary on Psalm 90*, in Fink, *Reformation Commentary*, 77.

4 Job Y. Jindo, 'On the Biblical Notion of the "Fear of God" as a Condition for Human Existence', *BibInt* 19 (2012): 433–53; see also Daniel J. Estes, *Hear, My Son: Teaching and Learning in Proverbs 1–9* (Leicester, Apollos, 1997), 35–39.

we are wholly dependent upon him – we will not learn wisdom, and will not be able to understand the book of Proverbs.

Indeed, it could be argued that the fear of the Lord is the key to understanding the whole of Scripture. The Holy Spirit enables us to understand Scripture (2 Corinthians 3:16–17), and part of that is giving us the right attitude to it. Scripture is not just like any other text that requires study and careful reading (although it is not less than that). It is God's word, and true understanding comes from recognising who we are in relation to God. It is an attitude of humility and obedience, which is only truly possible with the Holy Spirit. A certain level of understanding is possible for anyone with a brain, but where the heart is stubborn the brain will misunderstand. Anyone who has studied the Bible with an intelligent but determined unbeliever can testify to this; some of the simplest axioms can remain hidden.

Such right fear of the Lord includes both knowledge of the mind and attitude of the heart. It is something we can learn (Psalm 34:11) through studying the law, statues, commands and ordinances of the Lord and obeying them (Psalm 19:7–9). But it is more than just knowledge, or even knowledge and actions. Fear of the Lord is also emotional, a combination of love, awe and devotion.[5] It is linked to humility (15:33; 22:4). Both love and fear of the Lord are rooted in faith.

The purpose of Proverbs

The book of Proverbs will teach wisdom. Humans are notoriously better at knowledge. We have been given great capacity as God's regents (Genesis 1:27–8). The rise of modern science demonstrates how successful we have been at using that capacity. From tool users to farmers to miners to creators of technology to the modern scientific-industrial complex and space exploration, we are extremely good at knowing things and inventing things.

5 'For if we fear God, we know him; if we know him, we love him; and if we love him, we can be sure that he loves us: for we cannot love him first.' Cop, *On the Proverbs of Solomon*, in Fink, *Reformation Commentary*, 14.

We are much less good at wisdom – at using our capacities wisely and for the good, at having the humility to fear the Lord and set obedient limits on our capacity. We create great comfort and wealth and use it to accumulate unspendable riches for the few, rather than better lives for all. We create instant worldwide communication and use it to gossip and belittle and bully. We put immense effort into creating artificial intelligence which is immediately used to deceive and cheat. We are very poor at using our God-given capacity for rule when it comes to achieving equity, fairness and integrity (see 1:3).

This is partly because growing in wisdom requires correction and reproof, which our pride hates to hear. Yet pain is part of learning. We would rather, understandably, be without pain. Yet God teaches our greatest lessons through suffering, and grasping this truth is key to surviving any suffering and growing through it.

Proverbs will teach wisdom through sayings. Working out how to read such literature is a skill worth having. There is educational theory here. It is not, again, just a matter of knowledge. That could be given more easily through a lecture. It is knowledge that must be grasped, pondered upon, absorbed and thought over, for the purpose of making right decisions and acting well. It must be contemplated, but it is for the living of life, not just for contemplation; it must result in good character with right values which will be expressed in right action. It is also for life in community, where equity and fairness apply. We need to deal with each other well. We need to treat each other properly, and if disputes arise, to settle them fairly, without revenge or rancour, acting with integrity and character. Life is not about fame or wealth. It is not about proclaiming one's rights as an aggrieved victim, or gathering likes and followings, or accumulating capital and material goods. Integrity and treating others fairly are the true measures of life success, the point of wisdom.

This is what the young and naïve need to be taught. Those who have already gained some wisdom will be all the more eager to embrace it. It will require, first, a right attitude towards God. That is simple common sense; if God is, as he is, the utmost good, perfect wisdom and the most important being in existence, then to start any scheme of knowledge without acknowledging that is simply ignoring reality. To ignore God is foolish; to treat him as less than he is, is foolish. Any such view is wrong in its most basic principles and attitudes towards the world. It has made the biggest mistake possible. God – and not just any God, but the Lord, Yahweh, the God of Israel – is there, and without recognising this, there will be no true wisdom. The most successful Oxbridge or Harvard scholar, the most accomplished musician or artist, the wealthiest multibillionaire: without fear of the Lord, none of these people can be considered at all wise.

The person who listens, who is prepared to receive wisdom in this way, will have the best character (1:3) and will know how to go successfully in the world, which is often confusing and deceitful (1:4). It will require effort and putting up with reproof. It will require humility and acknowledging reality as it is, not as we would like it to be (1:7).

2. Pay attention • Proverbs 1:8–9

Given the importance of wisdom as expressed in the first seven verses, it is not surprising that the father urges his son to start learning. This teaching should be listened to; the whole of life depends upon it (1:8–9). This is what children need. This is what parents should teach.

Prologue: exhortations to embrace wisdom

Warning against the invitation of sinful men

8 Listen, my son, to your father's
instruction
and do not forsake your
mother's teaching.
9 They are a garland to grace
your head
and a chain to adorn your
neck.

Why should we listen? The reason, 'for' (*ki*), links verses 8 and 9: you should listen *because* your father's instruction and your mother's teaching (1:8) are adornments, the things that make a person beautiful (1:9).

This is probably not something that many Christian audiences are used to. We accept Proverbs as Scripture; in good churches we will probably hear a sermon series on it sooner or later, or perhaps study it in small groups. It is the sort of literature, however, that tends to make up a summer series or to fill in a slot where nothing else more mainstream is being taught. When we do study it, it is probably with a sense of indulgence and some puzzlement. It's hard enough to understand Old Testament law in Christian doctrine – and the teaching of Proverbs does not even have the definite status of law. For the most part, it seems to be on the level of just-so stories or Aesop's Fables. Certain trite truisms are included, and the encouragement to have God as our foundation of understanding is welcome, but do we really regard this book as teaching what is absolutely fundamental and essential for a Christian life?

Conclusion to Proverbs 1:1–9

It is worth spending some time thinking about the purpose of the book of Proverbs as we begin our study of this book. Just what is this wisdom that is so important? What is this that fathers and mothers are meant to be teaching, so that their children are adorned? If we forsake it – as Christians in their attitude to Proverbs are often in danger of doing – what does that say about our understanding of God's work in the world, and in us? Just what is it we are missing out on? Pray that as we study Proverbs, we will be prepared to accept it on its own terms – as sayings that may be puzzling at first, but which need to be pondered and understood if we are to live the lives that God would have us live.

3

Teaching the Young

PROVERBS 1:10–2:22

We now embark upon a series of lectures in the form of a father teaching his son (1:10–19; 2; 3; 4:1–9, 10–19, 20–27; 5; 6:1–19, 20–35; 7), with two sections of wisdom, personified as a woman, speaking directly.[1] There are many connections between the parts of chapters 1–9. Proverbs 1:2–7 links with 2:1–8; 1:8–33 is parallel with 2:12–22. Wisdom calls and raises her voice (1:20–21); the son is invited to call to her (2:3). There is unity throughout these lectures, as the same motifs reappear: the need to listen to father's and mother's teaching, the need to listen to wisdom, the warning against alternative paths. The words of evil men (1:11–14) and an evil woman (7:14–20) are in contrast to the wise words of the teacher that appear between them.

1. Don't listen to peer pressure • Proverbs 1:10–19

First, the father/teacher tells the son/student most strongly not to follow persuasive sinners.

10 My son, if sinful men entice
you,
do not give in to them.
11 If they say, 'Come along with us;
let's lie in wait for innocent
blood,
let's ambush some harmless
soul;
12 let's swallow them alive, like
the grave,
and whole, like those who go
down to the pit;
13 we will get all sorts of valuable
things
and fill our houses with
plunder;

1 Exactly how these lectures are divided varies between commentators.

14 cast lots with us;
we will all share the loot' -
15 my son, do not go along with
them,
do not set foot on their paths;
16 for their feet rush into evil,
they are swift to shed blood.
17 How useless to spread a net
where every bird can see it!
18 These men lie in wait for their
own blood;
they ambush only themselves!
19 Such are the paths of all who
go after ill-gotten gain;
it takes away the life of those
who get it.

The father's emphatic advice is, don't just go along with the gang. That is not the path to tread (1:10). These sinners have a specific and enticing agenda: they promise easy wealth. They plan to set a trap to attack and kill innocent victims and steal their money. So, come with us, they say to the youth; the language is communal, creating a sense of shared identity – 'we', 'us', 'let us' (1:11–13) – with a promise that all will receive an equal share in the booty (1:14). Come on, we're all doing it. It will be fun. Don't be the outsider. And look at the money you'll make! The teacher knows that this is attractive; especially when it will be seen that the alternative way is to develop a law-abiding character, which may well be rewarded with wealth, but not immediately.

The teacher opposes this with a warning: do not walk with these people (1:15)! They are evil. Walking together sounds positive, but can be a disastrously wrong thing to do if you're not careful about your companions (1 Corinthians 15:33; Psalm 1:1; see also 2 John). Their feet are actually going the wrong way (1:16), and in the end, justice will prevail. They will be caught, for although they think they are expert trappers, they themselves will be snared. They will fall for the very traps they set for others (1:17–18).[2] They are actually fairly stupid; this is the folly of sin, in that people do not see the consequences that will come. A violent way of life like that will not prosper (1:19). The student is given a long view: whatever riches this gang might offer in the short term, that path will not lead to profit in the end,

2 'The greater the wealth, the greater spoil awaits a person,' comments Puritan John Trapp (1601–69) of this passage: 'Covetousness is daring and desparate: it rides without reins.' *Solomonis ΠΑΝΑΡΕΤΟΣ: Commentarie upon the books of Proverbs, Ecclesiastes, and the Song of Songs* (London, 1650), 6–7.

but only to death. The teacher names the murderous gang for what it is: evil. Yet this is not just blanket condemnation; he also points out the pragmatic problems with this way of life. It will not work.

2. The alternative call: wisdom • Proverbs 1:20–33

In this first of her speeches, the personified woman of wisdom is described. She is now given her own voice to convince the student of why she is worth following. She speaks loudly, calling clearly above the clamour of daily life.

Wisdom's rebuke

20 Out in the open wisdom calls
aloud,
she raises her voice in the
public square;
21 on top of the wall[d] she cries
out,
at the city gate she makes her
speech:

22 'How long will you who are
simple love your simple
ways?
How long will mockers delight
in mockery
and fools hate knowledge?
23 Repent at my rebuke!
Then I will pour out my
thoughts to you,
I will make known to you my
teachings.
24 But since you refuse to listen
when I call
and no one pays attention
when I stretch out my hand,
25 since you disregard all my
advice
and do not accept my
rebuke,
26 I in turn will laugh when
disaster strikes you;
I will mock when calamity
overtakes you –
27 when calamity overtakes you
like a storm,
when disaster sweeps over you
like a whirlwind,
when distress and trouble
overwhelm you.

28 'Then they will call to me but I
will not answer;
they will look for me but will
not find me,
29 since they hated knowledge
and did not choose to fear the
LORD.
30 Since they would not accept
my advice
and spurned my rebuke,

31 they will eat the fruit of their
ways
and be filled with the fruit of
their schemes.
32 For the waywardness of the
simple will kill them,
and the complacency of fools
will destroy them;
33 but whoever listens to me will
live in safety
and be at ease, without fear of
harm.'

---

d 21 Septuagint; Hebrew / *at noisy street corners*

The woman of wisdom goes out; she does not just wait at home for people to come to her (1:20). And she's not content with gentle urging: she shouts, she cries out, she makes a speech (1:21). This is important. She criticises three groups: the simple, the mockers and fools (1:22). The simple are simply ignorant, but they should not love that state – instead, they should seek knowledge. Mockers and fools are worse; they are actively rejecting knowledge. How long will they continue to do so? It seems she has been calling for some time. She offers to educate the gullible (1:23) – note she is *not* actually addressing her invitation to the mockers and fools, whom she knows will not listen, because they don't want to know. The simple, however, still have a chance.

However, they are all refusing what she offers so generously as she stretches out her hand (1:24). They ignore her counsel (1:25). But when disaster comes – as it will, in this world – it will be too late, and she will not help them. She will laugh, not mocking their distress, but because it will be the victory of right over wrong. If they continue to reject her, they will face eventual disaster, and that will be justice. The repetition emphasises the seriousness (1:26–7).

The change to the third person in verse 28 probably indicates a distancing from those who reject wisdom. When these mockers and fools finally wake up to their need for wisdom, they will call out to her, but it will be too late. When she called in verse 24, they did not listen; now they will call, but she will not answer. She will not be found. They did not choose fear of the Lord (1:29) and so will remain fools. Having rejected wisdom (1:30), they will now suffer the consequences (1:31). Their sentence is just.

Wisdom concludes with a summary: naïvety and foolishness will lead to death (1:32), but those who listen to wisdom will have resources to survive when danger comes (1:33). They will have security. Presumably the fools feel secure – why else would they ignore her warnings? But that will prove to be an illusion.

It is bad to be foolish and to reject wisdom. Those without knowledge should seek it. 'I just don't know,' an agnostic once said to me – an honest admission of ignorance about God. 'That's not good enough,' is wisdom's answer. If you don't know, then find out – knowledge and understanding are available. Those uncertain or ignorant about God have every opportunity in most places in the world to find out the truth, especially in the so-called progressive West, with its abundance of literature and availability of communication. Even under the most oppressive of cultural circumstances in some parts of the world, anyone can pray for wisdom, and God will give it; he is capable of bringing the truth to anyone. Those who refuse to accept knowledge, who wish to remain ignorant, who scoff at the wisdom that is offered and refuse to fear the Lord who is clearly before them; such people only have themselves to blame when they have no answers in the face of calamity, and nowhere to turn.

The warning is clear. Grasp hold of wisdom's hand. Take up her offer. For life will be hard, and we must not be the fools who reject the chance to learn how to live well within it.

3. The benefits of wisdom • Proverbs 2

If you have listened so far and chosen wisdom over the lure of quick (and violent) riches, that is an excellent first step. Now we see listed the enormous value of wisdom as a life path. That first step, of accepting that this is the better way, must be followed up. Wisdom must be sought, searched for as for treasure; one must have the right attitude, understanding that wisdom is worth determined pursuit. All sorts of benefits will result, in regard to both knowing God and in human relationships, as well as in life in general.

This chapter is a single sentence in twenty-two verses, the number of letters in the Hebrew alphabet, perhaps suggesting completeness.[3] The sentence follows the form: if you really seek wisdom (2:1–4), then you will have true understanding from God (2:5–8) and the right moral attitudes that come from it, with life benefits (2:9–22). It is a highly ordered and structured poem, and presents an order in the world: seek learning, and the Lord will give wisdom, which protects. It is structured as a logical argument; we have a series of 'if–then' statements to prove the assertion that wisdom is worth it.

Moral benefits of wisdom

2 My son, if you accept my words
and store up my commands within you,
2 turning your ear to wisdom
and applying your heart to understanding -
3 indeed, if you call out for insight
and cry aloud for understanding,
4 and if you look for it as for silver
and search for it as for hidden treasure,
5 then you will understand the fear of the LORD
and find the knowledge of God.
6 For the LORD gives wisdom;
from his mouth come knowledge and understanding.
7 He holds success in store for the upright,
he is a shield to those whose way of life is blameless,
8 for he guards the course of the just
and protects the way of his faithful ones.

9 Then you will understand what is right and just
and fair - every good path.
10 For wisdom will enter your heart,
and knowledge will be pleasant to your soul.
11 Discretion will protect you,
and understanding will guard you.

12 Wisdom will save you from the ways of wicked men,
from men whose words are perverse,
13 who have left the straight paths
to walk in dark ways,
14 who delight in doing wrong
and rejoice in the perverseness of evil,

3 Waltke, *The Book of Proverbs*, I.216.

15 whose paths are crooked
and who are devious in their
ways.

16 Wisdom will save you also
from the adulterous woman,
from the wayward woman with
her seductive words,
17 who has left the partner of her
youth
and ignored the covenant she
made before God.[a]
18 Surely her house leads down to
death
and her paths to the spirits of
the dead.
19 None who go to her return
or attain the paths of life.

20 Thus you will walk in the ways
of the good
and keep to the paths of the
righteous.
21 For the upright will live in the
land,
and the blameless will remain
in it;
22 but the wicked will be cut off
from the land,
and the unfaithful will be torn
from it.

a 17 Or covenant of her God

First, listen to what the teacher is saying (2:1) – treat these words as treasure. Do this by putting effort into understanding, realising that this is a matter to be applied to the heart (2:2). Call out to wisdom, just as she has been calling (2:3); seek wisdom with as much diligence as you might put into searching for riches (2:4); then valuable benefits will follow. The 'it' (actually 'her') of verse 4 groups wisdom, insight and understanding together, all describing the same thing to be sought.

What follows from seeking these things above all else? First, there is benefit in regard to God. You will gain that fear of the Lord that we have already been told is the beginning of wisdom (2:5; see 1:7). Indeed, knowing the Lord is the most valuable thing anyone can have, anywhere. It is not just knowing theology, but knowing God personally and rightly, submitting to him as who he is. Why is the right attitude towards God so important? Because it is the Lord who gives wisdom (2:6). God's name is actually the second word of the line, creating emphasis. As we will see as the book unfolds, there is wisdom inherent in creation itself, which anyone in the image of God is able to apprehend to some degree. Indeed, even animals have some wisdom by instinct (30:24–8); people can gain useful wisdom just by observing the rhythms of the world (Isaiah 28:23–9). But such knowledge ultimately comes from Yahweh and is always a gift (Job 28:12–28; Daniel 2:21–2).

The result of knowing God like this and obtaining his wisdom is success, which is developed in terms of morality: keeping to justice, understanding what is right and fair. Having this wisdom is to gain God's defence in life (2:7). He will protect those who are devoted to him (2:8). What kind of protection? He will keep them on the right path, which means life, not death. This metaphor of walking, so important to Psalm 1, will be developed later in Proverbs (see chapter 4).

We then see the second benefit that comes from seeking wisdom with diligence: an understanding of what is right, of true moral character. You will know justice and fairness (2:9), the successful life that was promised for the wise in 1:3. This will not just be head knowledge; you will also gain a heart-and-soul-deep understanding of morality (2:10).

The ancient philosopher Aristotle saw this essential integrity as the goal of ethics, with motives and affections aligned in pursuing what was good; he thought it something obtained only through long habit and training from childhood.[4] The Hebrew wisdom tradition also commends such training, but with this extra dimension: that God grants wisdom. In the New Testament we find that truly transformed hearts only come as a result of the Holy Spirit, through Christ; in that way God will fully fulfil his promise of granting wisdom (see, for example, 2 Corinthians 3; Galatians 4:6; Ephesians 1:17–18). The prophets looked for this new heart, which would be transformed (Jeremiah 24:7; 31:31–4; 32:37–41; Ezekiel 36:27).

Wisdom will bring a certain protection amid the problems of life (2:11). It enables forethought and discretion, which help in choosing the best options as they are presented by life. Temptation can be resisted and the right way chosen.

The kinds of protections that wisdom offers are now spelt out in a little more detail (2:12–19). One is protection against the wicked,

4 Aristotle, *Nichomachean Ethics*, Book X.

those who are not upright and might seek to deceive or confuse us (2:12), as the gang did in chapter 1. These are people who are not honest, but prefer 'dark ways' (2:13), because they have abandoned good. They actively enjoy doing what is wrong and rejoice in evil (2:14). Just reading the news each day provides ample evidence that such people are as active today as they ever were. The protection against their schemes is wisdom, an ability to evaluate offers with an awareness of the depth of wickedness that people can willingly practise. Wisdom will also provide some protection against our innate greed, which can make fraudulent offers all too attractive. Such people inflict harm, but will often harm themselves too, the Hebrew suggests, since their paths are so crooked (2:15). It is the kind of path that trips people up (4:12; 22:5).

Another protection offered by wisdom is against adultery. We will see throughout Proverbs that faithfulness – basically, keeping one's word – is fundamental to the wise and moral character. Adultery is an archetypal example of faithlessness, and the warnings against it could hardly be stronger. The adulterous woman, like the evil man, speaks tempting but deceptive words (2:16). Melancthon comments that 'the adulterous woman is understood to be a figure for any purported wisdom that draws our minds away from God'.[5] She has been faithless to her partner and to God (2:17), and she will suffer consequences herself (2:18). It will be tempting to follow her and her seductive words, but that is the way of death. The choice is stark; not just good and bad, wise or less wise, but life and death. Go that way, and you will not have the paths of life (2:19).

Wisdom, however, will lead you to the right path, the 'ways of the good' (2:20). It will lead you to healthy community. So choose and pursue wisdom; that is, how to become one of the upright who live in the land, who get to stay there. It is the way of security with all the overtones of blessing that mention of the land (2:21) brings with it – remember the glorious descriptions of Deuteronomy (6:3, 10–11; 8:9; 11:9–12 and so on). This is worth devoting one's life and all one's energies to, for the alternative is terrible: being cut off from the land (2:22).

---

5 Melancthon, *Exposition of the Proverbs of Solomon*, in Fink, *Reformation Commentary*, 25.

We in Christ no longer look for a physical land; we know that those promises are fulfilled in 'the heavenly Jerusalem' (Hebrews 12:22), the new heavens and earth in which we will dwell as God's people for eternity (Revelation 21:1–4). This only raises the stakes. Staying on *this* path is radically important. We want to enjoy the blessings that have been won for us, freely and undeservedly, in Christ. We have every incentive to follow the sage's advice.

Conclusion to Proverbs 1:10–2:22

Pursue wisdom, then, the pupil is being urged; go after it with all your energies; cry out for it. In this section of Proverbs, we have discovered some of the benefits of having wisdom. The rewards are immeasurable. Wisdom will bring you closer to God and will bring success and protection against the wickedness of life. We also find out a little more about the nature of wisdom. It is something that transforms the whole person; it is far more than just knowledge, extending to motivations and deep desires. It will help in developing instincts that warn against danger, even when it seems attractive and seductive. This kind of moral instinct is invaluable in negotiating a confusing world, where so many competing voices advocate various life paths. How to choose what is right? By pursuing wisdom, by fearing the Lord, by listening to wise teachers. By gaining this knowledge from the one who is the very source of wisdom itself.

Pursue wisdom with passion. It is not just a matter of intellectual preference or clever games. It is life and death. This world is dangerous, full of wicked and violent people who will try to entrap you. Don't take this lightly; rather, make every effort to be the person who can see them coming and so avoid them. Be able to recognise those who are good, and so walk with them, relating to them rightly. We will see more of how to do this in Proverbs 3, the subject of our next chapter.

4

Whose Wisdom?

PROVERBS 3

So far we have been presented with a choice to make. Proverbs 1 showed that we can choose a get-rich-quick life with apparently easy gains to be made if we are prepared to be morally corrupt; or we can choose the harder, but much more valuable, way of wisdom. The benefits of wisdom have been extolled, and the worth of taking this harder path. The rewards of wisdom will be immense; in relating to God, the source of wisdom himself, and in ordinary life, as protection against the dangers and false paths that are simply part of living in this confusing world where evil people prey on the weak (the very invitation that was described in all its temptation in Proverbs 1).

If we have read this far, we have presumably chosen the path of wisdom, and the instruction in wisdom proper begins now. We have seen how important wisdom is, and in Proverbs 3 we get down to learning some specifics. Wisdom is still praised and commended; the pupil is never allowed to forget how valuable this path is. Such praise of wisdom divides the chapter into two sections, beginning at verse 1 and verse 13 – the next two lectures that the father is delivering to the son. The final two verses, 34 and 35, sum up with a comparison of foolish living versus wise living. In these two lectures, we see two foci: how best to relate to God and how best to relate to other people.

1. Do not be wise in your own eyes • Proverbs 3:1–12

The first half of chapter 3 carries on themes from the father's lecture in 2:1–11.[1] There, if the son listened to wisdom, he would

1 See Waltke, *The Book of Proverbs*, I.238.

have three spiritual benefits: he would understand what is right (2:9), find knowledge of God (2:5b) and understand the fear of the Lord (2:5a). Now, in this lecture, if the son does not let love and faithfulness leave (3:3), acknowledges the Lord (3:6a) and continues fearing the Lord (3:7), then there will be benefits for this world, as well as spiritual ones: to have favour in the sight of God and humanity (3:4), straight paths (3:6b) and health to his outer and inner being (3:8).

As well as the exhortations in general to seek wisdom, we now have particular instruction in how to live wisely. The pattern is to have a command (in the odd-numbered verses) with a reason or motivation for obeying (even-numbered verses). Keeping the father's commands brings life and peace; keeping steadfast love brings favour in the sight of God and humanity; trusting, fearing and honouring Yahweh brings straight paths, healing and plenty; and as a conclusion to this lecture, the son can know that the Lord's discipline should be welcomed because it shows the Lord loves him.

Wisdom bestows well-being

3 My son, do not forget my teaching,
but keep my commands in your heart,
2 for they will prolong your life many years
and bring you peace and prosperity.

3 Let love and faithfulness never leave you;
bind them round your neck,
write them on the tablet of your heart.
4 Then you will win favour and a good name
in the sight of God and man.

5 Trust in the LORD with all your heart
and lean not on your own understanding;
6 in all your ways submit to him,
and he will make your paths straight.[a]

7 Do not be wise in your own eyes;
fear the LORD and shun evil.
8 This will bring health to your body
and nourishment to your bones.

9 Honour the LORD with your wealth,
with the firstfruits of all your crops;

10 then your barns will be filled to
overflowing,
and your vats will brim over
with new wine.

11 My son, do not despise the
LORD's discipline,
and do not resent his rebuke,

12 because the LORD disciplines
those he loves,
as a father the son he delights
in.[b]

---

a 6 Or *will direct your paths*
b 12 Hebrew; Septuagint *loves, / and he chastens everyone he accepts as his child*

We begin this chapter with a reminder of how important it is to listen to the teacher. Wisdom comes from listening to the wise and paying heed to their words, while, as we will see, wisdom is in the warp and weft of creation itself; we need wise words to point out creation's lessons and interpret them for us. The teacher here reiterates why listening to him is so valuable for life: wisdom brings long life and good life, the kind of life that benefits humans (3:1–2). This is *shalom* life, not just a large number of days, but a full life with everything that is needed and 'inner contentment, delight, joy, and pleasure as a gift from God'.[2]

Verses 3–4 turn to general principles that will enable that flourishing life. Totally basic and essential to good living is love and faithfulness. This is a teaching we must always have with us, as if on a necklace, and written upon our hearts (3:3; see also 6:20–21; 7:1–3). We are to internalise this teaching, make it part of our inner being. The exhortation is similar to instructions about God's commandments (Deuteronomy 6:8) – the point is to remember them always. Christians often wear a cross around their neck, as an identifier and reminder that at the heart of our lives is Christ's death for us. What should identify us even more are the life principles that flow from being Christ's followers, the one in whom the secrets of wisdom are hid: we are to be people of love and people of faithfulness, just as God is. That is Christ's command. The cross (that many of us wear as a symbol) is proof of God's love and faithfulness to us; we should make sure we also live out these principles towards others. That is the true badge of our identity.

---

2 Waltke, *The Book of Proverbs*, I.240.

Our real adornment is not to be the physical symbol, but our character and actions.

Having steadfast love and faithfulness is the way to have the approval of both God and humans (3:4). We will be acting in a way that delights the Lord as we imitate his character – love and faithfulness characterise God in descriptions throughout Scripture. The Hebrew *sekhel*, the good thing we will have, has a sense that we will then *understand* what is good and right, what a truly moral life is. It will also bring us favour, in general, with humans (see Luke 2:52; Romans 12:17). There will, of course, always be difficulties as we try to relate to other sinners in this fallen world; there will be disagreements, small and large, and our love and faithfulness will not always be recognised by all, especially those who reject God and his wisdom. However, it is still the only way to live. Even if some refuse to see the good in our lives, those who love God will; and true living in love and faithfulness, seeking the good of others, keeping our word and remaining faithful to God's instruction are foundational to living such good lives among the pagans that they see our good deeds and glorify God (1 Peter 2:12).

In 3:5–6 we go on to specific teaching about how to relate to God rightly, putting love and faithfulness towards him into action. Right living as God's people is not just being committed to a theoretical system of ethics, but also a personal commitment to the living God. Without that commitment, any code of ethics – even one originally derived from Scripture – will go astray. Moving in circles of professional ethicists, I have sometimes come across people who say they are no longer Christian but want to maintain Christian ethics because they think it is an objectively good system. They are half right; it *is* an objectively good system. However, without a relationship with the God on whom the system rests, knowing his personal character, the system inevitably becomes rigid and loses either the kindness and love that is central to God's character or the commitment to God's standards of righteousness that are also inherent to him. Neither is acceptable. Current reports show that large numbers of American Christians are leaving church but retaining their political/ethical stance; the result appears to be that, without the constant reminders of God's character from his word, their positions become more rigid and extreme in one direction or the other.[3] We must never make the mistake of thinking that our way of life can be detached from its heart: devotion to the living God.

What does that devotion look like? First, we must have complete confidence in God (3:5). He is entirely trustworthy and will not let us down. Turning to him as default, instead of thinking we can work everything out for ourselves, and submitting to his word above our own ideas is a proper reaction to his faithfulness.[4] We must submit to him – meaning not just a vague nod in his direction, but knowing him through obedience and humility and full reliance (3:6). It is not that we will never have our own ideas. After all, this teaching in wisdom is precisely to instruct us so that we will have right ideas. But our thoughts and instincts are to be shaped by God's wisdom, not our own, and not the world's. God will thereby make our paths straight. It's a twisty world out there, and there are all sorts of paths before us. The answer is not, as the world would have it, 'Follow your heart,' but to follow God's heart. He is the one who knows. 'We also have the prophetic message as something completely reliable, and you will do well to pay attention to it, as to a light shining in a dark place' (2 Peter 1:19).

As we rely upon God, we are to have a proper attitude towards him, of reverence and respect, described as 'fear' of the Lord (3:7). Our world loves to preach self-reliance and human autonomy. This is a lie, and a dangerous one; we are not autonomous, and thinking so easily leads to evil (Judges 17:6; 21:25). In particular, it will likely lead us to putting our own desires and goals ahead of others' good (see James 3:14–16). Fearing God is the opposite. The first and most fundamental truth of the world is that he is God, and we are not. Getting that wrong sets everything else on a false footing.

Getting our attitude towards God right, however, brings a genuine hope that our deepest longings for health and wellbeing will be

---

3 Daniel K. Williams, 'What Really Happens When Americans Stop Going to Church', *The Atlantic*, 3 September 2023, www.theatlantic.com/ideas/archive/2023/09/christianity-religion-america-church-polarization/675215 (accessed 11 June 2024).

4 'This is understood in a threefold sense as referring to the knowledge of God, to morals, and to judgments of a practical nature.' Melancthon, *Exposition of the Proverbs of Solomon*, in Fink, *Reformation Commentary*, 31.

satisfied (3:8; see 15:30). The parallelism of 'body' and 'bones' in verse 8 gives a holistic picture: the outer body and the inner person are both nourished. Living rightly is *good for us*. God sustains us and gives us everything, and he loves to bless. We can trust him to work for our good (Romans 8:28).

We have so far seen two aspects of relating rightly to God: relying upon him and his word and humbling oneself before him, and now in verse 9 we see a third way of relating to God – honouring him by giving up the best of what was already his to give in the first place. This is the way to have plenty (3:10). God will be generous to those he trusts to be generous with his provisions. The image here is of abundance; barns overflowing, vats brimming over. Possessions are not to be hoarded (see Numbers 18:12–13; Ezekiel 48:14). God's gifts are for sharing, and he loves to bless. We should love to offer to him what we have, not as a religious duty, but because we enjoy sharing with him. In the Old Testament context this would have been through Temple offerings (Numbers 15:20; Deuteronomy 18:4; 26:2, 10; 2 Chronicles 31:5; Nehemiah 10:38; Ezekiel 44:30), but the sense of rightly honouring God in our use of possessions is a theme carried through to the New Testament (for example, Matthew 6:3–4; 2 Corinthians 8:7–15; 9:6–7; Philippians 4:10–19). It requires trust to do so, to trust that God will resupply what we give to him. It also requires humility and thankfulness, recognising that he is the source of all our goods. The three ways of relating to God go together and enable each other.

Is this hard to do? Some may find it so, and some may find themselves disciplined by God when they fail to heed his instructions. That, too, is part of God's blessing and so should be received thankfully (3:11). God disciplines us out of love, for our good. Discipline is never pleasant, and being humbled hurts our pride. When we consider the benefits of a right relationship with God, however, we can see that anything is worth obtaining it. God knows this; he values our holiness over all else, and will go to any lengths to achieve it. That is his mercy. God disciplines those he loves (3:12). Christ does it himself (Revelation 3:19; see also Job 7:17–19). Do not reject difficulty in your life, or think it evidence of God's powerlessness or lack of love. Suffering we face in this world may be God *keeping* his promises to love and bless us, for that is how he develops the most valuable thing we have – our faith in him.

This chapter has nine references to Yahweh (the Lord), demonstrating that relating well to God is clearly a central part of this wisdom teaching. The sage, the wise man, teaching a pupil to be wise, hammers home this lesson that knowing God rightly is essential. In modern western secularism, it is generally assumed that 'the wise' – the intelligentsia, the intellectuals – do not even accept the existence of God, let alone humbling themselves in mind, spirit and physical life before him. Yet Israel's sage knew better. If God is the creator, the sustainer, the absolute ground of all existence, the one who provides everything and controls all things, then not to recognise that fact is the absolute opposite of wisdom. It is ignoring the most important thing that can be known. Wisdom begins with right relationship with God, and God generously allows that relationship and gives wisdom as generously as he gives all other things.

2. *Wisdom's praise* • *Proverbs 3:13–26*

God's gift of wisdom is well worth having, as we see in the second section of praise to wisdom in verses 13–26. This begins the second lecture of the chapter. The teacher stops to remember just how amazing wisdom is, and once more exhorts the student to pursue it. Wisdom is valuable to humankind (13–18), to the Lord (19–20) and to the listener (21–6).

13 Blessed are those who find
wisdom,
those who gain understanding,
14 for she is more profitable than
silver
and yields better returns than
gold.
15 She is more precious than rubies;
nothing you desire can
compare with her.
16 Long life is in her right hand;
in her left hand are riches and
honour.
17 Her ways are pleasant ways,
and all her paths are
peace.
18 She is a tree of life to those
who take hold of her;
those who hold her fast will be
blessed.

19 By wisdom the LORD laid the
earth's foundations,
by understanding he set the
heavens in place;
20 by his knowledge the watery
depths were divided,
and the clouds let drop the
dew.

21 My son, do not let wisdom and
understanding out of your
sight,
preserve sound judgment and
discretion;
22 they will be life for you,
an ornament to grace your neck.
23 Then you will go on your way
in safety,
and your foot will not
stumble.
24 When you lie down, you will
not be afraid;
when you lie down, your sleep
will be sweet.
25 Have no fear of sudden
disaster
or of the ruin that overtakes
the wicked,
26 for the LORD will be at your
side
and will keep your foot from
being snared.

Wisdom is truly a blessing; true wisdom and knowledge are the best of achievements (3:13), worth more than anything else. The Bible tells us many times about what makes a person 'blessed' (*asher*), having the best life; Jesus continues the tradition in the beatitudes (Matthew 5:3–12). This blessing depends upon knowing the Lord, valuing him and his word, and living for him. Nothing else compares; certainly not worldly wealth (3:14–15). We cannot buy wisdom, but all things that we value – long life, riches, earthly glory, a pleasant and peaceful life (3:16–17) are offered by wisdom. She is, in fact, a 'tree of life' (3:18) and so a source of blessing in herself.

It is worth pausing a moment to reflect on the image of a tree of life. While this was a general ancient Near Eastern idea, describing wisdom in this way evokes the biblical tradition of *the* tree of life. That tree was the source of immortality in the garden (Genesis 2:9) and was lost through the fall (Genesis 3:22–4). There, humans wanted their own wisdom, without God; they wanted to decide good and evil for themselves, not to trust God's word on that. Doing so, humans overreached themselves and so lost their access to the tree of life. Now we are able to regain it through God's wisdom. Ultimately, we will have full access in the new creation (Revelation 2:7; 22:2).

Wisdom is that important, and so of course grasping wisdom and holding fast to it will result in blessing.[5]

Why is wisdom so monumentally powerful? Now we find out what wisdom means to the Lord as he created. For wisdom is tied up with the creator; she personifies the Lord's understanding in designing and ordering this glorious universe, and his present sustaining of it. God did not create haphazardly. Wisdom is part of his power. The mighty acts of creation are described in Genesis 1 purely in terms of his word – he spoke and creation obeyed, dividing according to his plan. Here in Proverbs we gain further insight into that power, as flowing from his wisdom and understanding (3:19–20). As we see from Genesis 1, God ordered creation according to his plan; setting up cause and effect, he made it a place that we could inhabit (Isaiah 45:18). He controlled the act of creation in the past, and continues to do so as he sends rain and dew (Proverbs 3:20).

The language could also be alluding to God's acts in judgment, as in the flood, when the depths were split open (Genesis 7:11); a similar phrase is used to describe God splitting open rocks in the desert to give water to his people (Psalm 78:15). God orders creation, and he can reorder it as he chooses; he does so knowingly and wisely. This is the power of wisdom; and this wisdom is being offered to us. These verses also tell us that wisdom and its moral commands are not a matter of human culture; they are part of creation itself.

Of course, then, we must pursue and grab hold of wisdom, and in verses 21–6 more benefits of doing so are spelled out. What a treasure to gain! The student is once more exhorted to hold fast to wisdom, the basis of discretion, the way to ensure successful living (3:21). Once again, we are given the image of wisdom as adornment, and the way of life itself (3:22). It is the means of getting through life well, not stumbling over the many potential pitfalls, but instead staying on the right path, safely and securely (3:23). Wisdom also gives the opportunity to avoid fear, and instead to enjoy the opposite: sweet sleep (3:24). This is what David enjoyed, even in the face

---

5 The English Presbyterian Francis Taylor (1590–1656) writes, 'So wisdom restores us to that which we lost in Adam, eternal life, but in a better place in heaven.' Francis Taylor, *An Exposition with Practical Observations*, in Fink, *Reformation Commentary*, 35.

of enemies and the betrayal of his own son (Psalm 3:5). There, the reason for his confidence that allowed him to sleep under the worst of earthly circumstances was his knowledge of God and trust in him. Wisdom is a consequence and cause of that knowledge, seen earlier in the chapter. Those who struggle with anxiety and fear long for a peaceful inner calm; here, we are told, wisdom is what brings that confidence. Sound sleep is a benefit of faith in God.

As I write, my mother is suffering from terminal cancer. It is a source of constant worry; I find it hard to sleep, or if I do sleep, I wake up, mind racing. At such times, in the darkness of the night, it is reminding myself of God's goodness that gets me through. Reciting Psalm 23, praying the Lord's Prayer: such reminders are what enable me to regain some measure of calm and to sleep again. In such bleak times, only the imbedded memory of such a great truth has the power to dispel darkness.[6]

This theme of avoiding fear is further explored in the next two verses – it is not a casual aside. Wisdom is the means of not panicking (3:25). We need not fear that the world will fall apart, for God is at our side (3:26). This is not an assurance that bad things never happen; rather, wisdom is the means of going forward and succeeding, even in the midst of confusion and evil. In particular, when we face God's judgment, the ruin of the wicked – when the world *will* fall apart – we need not fear, for God will spare those who are in Christ. Wisdom guides us and gives us security, for it is connected with God's sovereignty, in this world and the next. Follow wisdom, and have confidence in God.

3. Relating to others • Proverbs 3:27–35

After these commendations of wisdom, we now enter specific wisdom teaching again. We have seen what wise relating to God involves in the first half of the chapter; now we see how to relate to other humans.

6 See Kirsten Birkett, *Living Without Fear: Using the Psalms To End Your Worry And Anxiety* (Carlisle: Kirsten Birkett, 2022).

27 Do not withhold good from
those to whom it is due,
when it is in your power to act.
28 Do not say to your neighbour,
'Come back tomorrow and I'll
give it to you' –
when you already have it with
you.
29 Do not plot harm against your
neighbour,
who lives trustfully near you.
30 Do not accuse anyone for no
reason –
when they have done you no
harm.
31 Do not envy the violent
or choose any of their ways.
32 For the LORD detests the
perverse
but takes the upright into his
confidence.
33 The LORD's curse is on the
house of the wicked,
but he blesses the home of the
righteous.
34 He mocks proud mockers
but shows favour to the
humble and oppressed.
35 The wise inherit honour,
but fools get only shame.

There are three aspects of relating well to our neighbours (3:27–33). First, we should do good and be generous (3:27); don't be mean by postponing help when you're quite able to give it (3:28; see also Leviticus 19:13). If you can help your neighbour, then do so. Jesus would later tell the good Samaritan story in response to the question, 'Who is my neighbour?' Wisdom teaches how to be a good neighbour.[7]

Second, don't be malicious. Don't plot secretly against others (3:29) and don't manipulate the courts to charge someone unjustly (3:30). There is no place in wisdom for such evil and injustice.

Third, don't envy a violent person (3:31); such people are to be rejected and avoided, not emulated. Your inner character matters just as much as your outer actions, and envy is an insidious evil. Love does not envy, we are told in 1 Corinthians 13:4; the converse is also true that if you envy, you do not love. Envy is essentially self-seeking; it is saying, 'I deserve what you have.' It fails to be thankful for what God has given us. We should especially not envy the wicked, however attractive their current wealth may look. Their way is not how people should be relating to each other.

7 This is not a command to give what you can't (see 2 Corinthians 8:12; Galatians 6:10); in fact, you are not to put yourself up as security for a stranger (Proverbs 6:1–5).

These injunctions are based on God's character. He hates such perverse people, the wicked and violent, but if you are upright, you can enjoy his confidence (3:32). He curses the wicked and blesses the righteous (3:33; see also Deuteronomy 11:26–8).

Finally, this chapter is wrapped up with a comparison between the unwise and the wise. It is those who are humble who gain God's favour; those who mock him will be mocked in turn by God (3:34). Verse 35 makes a similar comparison; honour is for the wise, shame for the fools.

Conclusion to Proverbs 3

The essence of wisdom can be seen in how we conduct our relationships, not in selfishness or self-regard but being faithful to our neighbours, in generosity and honest dealing. This is rooted in our way of relating to God, recognising his power and greatness and responding to his generosity. We can trust him, he who ordered creation itself, who knows all things; and trusting him, we can have stability and confidence in life even when circumstances seem to be frightening and unstable. It turns out that wisdom consists of loving the Lord our God and loving our neighbour as ourselves.

5

Wisdom Through the Generations

PROVERBS 4

The NIV heading is 'Get wisdom at any cost'. This of course has been a theme already in the first three chapters of Proverbs, but is emphasised here. The father is strong in his exhortation: get wisdom and keep it. The teaching is further strengthened by the introduction of a deeper heritage: this is not just the teacher's insight, but the wisdom passed down from *his* teacher, his father. Generations are testifying that this is true wisdom, and that it is essential to life.

This chapter introduces the second half of the first major section in the book of Proverbs. Chapters 1–9 form the first major division of the book. We have seen that 1–3 are the teacher's initial stages in wisdom instruction, as he instructs his son. Chapters 4–9 consist of the wisdom gained from the generations, from the teacher's teacher, the sage's own father. As we will see, it involves teaching about right behaviour and listening to the right women. We are told what to do if we get it wrong; this matters, for getting this right leads to life.

Who is being taught? The address is singular (4:10, 5:1): this is the grandfather addressing our first teacher, the father. However, it is also plural (4:1; 5:7; 7:24) as the teacher has a wider audience, transmitting his inherited wisdom to a new generation. We may include ourselves in that audience, inheriting this wisdom teaching in our turn.

1. Listen to Grandad • Proverbs 4:1–9

In 4:1–9 we have the introduction to chapters 4–9. It contains the refrain that continues through the first nine chapters, commending wisdom and the importance of obtaining it. Both the teacher and his teacher are strong in this exhortation. Gaining wisdom is hard; it takes effort, and learning, and experience, and time. It is important that we are reminded of its value. This is something it is absolutely worth spending our life doing. If you plan to choose a life goal, consider making it 'the acquiring of wisdom'. It is what makes for the balanced life, rightly understanding God and rightly living with others, the way of personal flourishing, of confidence and stability in a chaotic world. It has always been of value; in our current world with its constant, monumental change, its overwhelming technology and influx of information, and its current insistence on redefining ethics, knowledge and indeed the definition of our being, perhaps wisdom is more important than ever. It will be wisdom that guides our path through this maze.

Get wisdom at any cost

4 Listen, my sons, to a father's instruction;
pay attention and gain understanding.
2 I give you sound learning,
so do not forsake my teaching.
3 For I too was a son to my father,
still tender, and cherished by my mother.
4 Then he taught me, and he said to me,
'Take hold of my words with all your heart;
keep my commands, and you will live.
5 Get wisdom, get understanding;
do not forget my words or turn away from them.
6 Do not forsake wisdom, and she will protect you;
love her, and she will watch over you.
7 The beginning of wisdom is this: get[a] wisdom.
Though it cost all you have,[b] get understanding.
8 Cherish her, and she will exalt you;
embrace her, and she will honour you.
9 She will give you a garland to grace your head
and present you with a glorious crown.'

a 7 Or *Wisdom is supreme; therefore get*
b 7 Or *wisdom. / Whatever else you get*

Verse 1 begins with a call to listen to a father's instruction – we are to pay attention! This is the way to knowledge. *Musar*, translated 'instruction', is actually quite strong, implying discipline: the teaching is strict, important and valuable (4:2), so don't ignore it. This is the teaching of the ages, coming down from the teacher's own teacher (4:3). It is not just one sage's opinion; it has been tested across generations. 'I too was a son,' he says, with the overtones not just of biological descent, but also of the obedient son listening to wisdom. He was young and unformed, and taught in a loving family.

What was the grandfather's teaching? He, too, commended wisdom (4:4). This is vitally important; we have a list of imperatives in verses 4–8. In the face of all the other things we might 'get', or acquire, in life – riches have already mentioned – we should put getting wisdom first. Don't forget this command, and don't ignore the teaching (4:5). Wisdom is what will protect you in life; so love her, do not leave her: this is language both of marriage and of commitment to God (4:6). And the first instruction in wisdom is to get wisdom (4:7). Above anything else, seek this.

Why do we need such strong, repeated commands? Presumably because we are only too likely to forget, or fail to prize this wisdom. Our natural, sinful inclination will be to be selfish, and only to exert effort in what will exalt ourselves. It is a wrong impulse; not just wrong in itself, but also not the way to reach a truly valuable life. The world teaches us to crave and seek status, fame, wealth and accumulated possessions. But wisdom is what we should desire. Some aspects of the western counterculture challenge worldly materialism, and to that extent come closer to wisdom; but all too often, what it prizes instead is still frequently very selfish – self-realization, self-fulfilment, a comfortable life through inner peace and positive mood.

So remember the sage's teaching. Cherish wisdom, as it is taught and defined here, and receive a right exaltation and honour (4:8). This is the real adornment, the real crown (4:9). Wisdom, again 'she', is the woman to follow.

2. *Walk this way* • *Proverbs 4:10–19*

Temptations to turn away from wisdom and follow evil will still be about. The alternative path may appear more attractive, lucrative, interesting and intellectually fulfilling, in line with the times or current fashion or whatever desirable face evil chooses to put on. In this section, as the teacher continues to relate what he himself was taught as a youth, he warns against this constant temptation. This will prepare the student for the subsequent wisdom teaching that will follow in chapter 5.

10 Listen, my son, accept what I
say,
and the years of your life will
be many.
11 I instruct you in the way of
wisdom
and lead you along straight
paths.
12 When you walk, your steps will
not be hampered;
when you run, you will not
stumble.
13 Hold on to instruction, do not
let it go;
guard it well, for it is your life.
14 Do not set foot on the path of
the wicked
or walk in the way of
evildoers.
15 Avoid it, do not travel on it;
turn from it and go on your
way.
16 For they cannot rest until they
do evil;
they are robbed of sleep
till they make someone
stumble.
17 They eat the bread of
wickedness
and drink the wine of
violence.

18 The path of the righteous is
like the morning sun,
shining ever brighter till the
full light of day.
19 But the way of the wicked is
like deep darkness;
they do not know what makes
them stumble.

In 4:10 the new lecture is introduced with a general exhortation to listen to wisdom, in the pattern we have seen established earlier. Here, we see the reason for following wisdom that has been mentioned before: it brings long life.[1] The verbs of verse 11 are in the past (perfect and pluperfect): the student already has a foundation in past teaching, which it seems he followed, walking on the right path. This was

1 German theologian Lucas Osiander (1534–1604) explains life-prolonging power of wisdom in part by wisdom allowing one to avoid the pitfalls of evil. Lucas Osiander, *Proverbs*, in Fink, *Reformation Commentary*, 43. Cop adds that the long life may be referring to eternity; on this earth, 'however short our life may be, it shall be so long as is expedient for the salvation of our souls'. Cop, *On the Proverbs of Solomon*, in Fink, *Reformation Commentary*, 44.

the way to be unobstructed, even when moving fast (4:12). This is the way to continue, taking heed of correction and instruction in verse 13, holding on to it (actually 'she' – wisdom), not letting go.

The good way has been commended, and reasons given for following it; now we have five imperatives, in verses 14–15. Do not go the wrong way. Do not follow evil. Avoid it. Don't go there. And if the youth is already going that way, verse 15, turn back.

Why? Two reasons, introduced with 'for' in verses 16 and 17. The people on this way are not just evil, but evil compels them; they cannot rest until they have achieved it. This tells us two things about wisdom. First, it is not just about knowledge. The wrong path is a *morally* wrong one, not just an ignorant one. Second, rejecting wisdom does not lead to autonomy. Turning away from God does not lead to 'free' thought or 'free' love. It leads to a lack of ability to think freely and act freely. Those who have chosen this path, verse 16 says, cannot rest, cannot sleep, until they do more evil. Evil has become their food and drink (4:17).

It is similar to the description of those who have turned away from God in Romans 1:18–32 who are so given over to evil that they will even invent new ways of doing it (Romans 1:30). People who turn away from God do not become neutral. Their minds become darkened and their morals are corrupted. The Bible is clear that wisdom is far more than just knowledge. A person can turn away from God and still know a good many things, even a good many true things. Even so, such a person becomes a fool. Truth becomes obscured as it is suppressed and exchanged for a lie. What follows is wrong worship and wrong morality. These things are not separate, and they do not bring freedom, but rather reduce freedom. Evil is its own addiction. Like food and drink, wickedness and violence become a way of life, a compulsion.

Yet so different is the way of the righteous – in context, those following wisdom, those seeking to fear the Lord. It's like the sunrise, which only gets brighter (4:18). This summer, I have been following the Swedish practice of *gottoka*, rising before 5 a.m. to walk outside and listen to birdsong. Here in the north of England the sun is already well up by then, and the light is magical. As it grows, the world seems to glow, and the Lord's creation simply grows in beauty.

It is an apt metaphor for wisdom. Following the Lord only becomes more and more rewarding. The light will continue to increase, and we can look forward to an eternity in God's light when we will not even need the sun (Revelation 21:23).

How stark, then, is the contrast of verse 19. As in 1:32–3, 2:21–2 and 3:35, a section of teaching is ended with a deliberate contrast between right and wrong. Here, the way of evil, the way of non-wisdom, is deep darkness. It is the way full of hazards that you cannot see, waiting to trip you up. This is a picture of the dark of night; not a glorious night full of stars and moonlight, but a deep night, with all light obscured, the time of stumbling unawares on dangers. Do not go there, the warning of verse 14 echoes. It is not worth it.

3. Stay straight • Proverbs 4:20–27

We continue with praise of wisdom, and some specific teaching on wisdom. Here the teacher, the sage, gives advice about living out the wise principles that have been recommended so far. The student is back on track, not following the evil people who seemed so tempting in the previous section, but willing to listen to some more wisdom.

This lecture contains a lot of 'body' language: the student needs not only to have right understanding and right morals, but these are expressed in how we live in our physical bodies. We are embodied creatures, not pure mind or spirit. Goodness is something that is lived, not just thought about; character reveals itself in the actions we take and the way we behave as we go about our embodied lives. It may require self-control; this particular fruit of the Spirit is very important in disciplining ourselves to live wisely, for bodies are unruly and want what they want. Yet they can learn, and the wise student will pay attention to controlling bodily behaviour. The teacher will return to the theme of right embodied behaviour again later in his lesson. The most important 'body part', however, is the heart, and it stands for what really controls the body, the inner driver that will either obey the word or reject it.

20 My son, pay attention to what I say;
turn your ear to my words.
21 Do not let them out of your sight,
keep them within your heart;
22 for they are life to those who find them
and health to one's whole body.
23 Above all else, guard your heart,
for everything you do flows from it.
24 Keep your mouth free of perversity;
keep corrupt talk far from your lips.
25 Let your eyes look straight ahead;
fix your gaze directly before you.
26 Give careful thought to the[c] paths for your feet
and be steadfast in all your ways.
27 Do not turn to the right or the left;
keep your foot from evil.

c 26 Or *Make level*

Wisdom begins with our eyes and ears. The student is to listen to these words with his ears, and pay attention (4:20). He is to observe them with his eyes. He is to engage his body in learning and remembering these lessons (4:21). Why? Again, we have our refrain of life. These words are not just interesting, but they also bring life; learn with your whole body, and you will have health to your whole body (4:22).

Especially, the heart is to be protected (4:23). The heart here stands for the inner being that controls behaviour: the decision-making centre. We could think of it as mind, or even will. It is similar to the sentiment of 2 Corinthians 10:5: 'take captive every thought'. This is actually the secret of true freedom of thought; being disciplined in where our minds go, so as to think truly. We must guard our inner life – still something that happens within our bodies, and subject to bodily weakness. Guarding the heart takes discipline and practice, just as any other habit of body, and these are essential to directing what our bodies do.

Our mouths must also be set right (4:24). The tongue is a fire, James says; it sets the whole course of one's life on fire (James 3:6). No human can tame it. What we say is hugely powerful; words can build up or cut down. We must tell the truth, speak honestly, say nothing perverse or corrupt, for with our words terrible evil can be spread. (But silence is not always the answer, either! Judging when to speak, and what to speak, certainly takes wisdom.) Our words also affect ourselves powerfully – through silent 'self-talk' as well as what we habitually say to others. As we speak, so we will be.

The eyes, too, must be disciplined (4:25). Look straight ahead, look where you are going. Don't glance aside, don't be distracted, and don't let your eyes stray to the wrong goal (see Matthew 5:28). The New Testament answer is, of course, as the hymn goes, to turn your eyes upon Jesus.[2] Where you are looking, both physically and metaphorically, will determine where you go. And watch your feet (4:26); think about where you are going and stay on the right path. Be steadfast; don't deviate from the path (4:27). Both physically and metaphorically, our keeping track of what our bodies are doing and exercising self-control are crucial to our gaining of wisdom.

Conclusion to Proverbs 4

The grandfather and the father, through the generations of teaching, have revealed the secret of wisdom: pay attention, first, to what you're thinking and believing, and then live it out. Right thinking comes from listening to the teacher; this is God's teaching. This right knowledge is true freedom.

2 Helen Howarth Lemmel (1864–1961), 'Turn Your Eyes Upon Jesus'.

6

Speaking of Bodies . . .

PROVERBS 5

Proverbs is about wisdom, about how to live the best possible human life. It emphasises the mind, knowing the truth and especially knowing the Lord. This truth is to be absorbed internally so it results in a changed heart, one that is inclined towards wisdom; and that changed heart is meant to lead to changed behaviour, in all aspects of our embodied life. True wisdom is what leads to moral behaviour, which is the way to a truly flourishing life.

A key theme of Proverbs is the emphasis on right relationships, and we have already seen that, in general, human relationships should be characterised by loving faithfulness. One of the major ways in which Proverbs applies this teaching is its emphasis on sexual morality. The poetic structures used in chapter 5 add to the emotional impact that helps to embed this teaching. Sex is one of the strongest human drives; it is here that we are prone to go spectacularly wrong. It should not be surprising, then, that Proverbs warns so strongly, and so repeatedly, against adultery.

Western culture is obsessed with sex. Governors of nursery schools are given government guidelines on teaching sexual health and well-being. Teenagers are presented with live naked couples and asked to discuss their relationships. A parent I knew asked her children's teacher if the curriculum included teaching on abstinence; the teacher in his answer revealed that he actually *did not know what that meant.* At all levels, western culture encourages maximal sexual experimentation and activity, with apparently no time for self-control or restraint, while at the same time trying to teach respect and deference to others' feelings – an all but impossible combination, as recent scandals have amply demonstrated.

It is not the way of wisdom. Wisdom recognises that we are sinful, and that there are very wrong ways to indulge sexual impulses. Those ways will not lead to happiness, flourishing or good relationships. Proverbs 5 develops this theme as it teaches the youth about the wrong, and the right, ways to go about sex. Marriage is what protects and nurtures human sexual relationships, faithful, lifelong marriage is the way of joy and fulfilment, delight and desire, and safe sex.

1. Body language • Proverbs 5:1–6

This new wisdom lecture starts with an introduction (5:1–6), and begins with the familiar exhortation to pay attention to wisdom, here specifically described as belonging to the father – that is not to say that it is not also divinely inspired wisdom, but that he is the one passing it on.

Warning against adultery

5 My son, pay attention to my
wisdom,
turn your ear to my words of
insight,
2 that you may maintain
discretion
and your lips may preserve
knowledge.
3 For the lips of the adulterous
woman drip honey,
and her speech is smoother
than oil;
4 but in the end she is bitter as
gall,
sharp as a double-edged
sword.
5 Her feet go down to death;
her steps lead straight to the
grave.
6 She gives no thought to the
way of life;
her paths wander aimlessly,
but she does not know it.

These are the words to listen to (5:1); and we are given a reason for the importance of wisdom. It is the way of discretion, of forethought. Having wisdom will enable one to make good decisions, to weigh up options and see the best way forward. This will become particularly relevant when considering when, and with whom, to have sex. Wisdom will also enable lips to preserve knowledge (5:2). This is in contrast to the woman's lips in verse 3, which will give the opposite. So, the teacher exhorts in the introduction, listen. The bodily references of the previous section are very relevant; this will be all about what to do with one's body.

The woman who is now presented is the reason why the son needs wisdom and discretion. She is 'strange', or 'forbidden'. She's not from around here, and is possibly exotic and enticing. The NIV translates this 'adulterous', since in the context that is clearly her intent. This woman initially sounds good. She is dripping honey from her lips – sweet and tempting (see Song of Songs 4:11). 'Free sex' does indeed seem tempting. It is what bodies want, after all. It is easy to present it as natural, normal and good to let bodies do what they want to do, what they seem to be made for. Any restriction is easily portrayed as repressive, even unhealthy. Yet free sex is not at all free; it has certainly not led western society to be tolerant, loving and happy. Instead, we see broken families, scarred adults and damaged children.

This is exactly what verse 4 predicts. In the end, following this path leads to bitterness. The outcome is bitter as gall and as sharp as a weapon of violence. Her feet are not on the path of life, but instead lead to death, which is precisely what a two-edge sword is designed for. She is going down to the grave, to Sheol, the place of the dead (5:5), and so following her will end there. In fact, it seems she does not even know how to pursue life (5:6). She's wandering aimlessly. She may seem to be offering something good, but she does not know where she's going (see Jeremiah 14:10).

The fact that this negative figure is a woman is not misogyny; there are plenty of evil men presented in Scripture as well. The Bible has equal-opportunity sinners. The trap of the seducer can come in male as well as female form, and the temptation can be for any orientation. The point is to be on guard (verse 2) and not to be deceived by appearances. Smooth words and attractive lips can be a facade that hides an option that actually leads to bitterness and death.

2. What happens if you don't listen? • Proverbs 5:6–14

We will now discover some of the consequences of following the negative figure. Those consequences can be dire.

7 Now then, my sons, listen to
me;
do not turn aside from what I
say.
8 Keep to a path far from her,
do not go near the door of her
house,
9 lest you lose your honour to
others
and your dignity[a] to one who
is cruel,
10 lest strangers feast on your
wealth
and your toil enrich the house
of another.
11 At the end of your life you will
groan,
when your flesh and body are
spent.
12 You will say, 'How I hated
discipline!
How my heart spurned
correction!
13 I would not obey my teachers
or turn my ear to my
instructors.
14 And I was soon in serious
trouble
in the assembly of God's
people.'

a 9 Or *years*

Having begun with such a strong warning, the teacher goes on to urge the son – and all sons following him (5:7) to pay attention to this warning, and then spells out what will happen if the son does not: social and financial ruin. Stay away from these immoral relationships. Do not go down the path of easy sex. Don't even visit the door of her house (5:8, possibly a double entendre). Don't even go there, both metaphorically and physically. As Jesus would say, don't so much as entertain the thought in your mind (Matthew 5:28). Adultery should be unthinkable; don't let it be an option, even in fantasy. Stay on a different path, far away.

For adultery – and what is being described is sex outside marriage between a man and a woman – has all sorts of bad consequences. Verses 9 and 10 are in parallel. Verse 9 talks about the loss of honour and dignity. It's not something to be proud of. The phrasing is slightly elliptical; it talks of merciless people taking your glory and years – a loss of valuable and intangible things (this could include reputation and mental health). Verse 10 applies this to more tangible assets, as strangers take your money and goods. Who are these strangers? Given that the adulterous woman is married, it could mean her husband's family; in any case, they are outside the son's community, where his wealth belongs.

People who have gone through divorce can testify to this very practical outcome of marriage breakdown; it's incredibly expensive. The emotional pain and injury go alongside considerable loss of finances, particularly for the vulnerable (and it is usually the wife and children who are the most vulnerable). It's moral and physical bankruptcy.

Such a life is one you will look back on with dismay (5:11). The body is worn out through the stress of immorality and the payment demanded by the cheated husband of verse 10. Verses 12 and 13 are in parallel, about the folly of not listening. No one likes hearing reprimand – and our world especially does not like hearing *this* reprimand – but, the teacher warns, you will regret not heeding it. These are words that our whole culture needs to hear. Calls to chastity, to protecting traditional marriage and rejecting sexual promiscuity are derided and, indeed, increasingly punished. Such reproof is heard as unloving and immoral. Yet they are the words of love and life. Ignoring them will lead to the lament of these verses, regret that warnings were not listened to, for the result was serious trouble, utter ruin (5:14) – in ancient Israel, maybe facing punishment under the law.

The voice here is of one looking back on youth, remembering teenage rejection of authority. This kind of adolescent unwillingness to listen is far more characteristic of our society than the mature adulthood it pretends to. We so often hear the narrative of history moving forward, that our culture is progressive, that we have grown out of old restrictions, that in these modern times we have advanced and grown up, and therefore everyone else should catch up. However, so often the behaviour of our culture is far more like the unruly adolescent who refuses to listen to reason, preferring to give in to physical impulses. What makes us think that, in this claimed ongoing march of history, the current era represents mature adulthood?

3. Drink from your own well • Proverbs 5:15–20

Yet it's not inevitable that we fall prey to the follies of youth. God offers a wonderful alternative.

15 Drink water from your own
cistern,
running water from your own
well.
16 Should your springs overflow
in the streets,
your streams of water in the
public squares?
17 Let them be yours alone,
never to be shared with
strangers.
18 May your fountain be blessed,
and may you rejoice in the
wife of your youth.
19 A loving doe, a graceful deer –
may her breasts satisfy you
always,
may you ever be intoxicated
with her love.
20 Why, my son, be intoxicated
with another man's wife?
Why embrace the bosom of a
wayward woman?

So what is the alternative? How can one resist the immense social pressure to take sex wherever and however you like, to satisfy bodily impulses as they arise? The answer is not actually about water fountains, but about marriage (5:15; see also Song of Songs 4:15). Drink from your own well: in other words, stay faithful to your own marriage. Marriage is the solution to burning with passion (1 Corinthians 7:9). Your marriage, your body, your sex, are for you and your spouse, not anyone else (Proverbs 5:16–17); and your spouse is for you and you are for your spouse, and neither of you are for anyone else. Stay there, where you belong. Pour your efforts and energies into enriching your married life. Rejoice in your partner; the language here is rich and flowing, similar to the delightful phrases of Song of Songs (4:5; 7:4). Invest in your marriage relationship and delight in it; be intoxicated with it (Proverbs 5:18–19) – a 'most sweet exhortation', as Melancthon describes it.[1] Take marriage advice, go on enrichment weekends, learn how to make your relationship better. It's not just the way to enjoy marriage more; it's also the way to avoid the disaster of adultery.

Given the delights of marriage, is there any reason at all to commit adultery (5:20)? Considering the arguments already presented, the answer to these rhetorical questions would have to be, 'No reason at all.' It's foolishness; it leads to disaster. It's the way of dissatisfaction, unhappiness and death.

1 Cited in Fink, *Reformation Commentary*, 49.

SINGLENESS

What if you are not married? What if that just never worked out for you? Or if you are widowed, or a spouse left you? What if you are same-sex attracted and choose abstinence? There are many reasons why someone may not be married, quite apart from choosing singleness for the sake of vocation or ministry.

In the Israelite context of the Old Testament, marriage was expected of everyone. Singleness as a blessed, godly option did not really exist. This was to change with the New Testament, and indeed is a very surprising innovation of the new covenant. Singleness becomes a blessed and valid option.

We know that marriage is more than just an earthly context for relationship; in Ephesians 5:31–2 we discover that it is a picture of eternity, when Christ will be married to his church. This earthly institution, then, has a symbolic function as well as a practical one. It teaches something about eschatology, what will happen in the new creation after Christ returns to judge the earth. It is a symbol of what eternity will be like.

The surprising new teaching in the New Testament is that singleness is also a picture of eternity, and the New Testament teaches something of what the new creation will be like. For there will be no human marriage there; we will be 'like the angels', evidently eternally single (Matthew 22:30). This most glorious, fulfilling, perfect heavenly life, without fear or tears or suffering of any sort, will be the single life. Singleness now is not just a practical option, freeing people from all sorts of earthly worries (1 Corinthians 7:32–5); it also teaches us about eternity.

This is something that is rarely recognised even in the church these days (it was otherwise in the early church), let alone in wider society. Being single and celibate is usually very much an unwanted option, among both Christians and non-Christians. But it is a heavenly option. Put like that, it is hardly surprising that Paul considers it better than marriage (1 Corinthians 7:38), even though marriage is not sinful. Churches would do well to take this seriously, for the benefit of their many single members, as well as the families.[2]

---

2 See Danielle Treweek, *The Meaning of Singleness: Retrieving an Eschatological Vision*

4. Staying safe • Proverbs 5:21–3

Chapter 5 has given us some powerful and countercultural warnings. The chapter finishes with the context that makes these warnings worth listening to.

21 For your ways are in full view
of the LORD,
and he examines all your
paths.
22 The evil deeds of the wicked
ensnare them;
the cords of their sins hold
them fast.
23 For lack of discipline they will
die,
led astray by their own great
folly.

In conclusion, the teacher turns to the wider reality of theology. God is sovereign, and he is judge. The Lord knows what we are doing (5:21; see also 2 Chronicles 16:9; Job 34:21; Psalm 33:13–15; Jeremiah 16:17; 32:19); he knows the paths we take. We might also remember that God created marriage and its joys, and he knows that sex outside that context will only damage us. He is the one who tells us what paths to take. That is why following the wrong path – following evil, following the way of adultery – will only entrap you; there are consequences to ignoring the right moral order (5:22). Ignore discipline, ignore reproof, and you will die (5:23). Consider adultery to be as bad as death. Your own folly will take you there. The word for 'intoxicated' in verse 19 is the same for 'led astray' in verse 23; if you are going to stagger around, let it be in overwhelming delight of your marriage partner, not in foolishness and evil.

Conclusion to Proverbs 5

Marriage matters, and the right way to conduct sexual relationships matters. If the church is criticised for being overly harsh about sex,

for the Contemporary Church (Lisle, Illinois: IVP Academic, 2023), for an excellent discussion of these issues. Note that the warnings against adultery in Proverbs apply to all sex outside marriage; it is all unworthy of humanity and means a loss of dignity and honour.

the teaching of Proverbs 5 puts it into context. Following this way is the way of life, of joy, of delight, of love, and the alternative is the way of death. How could any loving church preach otherwise?

7

Money and Other Pitfalls

PROVERBS 6:1–19

The teacher now embarks on a new topic, to do with work and money. Relationship with God (and therefore wisdom) has given us the framework so far, and sexual purity has dominated the practical topics. We now come to the next perennial problem for humans: the love of money, especially easy money. The temptation was already there in the background of chapter 1, as our student was urged to choose wisdom over the invitation to join the gang of muggers who offered riches. Now we see some further teaching on a similar topic. A stranger has come requiring a pledge of money; perhaps that this is some scheme that seems preferable to working hard for a living, which is why the student is then criticised for being lazy.[1] The sage has some very pointed advice for any student who would fall for such a scheme.

Yet it's human nature to do so, and millennia later people are still trying to scam others. Appealing to greed under a veneer of compassion is very powerful. The scams take on new faces, but they are still traps, offering something for nothing.

1. On your feet! • Proverbs 6:1–11

The context is still that the teacher is relaying the wisdom from his own teacher, the grandfather, the wisdom passed down the generations. In a world where generational wisdom seems to be lost, as families are far more mobile and likely to move away from grandparents, and family breakdown can easily mean that contact between

1 See Ansberry, *Proverbs*, on this section for more detailed discussion.

generations is broken, it is good to be reminded that it is right and beneficial to learn from past generations. An older teacher has seen it all, and knows better than to be taken in by an offer of easy money. The tone is fairly harsh, and becomes increasingly so through the course of the chapter, with commands and rebuke; this is an important topic, and the teacher evidently feels it needs emphasis.

Warnings against folly

6 My son, if you have put up
security for your neighbour,
if you have shaken hands in
pledge for a stranger,
2 you have been trapped by what
you said,
ensnared by the words of your
mouth.
3 So do this, my son, to free
yourself,
since you have fallen into your
neighbour's hands:
go – to the point of exhaustion – [a]
and give your neighbour no
rest!
4 Allow no sleep to your eyes,
no slumber to your eyelids.
5 Free yourself, like a gazelle
from the hand of the hunter,
like a bird from the snare of
the fowler.

6 Go to the ant, you sluggard;
consider its ways and be wise!
7 It has no commander,
no overseer or ruler,
8 yet it stores its provisions in
summer
and gathers its food at harvest.

9 How long will you lie there,
you sluggard?
When will you get up from
your sleep?
10 A little sleep, a little slumber,
a little folding of the hands to
rest –
11 and poverty will come on you
like a thief
and scarcity like an armed
man.

a 3 Or *Go and humble yourself,*

To start with, the son has pledged money, signed a contract of some sort on behalf of his neighbour. The situation seems to be that the son has taken on an obligation or offered security for another person, signed his name and shaken hands on it, and so has become financially vulnerable to others. This is not talking about a situation of generosity towards the poor, which is clearly encouraged in the Old Testament (Deuteronomy 15:7–11; Proverbs 3:27–8). It is warning against being a guarantor of a stranger's debt (although you could possibly secure yourself for your own debt, Exodus 22:26–7; Deuteronomy 24:10–13, 17). The problem recognised several times in Proverbs (11:15; 17:18; 20:16; 22:26) is giving a pledge for a stranger, someone not necessarily to be trusted (6:1).[2] This would make you liable to losing everything if the stranger defaults; he has made a promise without having any control over what happens. The youth has been trapped by his words, by what he has agreed to (6:2), through foolishness, or greed, or vanity, or whatever wrong motive.

So, what now? The youth thought he was just shaking hands on a deal, but he has actually fallen into this person's hands; the language seems to be deliberately reversing the significance of 'hands', from what was seemingly a friendly gesture to something sinister (6:3). How to free himself? The sage is emphatic: Go! Act immediately! Get on the case! The entrapped youth needs to extricate himself from this deal, and to do it now. He must deal with this, go to the neighbour, pester him and resolve the problem. Don't just leave it to fate, the teacher is saying: do something! Get yourself out of this situation!

It is tempting, when in difficulty, to want someone else to deal with it. It is a very human tendency to look to both someone else to blame and someone else to take responsibility for fixing the problem. Perhaps the welfare state exacerbates this human tendency. Yet the sage here does not allow for that. The youth got himself into this mess, and so he needs to get himself out of it. Even to the point of not sleeping, he must act (6:4) and free himself (6:5). Don't be lazy, he is urged, a point that will be taken up in the next section. In the first image of what will become a 'learning from nature' theme, the youth is urged to do what any animal would have the sense to do when in trouble: struggle, make an effort, deal with the problem. The gazelle springs away when hunted, the bird gets away from the fowler. They see the danger and they exert energy to act. Do likewise, the command says.

---

2 Luther, however, takes this as a prohibition of pledging surety for anyone, for in doing so 'he pledges and promises what is not his and is not in his power'. *On Trading and Usury*, in Fink, *Reformation Commentary*, 54.

But why did the youth fall into such a trap in the first place? The teacher now does not mince his words: you sluggard! You're lazy! Observe the ant – another part of nature to learn from. It's only a tiny insect, but one that can teach a lesson in diligence (6:6). Wisdom will come from observation of God's creation and how well it functions (1 Kings 4:30, 33 – although we need guidance as to what to observe and what to learn from it; see 7:7; 20:12). An ant, a mindless insect, doesn't have leadership, isn't told what to do (6:7), yet does something very wise – it works when food is plentiful to store up what is needed (6:8). No get-rich-quick scheme for the ant. It exemplifies, albeit unintentionally, good planning and disciplined hard work. This is what the youth should have been doing. Instead of entering some dubious deal with a stranger, a lazy way to make money, he should have worked sensibly for his livelihood. God is generous and provides food (Psalms 104:14–15 136:25; 146:7; 147:9) – this is a reason for working to enjoy it, not an excuse for avoiding work.

The student needs to stop lying around doing nothing, the teacher goes on (6:9). Get up! On your feet! Get to work! The words of verse 9 – 'How long will you lie there?' – suggest complacency, not genuine rest. This lying about has been going on for some time. This is the background problem, the reason why the youth fell into the trap at the start of the chapter. That was an immediate problem, and the teacher betrayed his agitation that the youth needed to get out of it, fast. But here we have the root problem – he is lazy.[3] He does not have the right attitude to work and money; he prefers idleness (6:10). But laziness will bring poverty (6:11). Poverty here denotes not just lack, but also destitution, being without food or other necessities.[4] This is not the poverty of the blameless poor, for whom the Lord has special compassion (19:17).[5] It is poverty owing to folly, to idle dreams and laziness. Money will not appear miraculously, and to think this way is to become vulnerable to

3 See 'The sluggard', in Kidner, *Proverbs*, 42–3.

4 Waltke, *The Book of Proverbs*, I.339.

5 Waltke points out that Proverbs does not address poverty owing to natural disasters such as famine or other calamity, as Job does. Not all poverty is owing to folly; this was a mistake of Job's comforters. Waltke, *The Book of Proverbs*, I.340.

unsound business deals. Poverty will come like a thief, like an armed man, like someone out to take you unawares, like the stranger who proposed the deal in verse 1.

So, the teacher says, you need to reform your ways – start having more sense in how you approach work. This is the more important lesson. The youth needs to take responsibility and get himself working, with forethought and organisation. Even ants are doing better.

We have seen here not just wise teaching, but teaching in a wise way. The immediate problem is put in the context of the underlying bad pattern of behaviour that made it possible. The teacher deals not only with the immediate application, but also with the general life principles that will stop the problem from occurring again. It is done emphatically, with illustrations from nature to capture the attention. One could take lessons here on how to construct a sermon.

2. The troublemaker • Proverbs 6:12–15

We now have a few verses on a new topic, about a troublemaker. This is the kind of person, a *beliyya'al*, who is against God and his people (Deuteronomy 13:13; 1 Samuel 2:12; Nahum 1:11, 15), against justice (1 Kings 21:10) and community (Deuteronomy 15:9; Judges 19:22; 1 Samuel 30:22; Psalm 101:3).

How do we recognise such a person? What characteristics will such a person have? Using five body parts, which the NIV brings out clearly, the teacher details what this disruptive person does, and then what the results will be. This description is both a warning not to be such a troublemaker and a warning to stay away from this kind of person. This is the kind of person who may well have started out by being lazy and wanting easy money. Such behaviour can easily escalate into worse.

12 A troublemaker and a villain,
who goes about with a corrupt mouth,
13 who winks maliciously with his eye,
signals with his feet
and motions with his fingers,
14 who plots evil with deceit in his heart –
he always stirs up conflict.

15 Therefore disaster will overtake him in an instant; he will suddenly be destroyed – without remedy.

This worthless person is summed up as morally corrupt. Why? First, he has 'a corrupt mouth' (6:12); his speech is twisted, not to be trusted. He is the sort of person who spreads rumours, speaks ill of others, gossips and slanders. His eyes wink (6:13); the implication is a malicious expression, conspiring behind someone's back. Even non-verbally he tries to signal evil and spread malice. His feet literally grind, or scrape, signalling something bad. His fingers point – apparently a gesture of ridicule in Egyptian and Sumerian Wisdom literature[6] – or this could be seen as accusatory pointing or giving instructions to fellow plotters. Externally, then, everything he does is antisocial.

What about internally? His inner being, his heart, is perverted (6:14). He is thinking about how to do evil, more ways of doing the things that his outer body is involved in, more ways of disrupting other people and sowing discord. Moreover, he is always doing this (see Genesis 6:5). It's his habitual way of being.

Calamity will come upon this person; those who create trouble are likely to make trouble for themselves. Moreover, this will happen suddenly, in a moment, and will be devastating. We can think up all sorts of scenarios in which a habitual troublemaker, a creator of mischief and social disharmony, will receive a comeuppance. It is the stuff of any number of stories. One who continually divides community and treats others badly will have no community support, but rather will create wrath. Some individuals may be able to get away with malice for some time, but it is a comfort to know that this way of life brings trouble for the one who lives it. For as verse 15 makes clear, the context is not just some implacable karma or an automatic rule of nature, but God's judgment. God hates this kind of behaviour and will provide justice, in this world or the next.

It is good to be able to recognise a person who simply wants to create trouble and so not be drawn into the conflict, or at least be wary of it. Part of wisdom is not to be gullible, to be able to

6 Overland, *Proverbs*, 131.

see such trouble coming. It is also a warning for us not to be that person, for it is surprisingly easy to fall into petty malice, to respond to the difficulties of life and other people's sin by becoming twisted oneself and eager to take revenge in all sorts of small ways upon others for one's own less-than-satisfactory life, or simply for the fun of it. Do not do it. Do not do it in your personal life, do not do it online, do not do it even if you are anonymous. Here, the warning depends upon the trouble that will come upon you as a result; later teaching will emphasise that regardless of outcome, such action is wrong in itself. Especially for the Christian, we have multiple warnings against creating social discord – in fact this theme dominates the moral teaching of the New Testament (consider Romans 12:14–18; Ephesians 4:2, 31; 1 Peter 3:8; 1 Timothy 6:4; Titus 3:3). Create harmony, do what is good for others and be patient with them; don't be the person who tries to mislead or create discord among others.

3. What the Lord hates • Proverbs 6:16–19

We have just seen how to recognise a worthless person. The next few verses tell us about someone even worse: a hateworthy person (6:16). This is not someone detested just by others, but by God. This heightens the impact of this section; the name of God is being invoked to emphasise the importance of what is said here.

16 There are six things the LORD hates,
seven that are detestable to him:
17 haughty eyes,
a lying tongue,
hands that shed innocent blood,
18 a heart that devises wicked schemes,
feet that are quick to rush into evil,
19 a false witness who pours out lies
and a person who stirs up conflict in the community.

This hateworthy person destroys others, and God hates it, finds it an abomination. This is strong language: we are talking about the covenant God, whose compassion and mercy are his leading characteristics, who is love itself. Whatever this God hates has to be what is at the other extremity of love, something truly terrible. These things are revolting to God; the language suggests they make him cringe.

Again, using elements of what bodies do, the wise teacher will tell the youth what an absolutely loathsome person amounts to, and just how bad such a person's effect can be. This is only a short section, but in this pithy sevenfold saying we have a depth of moral teaching that effectively sums up what the godly person should not be.

These things are six plus one, a numerical symbol for plenitude.[7] The seven things are set out in a symmetric pattern revolving around the mind, or heart, in verse 18a.[8] Outside the heart are hands/feet, tongue/false witness. The first and last elements are things that create conflict between people.

First, this person's eyes are 'haughty'; he looks down on people, he is condescending (6:17a). It's a sign of pride, of putting oneself above other people (Isaiah 10:12–14; Daniel 11:12). It denies God's authority (Job 21:22; 38:15; Psalm 101:5; Isaiah 2:11–17; 10:33). It is the opposite of what God's people should be, for God prizes a humble heart (Isaiah 2:11–17). The God who came to earth not to be served but to serve wants his people to follow his example, in humility valuing others above oneself (Philippians 2:3). The loathsome person is the opposite, valuing himself above other people. This is parallel to the seventh characteristic: he stirs up conflict, he creates controversy (6:19b). This is in contrast to what God wants of his people: we are entirely to avoid foolish controversies (Titus 3:9); it is the false teachers who have an unhealthy interest in controversies, resulting in envy, strife, malicious talk, evil suspicions and constant friction between people. This is a very strong element in the ethical teaching of the New Testament: do not be the person who likes to create conflict. It damages communities and people, and is entirely opposed to the character of God.

Characteristics two and six are also parallel. This detestable person has a lying tongue (6:17b) and is a false witness who pours out lies (6:19a). Lies are totally against God's character. It is the devil who is

7 Overland, *Proverbs*, 138.

8 Although Ansberry takes this as a linear pattern, working from the head down.

a liar and the father of lies (John 8:44). God destroys those who tell lies (Psalm 5:6); it is the wicked man who reviles the Lord whose mouth is full of lies and threats (Psalm 10:7). Throughout Scripture, telling lies is characteristic of God's enemies, the opposite of what his people should do; the eschatological vision of Zephaniah 3:13 describes the humble remnant as those who will tell no lies, for all liars will be consigned to the fiery lake (Revelation 21:8). Lies destroy, and it is no surprise that in our current times of cultural turmoil, a poor regard for truth is widespread, and the concept of being able to trust a person's word seems no longer to be a cultural value – while we still all hate being lied to, as parliamentary scandals show.

The third characteristic of the detestable person in 6:17c is 'hands that shed innocent blood'. This is parallel with the 'feet that are quick to rush into evil' (6:18b). His hands and his feet are both being used as weapons to destroy others. These hands are not just pointing at people, as in the previous section; now they are killing the innocent. The behaviour has escalated. With his feet he is not walking the path of wisdom as the youth has previously been advised; nor is this person merely strolling down the wrong path. He is rushing into evil; he can't wait to get there. He is using his body without constraint; he does not hesitate to find evil.[9]

In a culture that elevates the killing of the innocent to an absolute right through the campaigns in favour of abortion, and which seems to be accelerating in its enshrinement of immorality as uncriticisable, this description seems all too familiar. We can see the results in conflict, as the result is described in verse 19. Division in the church and in society is all too common and public, and debate descends into vilification and death threats, in those instances where it is not seeking to eliminate opposing views altogether by preventing speakers even from speaking to those who invite them. It is difficult to know how to defend truth when conflict is so rife. Yet as God's people we are to 'live at peace with everyone', as much as is possible (Romans 12:18). We must not respond to anger with anger, however hard it is.

At the centre of all this detestable behaviour is the heart, verse

9 See the parallels brought out by Ansberry between *Proverbs 6:12–19* and 16:27–30. *Ansberry, Proverbs.*

18a. Wicked schemes come from the heart. And all our hearts, in the end, are evil; deceitful above all things and beyond cure (Jeremiah 17:9); 'desperately wicked' in the King James Version. Wisdom will be to fight these tendencies of our hearts, which run to pride, violence and hurt; but the only cure is the new heart with the law written on it promised in Jeremiah 31:33, in the new covenant that will turn sorrow into joy. The heart of flesh promised by Ezekiel (36:26) is what comes with the gift of the Spirit in Christ Jesus. Walking in step with this spirit is characterised by all the things that are the opposite of the pride, violence, lies and discord described above; his fruit is 'love, joy, peace, forbearance, kindness, goodness, faithfulness, gentleness and self-control' (Galatians 5:22–3), the things that put others first and bring social harmony.

Conclusion to Proverbs 6:1–19

In just three short verses of Proverbs (6:17–19) we have a summary not just of this section, but of what God's people are not to be; the opposite of what we are called to be. The warning is profound and specific: do not be like this. Wisdom and God himself warn us that this is loathsome. The wise teacher could not put this more strongly. This is not just his own teaching as the result of long reflection and experience; this is the opinion of God himself. It reminds us that there is more to wisdom than just a fruitful way to live. We are dealing with the judge of humankind. These words matter.

8

The Cost of Wrong Desire

PROVERBS 6:20–35

Women feature a lot in the book of Proverbs, not just in the course of teaching about people but as teachers themselves. The pupil is told to heed his mother's teaching, as well as being taught by his father – her teaching is equated with the father's (see Exodus 20:12; 21:15, 17; Leviticus 19:3; Deuteronomy 21:18–21). Wisdom appears as a woman, teaching by word and example, offering guidance through life. Against her the adulterous woman also teaches but advises a completely different course of action, and tries by all means possible to persuade the student to follow her. For both good and evil, women are powerful teachers.

Throughout chapters 1–9 of Proverbs, Overland suggests that we can imagine the student asking his teacher a number of questions, to which he receives comprehensive answers. For 6:20–35 he suggests that the student asks, 'Sex between consenting adults . . . what's the harm?'[1]

It's a question both implicitly and explicitly asked frequently in western culture, and the culture's answer is an emphatic, unambiguous, 'Absolutely no harm at all.' Consent has come to be almost the only moral boundary when it comes to sex.[2] As long as both parties agree, it has to be all right – although we should have realised by now that consent can be severely compromised given power imbalances and other external factors, such as peer pressure and a generally sexualised atmosphere in society. The wisdom teacher has considerably more to say on the matter.

---

1 Overland, *Proverbs*, 140.

2 An age of consent exists in law in most countries, although in Britain at least there have been ongoing calls to lower it further since the late twentieth century. Sex with children, however, still remains taboo, although one wonders when this restriction will fall as well; presenting children with explicitly sexual material in schools is already well entrenched.

1. Wisdom as your guide • Proverbs 6:20–35

The teaching here expands on what God's law has already said: 'You shall not commit adultery' (Exodus 20:14). Why not? What's the harm? The teacher first presents the woman of wisdom, who will lead the student along the path of the law – we are working up to chapter 8, where wisdom's close relationship with the God who gave the law will be more fully worked out. In contrast, a picture of adultery is given, with analysis of what it is and the harm it does.

Warning against adultery

20 My son, keep your father's
command
and do not forsake your
mother's teaching.
21 Bind them always on your heart;
fasten them round your neck.
22 When you walk, they will guide
you;
when you sleep, they will
watch over you;
when you awake, they will
speak to you.
23 For this command is a lamp,
this teaching is a light,
and correction and instruction
are the way to life,
24 keeping you from your neighbour's wife,
from the smooth talk of a
wayward woman.

25 Do not lust in your heart after
her beauty
or let her captivate you with
her eyes.
26 For a prostitute can be had for
a loaf of bread,
but another man's wife preys
on your very life.
27 Can a man scoop fire into his lap
without his clothes being burned?
28 Can a man walk on hot coals
without his feet being
scorched?
29 So is he who sleeps with
another man's wife;
no one who touches her will
go unpunished.

30 People do not despise a thief if
he steals
to satisfy his hunger when he
is starving.
31 Yet if he is caught, he must pay
sevenfold,
though it costs him all the
wealth of his house.
32 But a man who commits
adultery has no sense;
whoever does so destroys
himself.

33 Blows and disgrace are his lot,
and his shame will never be
wiped away.

34 For jealousy arouses a
husband's fury,
and he will show no mercy
when he takes revenge.
35 He will not accept any
compensation;
he will refuse a bribe, however
great it is.

We begin this teaching with a reminder to the student to safeguard the wisdom he receives (6:20). What he learns from the teaching of his mother and father is to be heeded, not neglected, not ignored. On the contrary, it is to be bound on his heart, fastened around his neck (6:21), reminiscent of what the Israelites are to do with the Lord's commands in Deuteronomy 6:8–9 (also 11:8, 18–20). The point is that these teachings are precious, and for daily life; they are not something just to be kept in a reference book on the shelf or learned once for an exam and then forgotten. They are not a convenient Wikipedia entry to be accessed on a whim. No, they are to be right there with you, all the time, part of the very clothes you wear.

These teachings, this wisdom, are like your personal guide (6:22). The NIV continues to refer to the teachings impersonally – 'they will guide you'. However, the pronoun is feminine; the teaching is referred to as 'she' and so recalls the woman of wisdom who last appeared in chapter 3. It is she who will guide him, who watches over him when he is asleep and defenceless, and speaks to him when he is awake. The picture is one of care, and of reason: she talks to him; she is not the taskmaster who simply orders him around or yells at him like a TV weight-loss coach. She instructs in a way that engages his mind, so he can learn how to navigate the day (see Deuteronomy 11:18–20).

This wisdom is the one effectively holding the lamp (6:23a), which is what a commandment really is: a source of light, by which to see what is there, where obstacles are and where the right, safe path is (see Job 18:6; 29:3; Psalm 119:105). Neither God's commands nor the teacher's instructions are harsh; they are not trying to take away happiness or spoil fun. That is how God's commandments are often seen, especially when it comes to sexual ethics. They are not just presented as old-fashioned and repressive, but actually abusive, morally offensive and both physically and mentally unhealthy. On the contrary, the teacher says, the instruction – even the parts of it that are correction and reprimand (6:23b) – are light. They give life (6:23c). And one way they especially give life is to keep the student from adultery, no matter how attractive or necessary or life-giving it might seem.

The adulterous woman, the immediate contrast to the woman of wisdom, also speaks, but her talk is 'smooth' (6:24). She's slippery. She's not offering open, reasoned debate; she is using her speech to manipulate. The battle for wisdom is first fought in the mind. It begins there, and the student is warned about how important his mind, his internal life, is (6:25). The 'lust in your heart' is a mental battle; it is about fantasies and imagined plans, the very thing that Jesus warned not to do in Matthew 5:28 (see also James 1:13–15; Exodus 20:17; Deuteronomy 5:21). Thinking about adultery is the first step to doing it, so don't even start. What you think about matters; it is not just private musing, it will play out in your life, in your emotions and levels of contentment, in what you resent and what you aim for, and it will affect what you do. Don't start. Don't be captivated, even if she's beautiful and lovely; and eyes can be captivating. Look elsewhere.

Hearts are powerful, but can be taught; that is the point of learning wisdom, after all (4:23). Ultimately, we know that the Holy Spirit is required to renew and regenerate hearts, and he is available; ask, and he will be given (see Luke 11:13). We are to avoid sin in our hearts, which will be reflected in our behaviour, and we are given everything we need to do so. That is why we must make every effort to follow Scripture's wise teaching.

The teaching that follows gives reasons for avoiding sexual immorality. It will cost, in all sorts of ways. A prostitute requires a fee (6:26); this is not a discourse on prostitution or what might force women into it, or even at this point a discourse on the evils of prostitution for all involved, just an observation that there is monetary cost to the customer. Adultery, however, which appears to be without a fee, can cost your life (see 1 Corinthians 6:13–20; Galatians 5:19–21; Ephesians 5:5; 1 Thessalonians 4:1–8).

Anyone who has walked with those who have been caught up in or touched by adultery can testify to this. Adultery ruins relationships, it ruins families and it ruins people. The damage can last for generations. Marriage is a matter of trust – giving your word and keeping your word. Breaking those promises is a deep betrayal from which the relationship may never recover. No matter which partner it is who actually commits the adultery, both are damaged; and if there are children, they can be scarred for life and carry the damage into their own adult relationships. Marriage, meant to be lifelong, is a deep and profound bond, a picture of the strongest bond there is – that between Christ and the church, we are told in Ephesians 5. Yet even that bond, meant to be lifelong, can be broken by adultery. That is how devastating and serious adultery is.

This is precisely what the next few images in chapter 6 portray. It's like carrying fire – something insanely dangerous. It's like setting alight your own clothing (6:27). You just can't do it without being damaged, any more than you can walk around on hot coals without scorching your feet (6:28).[3] That's what it's like if you commit adultery (6:29). It's a terminally stupid thing to do, and you will be hurt; there will be punishment, of one sort or another.

Think about thieving, the next comparison goes (6:30). People might understand a thief, especially if they steal merely to eat when they are starving (see 30:9). Stories of the convicts who were sent to Australia during its days as a penal colony often tell of poor people with nothing, who stole merely to eat. Such stories are told to defend them: they weren't so bad, is the suggestion. (My own ancestor wasn't so pitiable; he stole some clothing and was deported, but since his family was relatively well to do, I've always wondered why he did it.) If you steal merely to eat, you won't be despised; but it's still a crime (6:31). Under Israelite law you're still obliged to pay back what you stole; you might even have to pay a fee as punishment, up to all your belongings (a poetic exaggeration of the law, Exodus 22:1, 7, 9; see also Luke 19:8 – seven times just stands for 'full compensation'). That's a tough punishment.

---

3 Waltke seems to suggest this may be a euphemism for a sexually transmitted disease. *The Book of Proverbs*, I.356.

Committing adultery, however, is far worse. It's senseless. It's self-destructive (6:32). It's shameful, and brings disgrace and harm (6:33). The suggested parallel is that stealing to eat may save you, but adultery will destroy you. It's socially disgraceful, and understandably brings wrath from an outraged husband who has been betrayed (6:34). This is the second comparison against adultery. Betrayal, bringing with it some of the deepest hurt possible, can also arouse some of the most furious anger possible. Such anger cannot be calmed with money (6:35). You have done something that destroys life; don't think that any payment can possibly make it better. The negative 'not' (*lo*) appears four times in verses 33–5, emphasising how inevitable and appalling the consequences of adultery are.

Conclusion to Proverbs 6:20–35

This is why wisdom is so important. What might seem at the start to be a good thing leads to destruction, wrath and injury. Faithfulness matters. Stay with wisdom, who will care for you while you sleep, not disgrace you. Adultery costs, far beyond any pleasure it may bring.

Are you listening? Possibly not, the teacher seems to think, for now he has a story.

9

Words of Life

PROVERBS 7

Now, in powerful and graphic language, the warnings given in earlier chapters are portrayed as a narrative. Whether it is a fictitious illustration or whether the father really did witness something like this, the detail is striking. The father is doing all he can to protect his son and warn him against danger. Like the stories of the criminals in chapter 1, the temptation is presented realistically and recognising all its attractiveness. Every effort is made to show how a deception can take place.

1. A story • Proverbs 7

We already know that our need for wisdom is immense; it cannot be overstated. Each time the sage begins a new teaching segment, he calls the student back to the importance of listening and following this instruction. Chapter 7, the tenth lecture, begins with another such exhortation. Consider what this tells us about the book of Proverbs. Any part of Scripture should be heeded; it is all inspired by God, and 'useful for teaching, rebuking, correcting and training in righteousness, so that [we] may be thoroughly equipped for every good work' (2 Timothy 3:16–17). Not listening to Scripture, not heeding it and doing what it says, is like looking in a mirror and then forgetting what you saw, James says (James 1:23–4) – it is like realising 'my face needs a wash' or 'my hair has glue in it' (as many a Sunday School teacher may experience) and then walking out to an important meeting without doing anything about it. Listen, take heed and do what it says. These are the words of life.

Warning against the adulterous woman

7 My son, keep my words
and store up my commands
within you.
2 Keep my commands and you
will live;
guard my teachings as the
apple of your eye.
3 Bind them on your fingers;
write them on the tablet of
your heart.
4 Say to wisdom, 'You are my
sister,'
and to insight, 'You are my
relative.'
5 They will keep you from the
adulterous woman,
from the wayward woman with
her seductive words.

6 At the window of my house
I looked down through the
lattice.
7 I saw among the simple,
I noticed among the young men,
a youth who had no sense.
8 He was going down the street
near her corner,
walking along in the direction
of her house
9 at twilight, as the day was
fading,
as the dark of night set in.

10 Then out came a woman to
meet him,
dressed like a prostitute and
with crafty intent.
11 (She is unruly and defiant,
her feet never stay at home;
12 now in the street, now in the
squares,
at every corner she lurks.)
13 She took hold of him and
kissed him
and with a brazen face she
said:

14 'Today I fulfilled my vows,
and I have food from my
fellowship offering at home.
15 So I came out to meet you;
I looked for you and have
found you!
16 I have covered my bed
with coloured linens from Egypt.
17 I have perfumed my bed
with myrrh, aloes and
cinnamon.
18 Come, let's drink deeply of love
till morning;
let's enjoy ourselves with love!
19 My husband is not at home;
he has gone on a long journey.
20 He took his purse filled with
money
and will not be home till full
moon.'

21 With persuasive words she led
him astray;
she seduced him with her
smooth talk.

22 All at once he followed her
like an ox going to the
slaughter,
like a deer[a] stepping into a noose[b]
23 till an arrow pierces his liver,
like a bird darting into a snare,
little knowing it will cost him
his life.

24 Now then, my sons, listen to me;
pay attention to what I say.
25 Do not let your heart turn to
her ways
or stray into her paths.
26 Many are the victims she has
brought down;
her slain are a mighty throng.
27 Her house is a highway to the
grave,
leading down to the chambers
of death.

a 22 Syriac (see also Septuagint); Hebrew *fool*
b 22 The meaning of the Hebrew for this line is uncertain.

The father gives urgent encouragement to listen to his words, which present the wisdom of God. We are to keep them and treasure them (7:1). In fact, 'Keep my commands and you will *live*,' the sage says in 7:2 (my emphasis), as opposed to the death following immorality (2:18; 6:26; 7:27). These words will be the safeguard against the 'seductive words' (7:5) and 'smooth talk' (7:21) of the adulteress. So guard these teachings 'as the apple of your eye' (7:2). Keep them as close to you as your eyes and value them as much, the father is saying; protect them as you would your eyes, the organ of illumination. Have them bound on your fingers, something you can never forget or ignore. Write them on the tablet of your heart; in other words, let these be part of your very self (7:3), which suggests memorising them. Make wisdom a member of your family, and insight part of your inner circle (7:4). That's how important listening to wisdom is. Remembering these words will save us from real danger (7:5).

For this is a high-stakes game. What the sage will go on to demonstrate – something we all know – is that feelings are powerful, and it is only too easy to let them overpower us. In the fairly explicit story that follows in this chapter, we see a perfect picture of seduction. It is how seduction happens. Whether the seducer is female or male, whatever form our passions take for each of us, it's very true that when our senses are engaged and we are promised fun without reprisals, there seems to be no reason not to. Bodies were made capable of easy arousal.

The teaching of this chapter is no different from the previous passage, but how much more powerful it is when in the form of a story. There is something about stories that captures our minds and emotions. We are social creatures, and so we relate to characters as they live out their lives; a story can grasp us, engage us and live in our memory far more than propositional logic or dry instruction. The dry instruction is necessary, as we don't always understand the point of a story, but we need stories to move us and capture our imaginations. It is why social movements thrive on storytelling, on personal narratives, on films and novels and biographies. Here the characters are all too real. The 'youth who had no sense' (7:7) – we all know plenty of young people like that; in fact, it is what we were all like. The 'woman with her seductive words' (7:5) – there are women and men like that the world over. Shifting to a story in this chapter makes the warnings against adultery all too real. It's not just theory; this is what happens when ordinary people follow their emotions without thinking through consequences. 'What were you thinking?' a friend of mine asked his colleague, aghast, having just heard that the colleague's marriage had been destroyed by adultery. 'I wasn't thinking,' was the sad answer. It is the same with the story here.

The details of place and situation draw us into stories as they start. Here, we are given the detail of the storyteller looking down at the street from his window (7:6). This is real life, the introduction implies. A group of young people on the corner, just socialising, just hanging out. One young man was impulsive; he 'had no sense' (7:7): look where he was heading! Down that corner, towards her house (7:8). It was dark (7:9) – that detail is part of setting the scene. We have the image of foolishness, a young person taking no care. The evening setting acts as a bit of realism; this is when socialising happens, after all, often lubricated by alcohol. But as well as that the emphasis on darkness provides atmosphere. This is something happening in secret, with a sense of foreboding.

And looked what happens. The camera pans to someone waiting; a bold figure, seductively dressed, waiting for this opportunity for conquest (7:10). Here, it's a wife looking for an affair while her husband is away. It could equally be a husband, looking for relief from the wife and kids in a workplace liaison. It could be the attractive profile on a dating site, someone presenting themselves as up for it. There will be seducers, and the young and hormonally charged will walk right into their invitations.

The woman is presented as seductively dressed, possibly hiding her identity (a prostitute's outfit could include a veil, Genesis 38:14); 'with crafty intent' (7:10), willing to deceive her husband and find another conquest. She's 'unruly and defiant', the metaphor suggesting not literal loudness, but restlessness (7:11–12); she's wandering around, on the prowl.

Then she finds her prey and starts her seduction (7:13–20). She grabs the boy and openly kisses him; no ambiguity here. It's fun. There's nothing to stop us, she says; there are no distractions, and you're just the one I was looking for. I'm actually a good person; look at all the good, religious things I did today! The bedroom is gorgeous, all the senses overwhelmed with indulgence. Let's have a good time. No one will interrupt us; no one will ever know. She flatters his ego and his senses, she has prepared an aphrodisiacal paradise (see Song of Songs 4:14), she assures him there is no threat of discovery. No revenge from an outraged husband to be feared here.

The 'persuasive words' work (7:21); given that this is a youth without sense, and probably by now without any other thoughts in his head at all, she doesn't have to try too hard! He follows her 'like an ox going to the slaughter'. Mindless following, but the narrative has suddenly taken a very dark turn. The images are of death; slaughter, being caught, an arrow in the liver (sounds very painful), the bird in a snare. Like all these animals trapped by the hunter, he is now helpless, not realising he was walking into death (7:22–3).

I can remember a preacher talking about what to do if you get to the point of adultery; what to do if you find yourself in bed with someone who is not your rightful marriage partner. What should you do? 'Run out of the house naked,' was his advice, rather than go through with it. Treat this as a matter of life and death. Even public humiliation would be better than immorality. It feels good, but it is deathly – spiritual death. Don't be the unwitting animal walking into the slaughterhouse.

So, listen, the teacher sums up (7:24). He is back in instructional mode now. You have heard the story; you can picture to yourself how easy it would be, how good it seems. Pleasing to the eye, and desirable, but still a trap. So don't! Don't do it! Don't let your heart turn to this way (7:25); instead, train your heart now, before temptation arises. Make sure you are prepared so that you do not stray into the wrong path, when the path presents itself. This kind of teaching and training needs to start young, and to be presented in a place of seriousness and calmness, before the moment of passion hits. Children do need sex education – the world is right about that. Proverbs shows us the kind of education they actually need.

'Many are the victims she has brought down' (7:26) – we can think of 'she' not just as the archetypical wicked woman, but as lust for the wrong thing in itself, and so just as applicable for women as for men. Don't let your lust take you the wrong way, whatever that way may be. Your capacity for arousal exists for a very good reason – for marriage, for the strengthening of that intimate, lifelong bond, and its rewards there can be great. Don't misuse it, for in the wrong context it will bring you down. It's a 'highway to the grave' (7:27). Literally, the highway to hell.

Conclusion to Proverbs 7

This chapter of Proverbs has been very carefully structured. The direct teaching begins and ends the narrative story. There are repeated words; *ishon*, the 'pupil' of the eye in verse 2 is the same word as the 'dark' of night in verse 9. The story starts with the teacher's house, moves to the seducer's house and finishes with the house as a highway to the grave. Life begins the story; death ends it. Good words are contrasted with slippery words. In many ways, we can see elements in the story that build up its intensity. Similarly, this story is a fitting conclusion to the build-up of teaching against adultery. The parallels between the introductions (2:15 and 7:5) and the conclusions (2:18–19 and 7:26–27) suggest that these chapters are a deliberate literary unit.

Most of all, we see a warning to avoid the danger, in the personifications of the two women. Listen to wisdom, who should be your sister, your relative, the one you love. Don't listen to the one sending you to death, even though that feels so good. The foolish youth lost his mind; he didn't guard insight and keep it close to him. Protect yourself. Don't go to the places where you are likely to be tempted. Beware of the justifications that make sin seem so right, so harmless: thoughts such as we're good people, we're just going where our hearts lead us, I need to do what's good for me. Beware of the power of your own senses, the pleasure that comes from beauty – a good thing, but powerfully dangerous in the wrong cause. Beware the claim that there will be no consequences, that nothing bad will happen. There always are consequences. Remember that this is not just harmless indulgence. God gives us these warnings for a reason. Treat sexual purity as important as your life itself.

Hold on to this wisdom; it truly is wisdom, and it is so worth having and clinging to, even if all your senses and every fibre of your body are telling you otherwise. Take wisdom deep within you. In the next chapter, we will see just how valuable this wisdom is.

10

The Call of Wisdom

PROVERBS 8:1–21

There are many directions we could take a discussion of Proverbs 8. It was prominent in early debates about the Trinity, as the similarity between wisdom as personified in this chapter and Christ is obvious. We could consider detailed arguments about what wisdom actually is in biblical teaching. Most importantly, however, we need to consider what the chapter teaches in the context of the book.

1. Wisdom's power • Proverbs 8:1–11

There are similarities between this chapter and wisdom's speech in chapter 2; once again, wisdom is calling publicly for people to learn from her. However, her teaching here is different, emphasising her ultimate origins and the nature of creation. We see a recapitulation of the earlier chapter, but also build upon it. This is the ultimate answer to the smooth seduction of evil presented so powerfully in the person of the adulteress of the previous chapter. How do we resist the lure of temptation? By understanding just how much better the alternative is. There is a far better woman to follow. She's a fantastic teacher, and she's taking on students right now.

Wisdom's call

8 Does not wisdom call out?
Does not understanding raise
her voice?
2 At the highest point along the
way,
where the paths meet, she
takes her stand;
3 beside the gate leading into the
city,
at the entrance, she cries
aloud:

4 'To you, O people, I call out;
I raise my voice to all humanity.
5 You who are simple, gain prudence;
you who are foolish, set your hearts on it.[a]
6 Listen, for I have trustworthy things to say;
I open my lips to speak what is right.
7 My mouth speaks what is true,
for my lips detest wickedness.
8 All the words of my mouth are just;
none of them is crooked or perverse.
9 To the discerning all of them are right;
they are upright to those who have found knowledge.
10 Choose my instruction instead of silver,
knowledge rather than choice gold,
11 for wisdom is more precious than rubies,
and nothing you desire can compare with her.

[a] 5 Septuagint; Hebrew *foolish, instruct your minds*

The teacher is calling you to class (8:1). She is wisdom; she is understanding; she is also insight (8:14). There she is, at the top of that hill, in that prominent place 'along the way' where everyone walks (8:2a). Now she's at the crossroads, perhaps also the metaphorical crossroads where people must choose their path (8:2b), and there she goes to the city gates, the most important part of the city where the leaders meet to discuss policy and government (8:3). She is not hidden away on a remote mountain, but out there in the city, willing to teach anyone and everyone, and they all need her. The lady of wisdom is about to make a speech; it's worth listening to. In fact, it's one of the most important speeches you will ever hear.

For this is a speech from wisdom, from understanding, from insight. This is the source of knowledge. As a species, humans are very hungry for knowledge; this is, no doubt, part of our God-given place as rulers of creation. Well, here it is; the best knowledge possible.

This is what the woman of wisdom offers us. But it is not just head knowledge, which is what most of us are after. She will offer far more than that, for she will tell us that there is much more to the world and even to theology than just facts. She will give us the inside story, the deep dive into understanding, not just how to think but also how to live, what to love and what to desire, how to be truly wise humans.

So what does wisdom say? First, she is talking to everyone, to all humankind (8:4). To all humans, wisdom cries out, and is doing so continuously. 'You,' she says; 'you there, I'm talking to you.' This is an invitation for everyone. Rich, poor, young, old, all races, all backgrounds. Wisdom is not something for the initiated elite, whatever form that initiation may take.

In the early church, groups of Gnostics carried out special rites to bring people further and further into supposedly higher knowledge. Knowledge was secret, only available for those who had undergone the right ceremonies, passed all the tests. Secret societies still abound, promising deeper, better knowledge the further you penetrate the organisation – usually with a higher fee at each level. Whether the secrets at the end are worth it may be up for debate, but the organisation leaders will certainly have profited by the time you get there.

The official knowledge industry also has its initiation rites; in order to qualify as truly knowledgeable, you need to go through the right process, the rite of obtaining a degree and then higher degrees, in the right discipline, at the right university. Only then can you give an opinion.

This is not to deride education or expertise – some topics are complicated and need long hours of study to master. Wisdom of any sort is not easy. But neither is it only for those wealthy enough or privileged enough to follow the world's educational structures. Wisdom will teach something far more important than the details of quantum physics.[1] More importantly, she will stop you from being simple and aimless; she will also stop you from being a fool (8:5). This audience she is especially concerned to reach. The 'malformed, uncommitted, and untutored gullible . . . [and] the spiritually dull and insensible fools', as Waltke calls them[2] – that is, most of us – are given the chance to change. Wisdom will teach prudence, that quality of character that means that life can thrive. What she says

1 Although such a detailed study of the world can certainly be done as part of wisdom.

2 Waltke, *The Book of Proverbs*, I.396.

can be trusted; she will speak of what is right, what is honest and trustworthy.

For wisdom is not just about knowing how the world works; or rather, how the world works is about much more than technical details. For reality is moral, and knowing morality is even more important than knowing factual details. And so wisdom herself is moral as she teaches. She speaks the truth and rejects wickedness.

This is something not often recognised in academic study of the world. Scientists have traditionally, and quite vehemently, insisted on value-free knowledge, asserted that scientific research is about the facts, and any neutral observer is capable of right knowledge. Concerns of morality are a matter of private opinion and should never impinge upon what happens in the lab.

Of course, most scientists would still balk at, say, obtaining experimental data through torture or murder, as happened in the World War II concentration camps. But there is still a strong sense that pure research should not be restricted by moral concerns over, for example, the rightness of experiments on embryonic cell cultures or suchlike. Knowledge itself is certainly seen as morally neutral. What *is* has nothing to do with what *ought*, the famous 'naturalistic fallacy' goes. Be as moral or immoral as you like outside the lab; knowledge itself is value free.

Yet philosophers of science have for decades been pointing out that no knowledge is ever neutral, and in fact the very practice of science depends upon the morality of scientists. For if scientists do not tell the truth, or cannot be trusted to tell the truth, the whole enterprise of science falls down. Scientific journals rely on scientists reporting their findings accurately and publishing them honestly. If scientists were to routinely lie in their publications, knowledge could never be accumulated.

Wisdom knows this; she speaks 'trustworthy things', high and important truths, and what is morally right (8:6). This is why people should listen to her. She will speak truth, and she will not speak wickedness (8:7). In parallel is verse 8 – her words are just, and not perverse. Those with insight themselves – those who have the right moral posture, who live according to God – will recognise them as such, and therefore benefit (8:9).

That is why her instruction is so valuable. Better than silver or gold (8:10), better than jewels *or anything else you may desire* (8:11) – a comprehensive commendation! This reminds us, of course, of something else that is better than silver or gold – the word of the Lord (Psalms 12:6; 119:72). This allusion is surely no accident, for as the chapter develops, wisdom will go on to describe just how close to God she is. But for now, let us see a little more about how valuable her words are: better than jewels, better than anything else you could desire.

It is nothing new for knowledge to be considered the highest good, better than any worldly wealth. The ancient Greek philosophers, although they disagreed on various details about what knowledge was and how to get it, generally agreed that seeking it was the best life possible. Aristotle and Plato agreed that the life of contemplation is the most noble, and the most satisfying – and also that it involves virtue, which they, unlike we moderns, did not separate from true knowledge. Wisdom agrees.

2. *Who is wisdom?* • *Proverbs 8:12–21*

We have a sense so far of the value of wisdom, and of what she can offer. We begin now to understand a little more of the nature of wisdom.

12 'I, wisdom, dwell together with prudence;
I possess knowledge and discretion.
13 To fear the LORD is to hate evil;
I hate pride and arrogance,
evil behaviour and perverse speech.
14 Counsel and sound judgment are mine;
I have insight, I have power.
15 By me kings reign
and rulers issue decrees that are just;
16 by me princes govern,
and nobles – all who rule on earth.[b]
17 I love those who love me,
and those who seek me find me.
18 With me are riches and honour,
enduring wealth and prosperity.
19 My fruit is better than fine gold;
what I yield surpasses choice silver.

20 I walk in the way of
righteousness,
along the paths of justice,
21 bestowing a rich inheritance
on those who love me
and making their treasuries
full.

b 16 Some Hebrew manuscripts and Septuagint; other Hebrew manuscripts *all righteous rulers*

Who is this wisdom? She is cleverness itself; she actually lives with prudence, the ability to make right and strategic decisions (8:12). She finds, attains, 'knowledge and discretion'. We already know from Proverbs 1 that wisdom starts with the fear of the Lord; we see further now that it is about hating evil, hating pride and arrogance, and hating evil behaviour and speech (8:13). It is about having a right stance in the world.

This, of course, makes sense if the world is indeed moral. The world is ordered – we know that from Genesis 1. God created it with order, with things reproducing according to their kinds, with regularities of times and seasons, with predictable patterns of growth and development. Yet more than that, it has a moral order; there are things that are right, there is justice and mercy, and these are not just invented concepts but truths about existence. All law actually depends upon that understanding; declarations of human rights assume it, and indeed any appeal to justice is based on a sense that justice is real, and matters. If that were not the case, then anyone could ignore claims of justice – why should I be fair? Why should I treat people equally? Why should I care about their feelings or their suffering or their lives? Why should I agree that any life matters? If we are simply pure accidents, and our concepts of justice were invented by human minds, then a human mind is free to reject them and do what it wants.

This vision of life is horrific, and we can praise God that we do not actually live in a universe like that. For justice is real; people do matter; concepts such as equality and dignity and care are not just fantasies invented by social theorists or idealists. Wisdom, knowing reality, is about knowing these things, not just about knowing how atoms work or how plants grow (good things to know, but there is more to reality than that). This is why it must begin with knowing and fearing the Lord, the creator of it all. For if we do not start with a recognition of this most basic fact about reality – who the most important being in reality is – then we will never get the rest of it in context.

Counsel and sound judgment come from wisdom (8:14). She has insight and power, for she is the true understanding of reality. So she is the place to go when you need these qualities. Only by having wisdom, this understanding of the morality in creation as well as the natural facts of creation, will kings rule well, will rulers be able to be just (8:15–16; see also Isaiah 11:2). It is wisdom who enables princes and political leaders to govern well. (If you ever wonder what to pray for our leaders, a prayer for wisdom is always relevant.)

Wisdom is also accessible. If you want it, if you seek wisdom, you will be able to find her. She will love you (8:17). Think about what you do concerning things that you love; you hold them in your heart, you think about them, you spend time on them. That is how we should be treating these words. Again, we see in verses 18–19 just how valuable wisdom is; if you truly want valuable riches, fine gold and choice silver, if you truly want honour and a good reputation, if you think those things worth having, then want wisdom more, for she is better. All the symbols of worldly wealth and wellbeing are encompassed here; and wisdom is more valuable than any of them.

And where will you find her? Along the paths of righteousness and justice (8:20). Walk where she walks. If that is what you are seeking, then that is where you will find wisdom, and she will reward you for it (8:21). Love wisdom, and you will have a full treasury.

Conclusion to Proverbs 8:1–21

As we go along further in the book of Proverbs, we will find that following wisdom – understanding how the world works, practically – will also, often, lead to physical riches and away from poverty. Knowledge is indeed power, as Francis Bacon (1561–1626) was famous for saying at the start of the scientific revolution.[3] When you know how the world works, you can work with it to gain great things; and

3 Francis Bacon, *Meditationes Sacrae* (1597).

knowledge and mastery of the world has indeed brought us many riches of technology, of health and better living – even as our lack of wisdom has seen such technology used unwisely, wastefully and inequitably. Knowledge with wisdom, in the way that this woman of wisdom will teach it, is what we need. For wisdom is part of the deep structure of creation itself, and this she will go on to explain in a passage that has dominated theological discussion for millennia.

11

A Grand Vision

PROVERBS 8:22–36

Now we reach out to the depths of primordial time and the vastness of the whole of creation as we start to grasp the extent of wisdom's power. Wisdom has cosmological significance. We find wisdom's ultimate eminence; it is no wonder that wisdom is so valuable and the basis of human thriving in this world. For wisdom stands before and above the whole of the rest of creation.

1. *Wisdom and creation* • *Proverbs 8:22–36*

We are entering the realms of the most profound understanding of God's work in the world. These verses have been pored over by scholars for centuries; they should leave us in awe at God's greatness, and his generosity to us. This is why we should listen to wisdom's call.

22 'The LORD brought me forth as
the first of his works,[c,d]
before his deeds of old;
23 I was formed long ages ago,
at the very beginning, when
the world came to be.
24 When there were no watery
depths, I was given birth,
when there were no springs
overflowing with water;
25 before the mountains were
settled in place,
before the hills, I was given
birth,
26 before he made the world or
its fields
or any of the dust of the earth.
27 I was there when he set the
heavens in place,
when he marked out the
horizon on the face of the
deep,
28 when he established the clouds
above
and fixed securely the fountains of the deep,

29 when he gave the sea its boundary
so that the waters would not overstep his command,
and when he marked out the foundations of the earth.
30 Then I was constantly[e] at his side.
I was filled with delight day after day,
rejoicing always in his presence,
31 rejoicing in his whole world
and delighting in the human race.
32 'Now then, my children, listen to me;
blessed are those who keep my ways.
33 Listen to my instruction and be wise;
do not disregard it.
34 Blessed are those who listen to me,
watching daily at my doors,
waiting at my doorway.
35 For those who find me find life
and receive favour from the LORD.
36 But those who fail to find me harm themselves;
all who hate me love death.'

c 22 Or *way*; or *dominion*
d 22 Or *The* LORD *possessed me at the beginning of his work*; or *The* LORD *brought me forth at the beginning of his work*
e 30 Or *was the master worker*; or *was a little child*

'The LORD brought me forth as the first of his works' (8:22), the NIV has it. The verb, *qanah*, has been highly controversial since early church history.[1] It can mean either to create or to acquire. 'Create' is argued for on the basis of some other Old Testament texts, and usages in Ugaritic. Other scholars, however, convincingly argue that 'acquire' is the predominant meaning, mainly on the basis of what this word means elsewhere in Proverbs concerning wisdom and in the Old Testament in general.[2] In any case, wisdom was with God from the beginning; we are talking about *God's* wisdom, not just some abstract ideal or standard of wisdom floating around in people's minds. God 'formed' this wisdom (8:23); he put wisdom together. This was before creation itself, before the earth, before the waters (8:24). Wisdom was right there as creation came into being (8:25–6); she pre-existed it all. Wisdom has priority over everything else, 'before'

1 See Overland, *Proverbs*, 127–8.
2 Waltke, *The Book of Proverbs*, I.408.

in time as well as in significance. When God made creation into a suitable habitat, limiting the sea from the land (8:27–9), wisdom was there, 'constantly' (8:30).[3]

There are echoes of Genesis 1 here, the careful forming of the different aspects of the world, consistent with the cosmogony described in Genesis. God's wisdom, then, is associated with this orderly progression of creation, the establishment of boundaries and categories in the world. Wisdom is associated with the idea that the world is not capricious and random; there is structure, and pattern, that holds even within all the marvellous diversity that is seen in nature. She was part of not just making the world organised, but also making it habitable.

One of the astonishing things about the world is how welcoming it is to life. Any student who has heard of the 'fine tuning' of the universe knows how staggeringly unlikely this is, just how delicate the balance of all sorts of natural forces need to be in order for the universe to exist at all, let alone be welcoming to life. Yet our world is, and that is no surprise for the biblical scholar, because we know that God made it to be inhabited. That is another aspect of wisdom; it welcomes life, and humanity. Wisdom was there when God was crafting the world so carefully to make it habitable.

Andrew Errington takes this to demonstrate the objectivity of wisdom.[4] It is God's wisdom, God's ability and knowledge, but wisdom has also become an objective characteristic of the world itself. It is something we can observe in the world, as well as something we are taught through words, and both are important; the words are pointing us towards something real.

What we also see about this wisdom in verses 30–31 is that it is about delight and rejoicing. Whether it is wisdom delighting (which would be in parallel with 8:30a and c) or God (ESV), we can see that celebration is in order. Creation itself is worth celebrating, and especially that it is a good habitation for humanity – unworthy as we are, yet in a place of great privilege by God's grace. The lowliest

3 The ESV translates this as 'master workman', but Waltke argues that 'constantly' is more likely. Waltke, *The Book of Proverbs*, I.417–18; see also Clifford's excursus (*Proverbs*, 99–101) on this word.

4 Errington, *Every Good Path*; see chapter 3.

person is someone that wisdom herself delights in; a truth well worth meditating upon in dark times of depression.

That God and wisdom are full of delight and celebration over creation significantly changes our attitude towards life. Gaining wisdom is, as we have seen, a matter of having knowledge about the world's workings, and also living in a moral way. However, if that were the end of it, if that were all, it could be a rather dry and cheerless pursuit, a matter of learning things and then gritting the teeth to act morally and avoid fun. It sounds like Stoicism, learning physics and then on that basis always acting rationally and never getting carried away with emotional reactions, believing that the only thing of value is virtue so anything else – even the death of one's child – can be accepted calmly without destroying happiness.[5] It's a view that has some similarities with Christian ethics, but is 'a form of godliness but denying its power' (2 Timothy 3:5). For one thing it lacks is a true understanding of what God values.

For God, in his wisdom, *delights* in the world. Wisdom laughs with joy. This is not just rational appreciation of a logical order; rather, it is a deep, genuine, emotional reaction to it – it's wonder, it's something to rejoice in. Wisdom loves the world, loves looking at it, contemplating it; and not just nature itself, but wisdom also delights in humans.

In a world where humans are increasingly seen as the villains, despoiling an otherwise delightful world, it is good to be reminded of this. God created us for good. That fundamental fact of our creation remains, despite the fall. God delights in us, and when we do our job in the world – ruling wisely over creation, in obedience to God, understanding it as his creation – then creation flourishes. We are meant to be here; we are not the enemy, however badly we go about our job of ruling. Eliminating humankind is not the answer, and neither is following a philosophy that either forgets God or equates him with nature. The answer to environmental problems is to take our place as God intended us to, and to rule with wisdom as creatures in his image.

So now, you humans, listen. Given all we have just discovered about

5 For example, Epictetus, *The Enchiridion*, 14, 16.

wisdom – her importance, her history, her closeness to God and her part in our own existence – listen to her! To listen to wisdom is to be blessed (8:32); this is the way to be truly human. This is the way to have God's attitude towards the world, his creation that he delights in. It's a blessing; it's the way to be fortunate, to be happy, to be flourishing, just as the person of Psalm 1 who is like a tree by streams of water. There the emphasis is on God's law; here it is on God's wisdom. They go together. This is the instruction that will bring the best way of being in this delightful world, the way of appreciating it and living a flourishing life within it. So we should listen to wisdom, to her instruction, and never disregard it (8:33, expanding 8:32a). Every day we should go to her gates, her doorway, and seek out what she would teach (8:34, expanding 8:32b). This is the way to life, wisdom declares in verse 35. It is the way to have the Lord's favour, for it is sharing in how God would have us view his creation that he formed for us to live in.

And heed the warning of verse 36; this is not an optional extra. It truly is life or death. Without God's wisdom, we are committing self-harm, we are loving death. In a culture where levels of teenage anxiety are skyrocketing, where euthanasia for any reason at any age is being proposed, we are starting to see such a world – one that harms itself, that loves death. It is a culture that has forsaken wisdom, for it has forgotten God and his ways. That is not freedom; it is death. Let us listen to wisdom. Let us love life, and rejoice.

WOMAN WISDOM – A TYPE OF CHRIST?

Who is the woman who appears in chapters 1 and 8? The guide (6:22), who calls for people to listen to hear, to enjoy her hospitality (9:1–6). Is she meant to be a prophetess, parallel to Judges 4:4 or 2 Kings 22:14? Or perhaps she is meant to be an example of a wisdom teacher, parallel to the 'father' who speaks so much of the teaching in Proverbs. She has been identified as a Platonic ideal, and as a goddess, or a female version of God, who can say 'those who find me find life' (8:35).[6]

---

6 Waltke, *The Book of Proverbs*, I. 83–5; see also Clifford (*Proverbs*, 23–8) for an extended discussion.

At least as early as Justin Martyr (AD 125), Christians almost without exception identified *sophia* (wisdom) in Proverbs 8 with Christ.[7] This passage therefore was part of the controversy over Christology; for instance, Origen (*c.* AD 180) saw wisdom's birth in 8:25 as Christ's 'continual coming into existence', against the Arians who held that the Son was created, albeit the most exalted creature, citing Proverbs 8:22. As we saw above, the verb *qanah* can mean either to create or to acquire. Nicene Christology, then had to recover 8:22 and argue that 'create' is not a convincing reading.[8] Athanasius (*c.* 293–373) achieved this in two ways: by emphasising that the Son was not 'created' but became incarnate, and that the creation of Wisdom was the creation of Wisdom's image in creatures.[9] This meant that Christ could be equated with Wisdom without question: someone pre-existing, an agent in creation (3:19–20; 8:22–31; see also John 1:3; 1 Corinthians 8:6; Colossians 1:15–16; Hebrews 1:3).

However, the New Testament does not follow the argument that wisdom is creator, Jesus is creator, therefore wisdom is Jesus. John does not equate Jesus with Wisdom; he never uses *sophia* with reference to *logos*. And *logos* in John is very different from the woman wisdom in Proverbs. For John, *logos* is God, creator, the light itself. Wisdom even in the late Jewish texts is not so exalted. Neither does Paul build his Christology on Proverbs 8 or the Wisdom literature. Christ as the wisdom of God in 1 Corinthians 1:24 is not connected with creation (the connection between Jesus and creation is in 1 Corinthians 8:6). Paul related wisdom to Christ's crucifixion, not his incarnation. Also, the woman wisdom has no role in atonement in Proverbs 8 or in Jewish literature.

Nonetheless, there are similarities between woman wisdom and Christ as he is portrayed in John: both existed with God before all things; both had some role in creation; both descended from heaven to dwell with humanity and were rejected by the masses; both teach heavenly wisdom, including to children; both lead to life and

7 Irenaeus (*c.* 135) identified Wisdom with the Holy Spirit. *Against Heresies*, 4.20.1.
8 See Clifford, *Proverbs*, 98–9. Reformation commentors overwhelmingly identified woman Wisdom as the preincarnate Son of God (Fink, *Reformation Commentary*, 21).
9 Waltke, *The Book of Proverbs*, I.127; see Athanasius, *Against the Arians*, 2.46, 78.

immortality, but to death for those who do not listen. Both offer blessings in symbols of food and drink.

But Christ is superior. He is the eternal Son, creator (not just witness to creation), judge (not one who will laugh at judgment), God himself. Also, there is no doubt that Jesus is greater than Solomon; the Queen of Sheba will testify to Christ's greater wisdom (Matthew 12:42).

Wisdom does have similarities to Christ, yet she is unique. Wisdom is a *type* of Christ, not to be identified with Christ. Waltke says Solomon identifies wisdom with his teachings, not with some heavenly being, even one representing God. Waltke therefore sees wisdom as primarily a personification of the teaching of Proverbs itself: 'There is every reason to think that "Wisdom" has the same meaning, intention, and source as in [Solomon's] opening statement, and none to think otherwise.' That is, she stands for 1:1–2. The gullible people and youths she speaks to are precisely what 1:1–7 addresses. She raises her voice in command and exhortation and plea, just as the father giving Solomon's teaching does. What she teaches – fear of the Lord, leading to faithfulness in marriage, sexual purity, honesty, rejection of violent or dishonest ways to make money – are exactly what Solomon's proverbs teach. She *is* 'the proverbs of Solomon and the sayings of the wise'.[10] This description, as well as seeing her as a type of Christ, seems to cover the way in which this woman is portrayed in Proverbs.

Conclusion to Proverbs 8:22–36

Humans have always sought wisdom; we just do not always know how best to find it. God lets us know. Wisdom is right here, right before us. It is no secret, not something hidden from us. It is built into creation itself, and it is good and lovely. It is life itself. Embrace the wisdom that God so freely gives.

10 Waltke, *The Book of Proverbs*, I.87.

12

Two Feasts

PROVERBS 9

The teacher of Proverbs 1–9 has been using various techniques to engage the student. We have seen his use of one particularly powerful technique in any teaching, whether from the pulpit or in the classroom: story. People remember stories. We are designed to relate to people, and the more we are moved by the personal emotions of a story, the more likely we are to remember the teaching point.

Several times so far we have seen the teacher using the stories of two women who compete for the student's attention: wisdom, the intelligent and godly woman; and another, at various times a prostitute, an adulteress or simply folly. Both women have power; both have considerable potential to capture a youth's allegiance, and both offer considerable reward. In these comparisons, the youth is required to evaluate the relative value of the rewards offered, as well as the reality of what each will actually deliver. Wisdom is clearly presented in a much more favourable light, but the teacher does not underestimate the lure of the alternative.

1. Banqueting with the right woman • Proverbs 9:1–12

The story continues in chapter 9, as now the two women prepare banquets in their houses and invite people in. Which invitation is worth accepting? What should the invitee watch out for? In this last chapter of the first section of Proverbs, those who do not yet have wisdom – the 'simple' who have no sense (9:4, 16) – are confronted with the two rival paths. On the surface, they can seem very similar, but the teacher will make clear that they will lead to very different places.

This chapter can be considered an epilogue to the whole of chapters 1–9; the choice between the two ways is brought to a climax with the imagery of two rival banquets, of life and of death. The banquet of life looks forward to the imagery presented by Jesus of the kingdom of heaven itself (Luke 14:15–24). Which banquet will we choose? Which listener will heed wisdom's call?

The chapter also acts as preparation for the collection of Solomon's proverbs to follow in 10:1–22:16, a banquet of teaching. The two ways to go – wisdom or foolishness, righteousness or wickedness – will be repeatedly contrasted in these proverbs. We are being given every opportunity to understand that the choice is real, ultimate and not always easy.

Invitations of wisdom and folly

9 Wisdom has built her house;
she has set up[a] its seven pillars.
2 She has prepared her meat and mixed her wine;
she has also set her table.
3 She has sent out her servants, and she calls
from the highest point of the city,
4 'Let all who are simple come to my house!'
To those who have no sense she says,
5 'Come, eat my food
and drink the wine I have mixed.
6 Leave your simple ways and you will live;
walk in the way of insight.'

7 Whoever corrects a mocker invites insults;
whoever rebukes the wicked incurs abuse.
8 Do not rebuke mockers or they will hate you;
rebuke the wise and they will love you.
9 Instruct the wise and they will be wiser still;
teach the righteous and they will add to their learning.

10 The fear of the LORD is the beginning of wisdom,
and knowledge of the Holy One is understanding.
11 For through wisdom[b] your days will be many,
and years will be added to your life.
12 If you are wise, your wisdom will reward you;
if you are a mocker, you alone will suffer.

a 1 Septuagint, Syriac and Targum; Hebrew *has hewn out*

b 11 Septuagint, Syriac and Targum; Hebrew *me*

The woman of wisdom, the 'personification of Solomon's teachings' as Waltke has it,[1] has gone to a great deal of effort in chapter 9. She has built her house (9:1), as her daughters will in 14:1 and 24:3, making its pillars. We are not sure whether there is significance to the 'seven', which is frequently a perfect number in Scripture (6:16; 26:16, 25); is it a symbol of the cosmos? The Temple? It could be that this just emphasises what a magnificent house it is (most houses would have had only four pillars).[2]

She prepares a delicious meal (9:2). Wisdom is, indeed, enticing. The promise of wisdom was part of what deceived Eve into taking the fruit – she took the wrong means to it, but wisdom was what she wanted. Here we are presented with the right route to wisdom. It is there, freely offered to those who need it, those without education. Wisdom is not just making her teaching available; she also advertises its value, she sends people out to bring in the needy,[3] she calls out from the highest point in the city, the point where she is most likely to be heard (9:3). Her metaphorical meal, symbolising teaching and knowledge, is being presented, and those without wisdom are invited to accept (9:4).

Will we accept the invitation? Will we be prepared to leave behind our simplicity, our ignorance, and come to this feast (9:5)? Will we change direction, be humble enough to repent and learn how to live with insight? (9:6)

It will not be easy, and it is easy to resent those who teach wisdom. Correcting and rebuking, perhaps especially when it is sorely needed, can create resentment, and in the central part of the chapter (verses 7–12), we see who is worth teaching. A teacher needs to appreciate this: those who are 'mockers', who do not recognise their own ignorance, who despise wisdom, will hate rebuke (9:7), so don't bother

1 Waltke, *The Book of Proverbs*, I.431

2 See Clifford, *Proverbs*, 105.

3 The people wisdom sends out are female servants – a small point, but another instance in which women are depicted as teachers of wisdom.

with them (9:8a). In fact, wisdom did not even bother calling them (9:4–6); she called to the simple, those with as yet no sense, who at least might listen and learn. They are worth rebuking. Also the wise, those already prepared to learn and become wiser, know the value of rebuke (9:8b). They want instruction, for they know that is the way to become wiser still. They are the ones worth teaching.

Early in my Christian life, a popular saying was that the church needs FAT Christians: Faithful, Available and Teachable. It takes humility to be teachable, but that is the only way to grow in maturity, with all its rewards of joy, Christlikeness and increasing closeness to God. If you are a Christian leader, pay attention to who is ready to learn, and invest in those people. They are not always the obvious candidates. It might be the shy, quiet one who simply faithfully listens during the sermon and takes the initiative to tidy away the hymnbooks afterwards. It might be the over-zealous new convert who criticises everything but is doing so out of genuine enthusiasm for Christ. No teacher has unlimited time; make sure investment is made into those who really will benefit and grow. Teach the wise and righteous (9:9); they have proved that they are willing to learn, and are able to continue to do so.

The first step, of course, is for the learner to start with the fear of the Lord (9:10). That's how you begin to be teachable, and that is what you should hold as foremost in order to be wise. This is where wisdom starts. Moreover, there will be personal consequences of being wise, or of being a mocker. Wisdom's rewards will be great: an abundance of life (9:11), and wisdom is a reward in itself – literally 'you are wise for yourself' (9:12a), the emphasis being on the fact that you are the beneficiary. The mockers, however, the sceptics who love to question but only in order to tear down, never to find truth, will in the end only hurt themselves (9:12b). The wise will learn from questioning and seeking, for their goal is knowledge. The scoffer, the cynical, the closeminded, will stay closeminded.[4]

4 And will be left lonely: 'Wisdom is the better route to take because things can only get better, whereas the mocker ends up alone.' Tremper Longman III, *Proverbs* (Ada: Baker Publishing Group, 2006), 220.

2. The second option • Proverbs 9:13–18

For all of us in this world, there will, however, be an alternative invitation.

13 Folly is an unruly woman;
she is simple and knows
nothing.
14 She sits at the door of her
house,
on a seat at the highest point
of the city,
15 calling out to those who pass
by,
who go straight on their
way,
16 'Let all who are simple come to
my house!'
To those who have no sense she
says,
17 'Stolen water is sweet;
food eaten in secret is
delicious!'
18 But little do they know that the
dead are there,
that her guests are deep in the
realm of the dead.

The woman of folly is unruly (9:13a); she is loud and outrageous, and that itself might attract visitors. Irreverence and shock are often the way to sell tickets. She offers entertainment, and like the wise woman she advertises clearly. She, too, has a prominent platform (9:14–15); she's there on social media, in the public eye, and she has a great advertising pitch, and to the same audience, the gullible (9:16). She's also offering a delicious meal – it has the added enticement of a certain secrecy, illicit glamour (9:17). It's a lie, of course; the 'stolen water' will not be sweet for very long, and actually doesn't compare with the richness of the meat and wine offered by wisdom. In fact, it's nothing; she has not actually prepared a banquet; it's all advertising and show. She has set herself up, but apart from that appears to have done nothing for her guests.

But she is a fool herself, and knows nothing (9:13b). She cannot actually help those she is calling in, because she has no wisdom of her own. She will only lead people to death (9:18).

Conclusion to Proverbs 9

There is certainly plenty of counterfeit wisdom on offer in our world; any and every pundit is offering courses, YouTube videos, blogs, books and mentoring in anything you like. Be wary, the teacher is warning us. The invitation of a fool can seem just as plausible as that of wisdom; it may even seem more enticing, more fun. But the stakes are high. Do not base your life on the wrong teaching. Start with the fear of the Lord, which will mean listening to his word. We must test the spirits, 1 John 4:1 tells us; there are false prophets who will attempt to exploit us with 'fabricated stories' (2 Peter 2:3). Know the truth from God, and do not be deceived.

Many Bible studies seem to end with the generic application, 'Pray more and read the Bible.' But there is a reason for this: God is the source of wisdom, and we must both ask his for his enlightenment and absorb what he teaches. In Proverbs 1–9 the teacher has taken pains to present the value of wisdom, and where we are to find it. Be prepared to humble yourself and accept it; even accept the rebuke and criticism that comes from challenging your own ideas with God's truth. Seeking wisdom without seeking God is nonsense. It is deliberately hobbling yourself from the start. It is a claim of wanting wisdom, but an action of avoiding it and staying in ignorance; any knowledge subsequently gained will be severely compromised.

We start off ignorant, but if we start with fear of the Lord, we can learn. Make the effort. It's worth it.

PART TWO

PROVERBS 10–24

13

THE PROVERBS OF SOLOMON

We now enter what might be thought of as Proverbs proper: this is the teaching of Solomon, the carefully constructed sayings that will educate us in wisdom. The style shifts away from storytelling and comparisons between the two figures, wisdom and foolishness. It now returns to the more didactic style of the early chapters, with a particular characteristic: these are gathered sayings, the content of wisdom, what most people think of as 'proverbs'. Most modern readers simply take them as largely unrelated pieces of advice; even preachers tend to preach on themes in Proverbs, rather than sequentially. However, there are patterns and structure in these chapters; the signposts of structure in chapters 1–9 continue. We see commendations of wisdom, the exhortations to keep going in the teaching that is being given, and, as in the first nine chapters, these exhortations often mark the beginning or the end of a section of teaching.

Historically, the whole of Proverbs 1:1–22:16 was considered one teaching unit. Proverbs 1:1 is the main heading, and 10:1 a subheading;[1] we are continuing with the teaching of father and mother to a son (10:1). What we have now are the 'proverbs and parables, the sayings and riddles of the wise' that were introduced in 1:6. The sharp contrast between wisdom and folly is introduced in the first nine chapters, and the second section ends with a recap of the warning against the unfaithful wife (22:14).

There is not so much overt encouragement to the student, not so much persuasion to seek wisdom – if you have come this far, presumably you have accepted the lesson that wisdom is worth having. What follow are teachings on wealth and life satisfaction, and how to teach others to get them.

Commentators disagree on how to best divide 10:1–22:16 into subsections, and whether this should be done thematically

1 Waltke, *The Book of Proverbs*, I.14.

or stylistically. However, in general we can see a progression in intensity and depth of teaching as the student advances in wisdom. The same topic might be revisited further on, but in a more advanced form.

14

Treasures Good and Bad

PROVERBS 10:1–22

The wisdom commendation of 10:1 marks the beginning of a unit, and structures the teaching within it, repeated five times. Five elements in 10:2–3 then reappear in 10:21–22: the moral person, abundance/enrichment, deficiency of something, what the Lord does, and the fate of death. The lecture covers the topics of true wealth, what brings (or does not bring) harm, and speech. There is an alphabetic poem with acrostic here, with twenty-two sayings.[1] What the acrostic letters spell is not entirely clear, but it may be referring to the cleverly designed nature of the text.

1. The best kind of wealth and how to get it • Proverbs 10:1–5

The teaching of Proverbs is practical, for real-life situations. It will tell us about physical wealth, the gaining of money. But it will also teach us about what is truly valuable; and money, while useful, is not ultimately worth striving for. This is wisdom. The wealth that is not monetary is actually far more valuable than the wealth that is limited to money. Money is not despised; it is part of life, and there is considerable teaching on what to do with it in both Old and New Testaments. It is part of life to consider how to gain it, and part of wisdom how to value it rightly.

---

1 See the discussion in Overland, *Proverbs*, 202. An acrostic is a poem in which certain letters (usually the first in each line) spell out something or are in some order.

Proverbs of Solomon

10 The proverbs of Solomon:

A wise son brings joy to his
father,
but a foolish son brings grief to
his mother.

2 Ill-gotten treasures have no
lasting value,
but righteousness delivers
from death.

3 The LORD does not let the
righteous go hungry,
but he thwarts the craving of
the wicked.

4 Lazy hands make for poverty,
but diligent hands bring wealth.

5 He who gathers crops in
summer is a prudent son,
but he who sleeps during
harvest is a disgraceful son.

Proverbs 10:1 gives us the introduction to this new section: the Proverbs of Solomon (10:1a). The section is introduced by a familiar statement about the importance of listening to teachers, and the most significant teachers will probably be parents (10:1b). This teaching that harks back to the first nine chapters eases us into this new section where the teaching is more aphoristic and so harder to parse. Now more than ever we need to listen to the teachers. Parents are meant to teach wisdom to their children. Children are meant to listen. Parents rightly desire life wisdom for their children, and it is a delight when they see it. Do you want to bring joy to your parents, rather than grief? Then gain wisdom. Do you want to be the sort of parent who rightly delights in their children? Value their growth in wisdom above all else.[2]

One of the saddest condemnations of modern western society in its individualism and family breakdown is the lack of intergenerational wisdom, the failure to pass on knowledge from grandparent to parent to grandchild.[3] The idea that parents are meant to teach children, and that

2 Both sides, of course, are necessary. A child who gains wisdom – i.e., follows Christ – may, sadly, face rejection from parents who do not. Christ teaches us to honour parents but says we must love God more (Matthew 7:21; 10:32–3, 35, 37; 15:4; 23:9; Luke 9:60).

3 Fortunately, this is not necessarily the case in other cultures; for example, see Ignatius Nnaemeka Onwuatuegwu and V. S. Paul-Mgbeafulike, 'African traditional educational framework: Unveiling the wisdom beyond western education', *Nnadiebube Journal of Philosophy* 6.2 (2023), 48–63. However, cultures that still have such a tradition need to work to preserve it; see also Habtu, 'Proverbs', 779.

children should listen and obey, is not just frequently not followed but can also be openly mocked. It is assumed that real parenting wisdom comes not from parents, but from technical experts. I can remember reading a research paper on teenagers, published in a peer-reviewed journal, that began with the astonishing claim that there was up until that point no wisdom on how to raise teenagers. What the authors meant was that they had found no published research papers on the particular idea they were researching, but what a claim! As if scientific research is the *only* way to understand how children develop, and the best way to guide them.

Biblical wisdom paints a different picture. Biblical families were generally much wider than the modern nuclear family of one parent, (optional) second parent, and children. The biblical family, in contrast, had not only married parents, but probably many other relatives and generations living in the same house. It is western culture that is unusual in this respect. 'Scholars who work on parenting and childrearing have consistently shown that, outside populations defined as WEIRD (white, educated, industrialised, rich and democratic), children are taken care of by multiple people, not solely their mothers.'[4] With families come accumulated wisdom, something we are at peril of losing as we lose the family.

Now, in 10:2–5, framed by the idea of the wise/foolish sons in 1b and 5, we turn to some specific instructions about wealth. We will find that it is worth seeking, but if the point is to live well – and what other point for riches can there be? – then the morality with which the wealth is obtained is what really matters. There is a theological and ethical basis for understanding the nature of wealth. Treasures obtained in a guilty way are no true profit (10:2a). True security comes from living righteously (10:2b). Why? Because life is in the hands of the Lord (10:3). It is God who makes riches possible, or keeps them away – and ultimately will reward the righteous, whatever the present may hold.[5] Seeking to please God, then, is more important than the sheer pursuit of wealth.

This is not a promise that God will never let a righteous person ever feel hungry (see Deuteronomy 8:3; Revelation 7:16); and Psalm 49

4 Francesca Mezzenzana 'Amazonian childcare: Why my Runa Indigenous family and friends found my child-centred, "natural" parenting practices so strange and troubling', *Aeon*, 20 June 2023.

5 The phrase translated 'have no lasting value' in verse 2 has the sense of eternal value; this is talking about the ultimate future, not just the present.

demonstrates that no wealth, even that gained righteously, will stop death. But God can redeem from death, and verse 3 is teaching about what really matters. To start with, we know clearly from both Old and New Testaments that no one is actually righteous (Romans 3:23). All wealth that is given by God is going to those who do not deserve it. Moreover, those whom God loves he may discipline, sending them through hardship precisely because this is a loving thing to do, for it develops perseverance, faith and hope, far more truly valuable than any temporary comfort that might otherwise have been present (Romans 5:3–5; 1 Peter 1:7; James 1:2–4). Proverbs is presenting the principle behind all wealth: it is God who owns it, and seeking to please God is what matters.

Now we turn to the advice for achieving riches, physical or otherwise. The basic lesson for getting *money* is: work. Be diligent. Don't be lazy (10:4). Lazy hands bring poverty, or poverty brings poor work.[6] The contrast, however, is important – diligent hands will bring riches. Be the prudent son, who gathers crops in summer; not the one who sleeps and skives off (10:5).

2. *Diligent living • Proverbs 10:6–17*

We are meant to work. It is the way to earn our own money, so that we do not sponge off other people, and so that we do not steal (Ephesians 4:28). Instead of taking from others in this way, we should make sure we have the means to be generous and give to others. We are to be diligent, and not lazy, minding our own business. We are not to be busybodies, idle and disruptive (see also 1 Thessalonians 3:10; 4:11).

6 Blessings crown the head of
the righteous,
but violence overwhelms
the mouth of the
wicked.[a]
7 The name of the righteous is
used in blessings,[b]
but the name of the wicked
will rot.
8 The wise in heart accept
commands,
but a chattering fool comes
to ruin.

6 The causal sequence is discussed in Overland, *Proverbs*, 199.

9 Whoever walks in integrity
walks securely,
but whoever takes crooked
paths will be found out.

10 Whoever winks maliciously
causes grief,
and a chattering fool comes to
ruin.

11 The mouth of the righteous is
a fountain of life,
but the mouth of the wicked
conceals violence.

12 Hatred stirs up conflict,
but love covers over all wrongs.

13 Wisdom is found on the lips of
the discerning,
but a rod is for the back of one
who has no sense.

14 The wise store up knowledge,
but the mouth of a fool invites
ruin.

15 The wealth of the rich is their
fortified city,
but poverty is the ruin of the
poor.

16 The wages of the righteous is
life,
but the earnings of the wicked
are sin and death.

17 Whoever heeds discipline
shows the way to life,
but whoever ignores correction
leads others astray.

a 6 Or *righteous, / but the mouth of the wicked conceals violence*
b 7 See Gen. 48:20.

Moreover, work *well*, meaning morally, as the next two verses emphasise what matters most (10:6–7). Part of the reward of right working is a good reputation, blessings on one's head (10:6), which is something good to have. The New Testament advice on work similarly encourages us to be positively viewed by the watching public (for example, 1 Thessalonians 4:11–12). We should be seen as those who are moral, diligent, honest and not lazy. The approval of the community – for the right reasons – is a good thing to have. We will not be able to avoid some worldly disapproval or even persecution when we follow Christ, for as he warned us, they first hated him (John 15:18). However, it should never be our personal conduct that gains such disapproval; we should not be the people speaking (having the mouth of) violence (10:6) or of wicked name (10:7). On the contrary, we should live such good lives in deed and speech that people, if they view us honestly, are forced to praise God (1 Peter 2:12). So work honestly and morally, and have a good name.

Wisdom also means accepting instruction, another kind of good speech, instead of using speech to be a 'chattering fool' (10:8). This is what the 'wise in heart' do – they are not 'wise in [their] own eyes' (3:7). The Christian is one who listens, and obeys authority, respecting even ungodly authorities if they are duly instituted (Romans 13:1–7), and do what needs to be done. We are to aim to live quiet and peaceful lives. There may be times when protest is necessary, against ungodly laws or immoral impositions. But it should not be our first instinct to rebel. The anti-authoritarian rabble-rouser is not to be our nature. Wisdom means being willing to take orders and obey them, not to speak foolishly.

For what we do matters, and here we have a series of instructions concerning how we walk, talk and act that emphasise the rightness of controlling ourselves in mind and body, and the rewards that can be expected from doing so.

There are definite wrong ways to speak and act. Reward will not come from being devious, taking 'crooked paths' (10:9b). Grief and ruin come from malice towards others in word and action – malicious winks or foolish chatter (10:10). Wicked words reveal a violent inclination (10:11b), so don't use them. Have integrity of character and words. This is the thrust of Jesus's teaching in the Sermon on the Mount (Matthew 5–7). Do what is right, but don't let it be just a matter of outward action; make sure it comes from right thoughts and motivations. Yes, refrain from murder, but refrain from hate as well. Even if you don't act in violence, the violence in your heart may be revealed by your words. Don't have either. For such hatred will only breed more hatred, and conflict (10:12a).

Security, on the other hand, comes from acting with integrity (10:9a). Right action means becoming a fountain of life, a blessing to others, with the morality of what you speak (10:11a). Be the one who loves, not hates, for that brings the opposite of conflict (10:12b).

But not everyone will want to hear this. Those who already have some wisdom, some discernment, will listen to and speak wisdom;

those who reject it will simply find it a punishment in itself (10:13).[7] The wise will become wiser, while the foolish, instead of speaking wisdom, will speak their own destruction (10:14). Wisdom is the way to wealth and security, we have seen, while foolishness leads to poverty (10:15). But even the fortified city is not where true security lies (see 18:10, 11). The wealthy are storing up the wrong thing, money rather than knowledge, leaving the poor ruined. Far better wages come from the morality that leads to life, while the wicked will go towards sin and death (10:16–21), and along the way we see more about how words are the tools of either the wise or the foolish as they proceed along these two conflicting ways. The effect of the language is not a promise that life automatically follows righteousness and sin and death automatically follow wickedness; it is a statement of a tendency, the direction that these two choices represent.

There will be exceptions and twists along the way, for we live in a fallen and broken world in which the wicked might prosper (Psalm 37). But the commendation of wisdom remains. It is still better to be moral and upright, to seek God and to act for the benefit of others, for righteousness brings life, and wickedness death (10:16). The mention of 'sin' puts this in the context of spiritual life and death. It is still better to do good and speak wisely and offer blessings to others. It is valuable in itself to live like this, whatever the outcome. Being willing to learn is the way of life and helping others, rather than leading them astray (10:17); this also brings us back to the context of being taught, as we began in 10:1.

3. Speak well • Proverbs 10:18–22

We have seen so far that the way we are instructed, and how willing we are to learn, has an effect on us; now we turn to the effect on others.

18 Whoever conceals hatred with lying lips | and spreads slander is a fool.

7 Waltke takes 13b as indicating that the senseless will not listen, and need physical correction to go the right way. Waltke, *The Book of Proverbs*, I.452.

19 Sin is not ended by multiplying
words,
but the prudent hold their
tongues.

20 The tongue of the righteous is
choice silver,
but the heart of the wicked is
of little value.

21 The lips of the righteous
nourish many,
but fools die for lack of sense.

22 The blessing of the LORD
brings wealth,
without painful toil for it.

In 10:18–21 the topic again is speech, and its effects. What we say matters tremendously: hatred brings lies and hurt to others (18–19a); good speech, on the other hand, will be timely and moral (14, 19b; 13:3; 17:27–8; 21:23; Ecclesiastes 5:2–7). The prudent restrain themselves when they speak. Words reveal what is in the heart, which can produce speech that is either silver or worthless (10:20; see also Matthew 12:34). And the result? Nourishing many, or having so little that you die (10:21). The effect is clear: don't be the fool who dies for lack of sense. Instead, seek the blessing of the Lord, for that is true riches, true wealth, and he gives it willingly.

Conclusion to Proverbs 10:1–22

Consider how this lecture from Solomon has developed its thought. It is not at all a random collection of sayings. Its six wisdom commendations (1, 8, 13, 14, 17, 21) show the different forms of wisdom and the consequences that follow it, both increasing in intensity. The types of wisdom start from respect for parents (10:1), then move to willingness to listen (10:8), then ability to teach others (10:13), learning when not to speak (10:14) and willingness to accept reprimand (10:17); while the consequences develop from bringing joy to parents to nourishing many, as opposed to grief (10:1), finally ending in death (10:21). Notice that the opposite of the righteous person in verse 21 is not an immoral person (although that is true), but a fool without sense.

We have been presented with a carefully constructed lecture that shows how to get worldly wealth, but greater value lies in righteousness and how it helps community; that kind of wealth comes from listening to instruction, showing love and mercy, and valuing wisdom.

15

Ensuring the Right Future

PROVERBS 10:23–30

Verse 22 can be taken as the conclusion and summation of the previous section, or as a link emphasising that we now turn to the outcomes of righteous (or wicked) living. A wisdom commendation in verse 23 gives us a future focus. Part of wisdom is planning for the future, and morality affects how effective that planning is. Verses 23 and 30 begin and end this short section on the future, by introducing the idea of planning (10:23) and stating its aim (10:30). Both are linked with moral conduct: wisdom and righteousness. What the righteous gain is the ultimate security – being able to stay, for ever, in God's land (understood, 10:30). The wicked, on the contrary, will not stay there, the ultimate doom.

SHOULD WE LOOK FOR FUTURE REWARD?

We know, after Christ, that the true land is not the physical Israel, but the kingdom of heaven itself. We do not enter the rest of being settled in the land, but a better rest for the people of God (Hebrews 4:9); we enter not the earthly holy place that was in Israel, with the golden altar of incense and the Ark of the Covenant (Hebrews 9:4), but the greater and more perfect one, not of this creation, because Christ has gained us entry (Hebrews 9:11; 10:19–22). We will receive this eternal inheritance, because Christ's death was the perfect sacrifice that won it for us.

What, then, do we do with the wisdom teaching that says it is moral conduct that gains us this reward? Is this no longer applicable? Do we reject it as the old covenant way of works, something that is instructive in pointing to Christ but nothing more? Is Proverbs simply something we read for historical interest, not for present teaching?

It is still the way of wisdom to aim for that eternal security, even if now we understand more fully what that security is. It is still wise to do whatever is necessary to gain that future goal – this appears to be what Jesus, in whom God's wisdom resides, commends in a number of parables about the kingdom (Luke 16:1–9; Matthew 13:44–46). The kingdom is worth everything we have, and more, and should be our overriding goal in all things.

It is also true that it was never moral conduct that won the land for Israel, even in the Old Testament. It was given to the people by the grace of God, not by their might or their moral desirability – that is made abundantly clear in the Pentateuch, Joshua and Judges. The land came by promise, and even when God's people were exiled because of their sin, God kept his promise and restored his people, little though they deserved it. They waited for his promise of the resurrection and the gloriously renewed land spoken of in prophetic visions in Ezekiel, Isaiah and the other prophets, and that promise was eventually fulfilled in Jesus, who will take us to the new creation where there will be no sin to mar that vision.

The difference now is that we know how God has dealt with the fact that no one ever lived up to the fullness of the wisdom teaching, the true moral conduct and righteousness that wisdom commends. He has paid for our sin, and so we can draw near in full assurance of faith with our hearts sprinkled clean (Hebrews 10:22). That is not a reason to be less zealous in pursuing moral righteousness; on the contrary, it is a reason to follow it even more fully, for now we have confidence that it is truly worth it. As the writer of Hebrews urges us, let us hold fast, *because* 'he who promised is faithful' (Hebrews 10:23). For that reason, we stir one another up to love and good works, and keep ourselves from sinning deliberately, because we know what has been won for us and what we have been saved from. Hebrews 11 goes on to commend perseverance in faith, staying true with our eyes fixed on the goal, just as the faithful of the Old Testament did. Indeed, we have even more reason to do so, precisely because we are surrounded by them, that 'great cloud of witnesses' (Hebrews 12:1). Christ is our example and our power to keep going, even in the face of difficulty; and so we make straight paths for our feet (Hebrews 12:13), picking up the exact image of Proverbs.

Both the future focus of Proverbs 10:23–30 and the way of staying true to it are entirely relevant in our Christian lives now. It is wisdom to want to be for ever with Christ, and wisdom to live as he would have us live as we walk towards that ultimate future, with confidence to keep going, knowing that it has already been secured for us.

1. Where righteousness and wickedness lead • Proverbs 10:23–30

This short section is all about future planning,[1] and how righteousness affects our approach to the future. It is better to be moral as we go forward. The references to the Lord show who is the ultimate guarantor of this scheme of things. The world does not always react to our good intentions as it should, but we can trust the Lord that this is, indeed, the best way.

23 A fool finds pleasure in wicked
schemes,
but a person of understanding
delights in wisdom.

24 What the wicked dread will
overtake them;
what the righteous desire will
be granted.

25 When the storm has swept by,
the wicked are gone,
but the righteous stand firm
for ever.

26 As vinegar to the teeth and
smoke to the eyes,
so are sluggards to those who
send them.

27 The fear of the LORD adds
length to life,
but the years of the wicked are
cut short.

28 The prospect of the righteous
is joy,
but the hopes of the wicked
come to nothing.

29 The way of the LORD is a
refuge for the blameless,
but it is the ruin of those who
do evil.

30 The righteous will never be
uprooted,
but the wicked will not remain
in the land.

1 Following Overland, *Proverbs*, 211.

Proverbs 10:23 opens these few verses with a seven-word Hebrew saying, the central word of which is 'planning', even though this is not brought out in the NIV. The fool doesn't plan properly, and instead wastes time in wicked schemes; the wise person knows better, delighting in what will be constructive. We then see how the plans just stated will come about, with two verses contrasting the wise and foolish attitudes towards the future. The guilty or wicked can only look forward to what they dread, and will be blown away in a storm. They have no security for the future. The righteous, on the other hand, receive what they long for (10:24). This prospect is not just immediate, but eternal; the storm has overtones of final judgment, through which the righteous stand firm, and for ever (10:25).

Verse 26 may seem a sudden change of topic, but it still concerns this theme of future planning. If you send someone ahead who is lazy and incompetent, then you will suffer; the emissary will do a bad job. It will be as irritating as vinegar on the teeth or smoke in the eyes. The alternative is in 10:27 – prepare for the future with reverence.[2] Verses 28 and 29 emphasise this future hope for the righteous: joy and refuge, ending in the eternal security of verse 30, as opposed to the short life, dashed hopes and ruin of the wicked. The stakes have been raised from simply having successful (or unsuccessful) plans in 23–4; now we are talking about life-affirming hope and joy, as opposed to the death of hope, and we end with eternal security or eternal rootlessness (10:30).

Conclusion to Proverbs 10:23–30

So how do we plan for the future wisely? Storms will come, but the way to survive them is through our moral conduct. This will bring hope and joy along the way, and ultimately ensures our security. We have placed this section in the context of eternal life, as the statement of verse 30 (and the 'for ever' of verse 25) gives us that context. However, even in this life the principles are sound. Moral behaviour

2 Overland (*Proverbs*, 216) sees conduct itself as this emissary to our future life. That is how to ensure a good future: by sending a good emissary – i.e., by acting in righteousness.

builds community and relationships, it avoids greedy risk-taking and vain ambition, and so it will tend to bring security as much as it is available in this world. We know that our ultimate destiny is secure, but we can also expect some benefits of righteousness in this life, too. Our moral conduct as Christians does not rest on what we will gain from it, but the gains will be there, for the most part – and for those who fall foul of a fallen world, eternal security awaits.

16

Honest Wealth

PROVERBS 10:31–11:31

We can take 10:31–2 as either a conclusion to the previous section or a wisdom commendation which is the beginning of a new one.[1] The new topic is wealth, particularly resisting the temptation of gaining it immorally. There are so many ways that we could gain wealth just a little dubiously: from not declaring something on our tax return to taking a few extra stationery supplies from the office, moonlighting on office time to pursue a side hustle, there are any number of apparently no-victim ways of making a little more money. If money itself is good – and the things we can do with it, such as supporting a family or even being generous, are definitely good – is it all that wrong?

1. True riches • Proverbs 10:31–11:13

This next section of Proverbs attacks that temptation, along with teaching on the importance of righteous words and the effect they have on others. We saw in the previous section how much more valuable non-monetary wealth is than physical wealth, beneficial though that may be; now the teacher expands upon this. True wealth comes from seeking to please God. Immoral riches are not worth it; but doing good, especially good to others, is.

31 From the mouth of the righteous
comes the fruit of wisdom,
but a perverse tongue will be
silenced.

32 The lips of the righteous know
what finds favour,
but the mouth of the wicked
only what is perverse.

1 As Overland does; *Proverbs*, 218.

11 The LORD detests
dishonest scales,
but accurate weights find favour
with him.

2 When pride comes, then
comes disgrace,
but with humility comes
wisdom.

3 The integrity of the upright
guides them,
but the unfaithful are
destroyed by their duplicity.

4 Wealth is worthless in the day
of wrath,
but righteousness delivers
from death.

5 The righteousness of the blameless makes their paths straight,
but the wicked are brought
down by their own
wickedness.

6 The righteousness of the
upright delivers them,
but the unfaithful are trapped
by evil desires.

7 Hopes placed in mortals die
with them;
all the promise of[a] their power
comes to nothing.

8 The righteous person is
rescued from trouble,
and it falls on the wicked
instead.

9 With their mouths the godless
destroy their neighbours,
but through knowledge the
righteous escape.

10 When the righteous prosper,
the city rejoices;
when the wicked perish, there
are shouts of joy.

11 Through the blessing of the
upright a city is exalted,
but by the mouth of the
wicked it is destroyed.

12 Whoever derides their neighbour has no sense,
but the one who has understanding holds their tongue.

13 A gossip betrays a confidence,
but a trustworthy person keeps
a secret.

---

a 7 Two Hebrew manuscripts; most Hebrew manuscripts, Vulgate, Syriac and Targum *When the wicked die, their hope perishes; / all they expected from*

To begin, we have our introductory commendation of wisdom (10:31–2), which comes from morality or righteousness. Wisdom and right behaviour go together; righteous speech brings wisdom, just as wickedness and perversity go together. There is also a sense of the effect on others; the lips of the righteous will know what is acceptable and will bring approval from others, whereas wicked speech will not. Wisdom, and the righteous speech and behaviour it brings, matters.

So moral behaviour in one of our areas of great temptation (money) matters greatly as well, as we see in 11:1. The Lord *detests* dishonest scales. He *hates* them (see also Leviticus 19:36; Deuteronomy 25:15). Cheating is not just a minor infringement; God abhors it. On the other hand, if you want to delight God, be honest in your financial dealings (see Matthew 7:12; 1 Corinthians 6:8; 1 Thessalonians 4:6). Moreover, be honest with humility (11:2). Avoid pride, which is what so often allows us to justify our cheating (I'm special; I have special circumstances; there's a special reason why I am justified in doing this thing even if other people are not). We're not told the mechanism by which social disgrace can follow pride, although Scripture has many examples (Genesis 11:5–8; Numbers 12:2, 10; 2 Chronicles 26:16–21; Esther 5:11; 7:10; Daniel 5; Luke 18:14; Acts 12:22–3). Modesty, a quality that the world sorely needs, is much better; pride in oneself is not the way of wisdom, whatever western individualist culture may preach. Be guided by honesty and integrity, be one of the honest, the *yesharim*, the straight; don't follow treachery which is crooked and will ultimately destroy you (11:3).

For, ultimately, it is not money that matters (11:4). It is not what brings a true profit; 4b repeats 10:2b. Sacrificing your integrity for the sake of wealth is a terribly bad bargain. Follow righteousness instead; however difficult it might be in the short term, it is what is worth pursuing.

Now we see a short progression in the next three verses (11:5–7). Neither morality nor immorality stays static. Righteousness keeps us walking straight, delivers us from danger and ultimately (the understood corollary of verse 7) preserves life. Wickedness, on the other hand, brings falls, captivity and death, and all the promises of ungodly wealth turn out to be false. That lust for wealth will not save; it will always let people down. Verse 8 sums up which kind of character is the more worth having: be righteous, not wicked. Examples of God enacting this kind of justice are throughout Scripture (Esther 5:14; 7:10; 9:1–10; Daniel 6:23–4; Luke 16:25) and, of course, eschatologically it will be true for everyone.

So what sort of wealth does righteousness bring? It brings the better kind of wealth, which goes beyond the value of money, especially through the power of speech. Wisdom will benefit you by allowing you to be spared from the trouble that godless people try to bring through their wicked speech (11:9). Moreover, wisdom brings benefit to one's city, and people will rejoice in the righteous, in their goodness and prosperity (which the righteous will be using for the good of others) (11:10). The city will enjoy the triumph of good over evil. (This is still what people want. Think of how popular are the novels or films in which good triumphs; the detective discovers the murderer, the action hero destroys the evil organisation, the good guy beats the bad guy.)

There are even more tangible reasons for a city to rejoice in the righteous: they bless the city (the blessing of the righteous could mean the blessings God gives them – which they will no doubt share – or the way in which the righteous bless others; either way it helps the community) and raise its reputation, as opposed to being torn apart or thrown down by wicked words (11:11). Anyone who has experienced the dreary effects of backbiting and factions in a local council, for example, will know this well!

Finally (11:12) lack of wisdom in derisive speech hurts the neighbour, but individual wisdom and discretion in speech helps others. Silence can be golden; the quiet, trustworthy person (11:13), the one who has self-control, is a far better friend than the loudly contemptuous or slanderous person who cannot be trusted. Human beings, evidence would suggest, are natural gossips and slanderers; we love scandal, and we especially love being able to be the person who can first report it to others. Social media algorithms are designed to encourage us in this tendency. We must resist it; online or in real life, care with our speech and the ability to keep a confidence are the ways to be loving.

2. The benefit to relationships • Proverbs 11:14–31

If we are loving in the way that Proverbs has been teaching us, we will reap great benefits. We were made to relate to others, and it matters that we do so wisely.

14 For lack of guidance a nation
falls,
but victory is won through
many advisors.

15 Whoever puts up security for a
stranger will surely suffer,
but whoever refuses to shake
hands in pledge is safe.

16 A kind-hearted woman gains
honour,
but ruthless men gain only
wealth.

17 Those who are kind benefit
themselves,
but the cruel bring ruin on
themselves.

18 A wicked person earns deceptive wages,
but the one who sows righteousness reaps a sure
reward.

19 Truly the righteous attain life,
but whoever pursues evil finds
death.

20 The LORD detests those whose
hearts are perverse,
but he delights in those whose
ways are blameless.

21 Be sure of this: the wicked will
not go unpunished,
but those who are righteous
will go free.

22 Like a gold ring in a pig's snout
is a beautiful woman who
shows no discretion.

23 The desire of the righteous
ends only in good,
but the hope of the wicked
only in wrath.

24 One person gives freely, yet
gains even more;
another withholds unduly, but
comes to poverty.

25 A generous person will prosper;
whoever refreshes others will
be refreshed.

26 People curse the one who
hoards grain,

but they pray God's blessing
on the one who is willing to
sell.

27 Whoever seeks good finds
favour,
but evil comes to one who
searches for it.

28 Those who trust in their riches
will fall,
but the righteous will thrive
like a green leaf.

29 Whoever brings ruin on their
family will inherit only wind,
and the fool will be servant to
the wise.

30 The fruit of the righteous is a
tree of life,
and the one who is wise saves
lives.

31 If the righteous receive their
due on earth,
how much more the ungodly
and the sinner!

Wisdom, and the true riches it brings, benefits different levels of relationships, as we see in the next few verses (14–18). Lack of wisdom (which includes greedy pursuit of wealth as well as slanderous speech) leads to the collapse of a community (11:14). Wise counsel, on the other hand, will keep it safe. This is evident in any civilisation. Where there is great social injustice, a large disparity between the rich and the poor, especially if it comes from the exploitation of the poor by the wealthy, community becomes unstable and less safe. It is also the sort of community that brings God's wrath, as the frequent criticisms Isaiah makes of his people show: God's judgment comes on leaders who fail to bring social justice (for example, Isaiah 1:21–5).

If we put community before monetary gain, however, we benefit (11:15). Don't guarantee loans for strangers, even if the rates are good; that kind of risk brings harm. We see it also in male–female relationships (the relational context here suggests 'wife', not just 'woman'). The woman who is gracious deserves commendation, as opposed to the violent who ruthlessly seek wealth (11:16) and so will put money above people. Similarly, in parallel with verse 16, the man who is kind does better than the one who is cruel (11:17). Both verses emphasise that right behaviour helps you yourself. Work for honest wages, don't deal falsely (11:18); the moral way, 'sow[ing] righteousness', is the way to reward.

Wisdom, then, benefits the self and others. The stakes are high; in contrast to evil, the wages that wisdom earns are life itself (11:19). That is because (11:20) it is what the Lord wants. He hates crookedness, as we saw in 11:1. He loves those who go the right way, walk the right path; they are his delight. We can trust him to punish evil (11:21); that is what guarantees the benefits of being righteous.

The philosopher Immanuel Kant (1724–1804) wanted morality to be rational. He wanted the good to be rewarded and the evil punished. The problem is that however much we want this to be true – and we have already observed that people do want this to be true – the world doesn't always work that way. If we only have this confusing, fallen world to observe, we do not always see righteousness triumphing or being rewarded. News media always want to highlight the bad and shocking, for that is what gets hits, but even so it does seem that things go from bad to worse. Whether the disaster of the day is environmental, the disintegration of government services, collapse of community and the integrity of politicians, social injustice or rising crime, it often does not look like righteousness is rewarded. It certainly didn't seem so for Kant, and for that reason he had to postulate that God exists even though his philosophy taught that we cannot know that. It was the only way that Kant could see to make ethics work.

It's actually true, even if Kant rejected the revelation that proves it to be true. Proverbs points out the real-world benefits of integrity, but ultimately it is knowing God that makes sense of the worth of integrity. After all, he is the one who is in charge of temporal riches and benefits as well as eternal ones. In any case, blessing one's fellows and community through honesty and the valuing of relationships will always see one reward, for we were created for relationships. Fallen as it is, the world was created on the principles of wisdom, and so we should not be surprised that following the ways of wisdom actually works.

In fact, following worldly wealth instead of integrity is ludicrous. An attractive woman – someone who has what is a very valued kind of worldly wealth – yet who lacks discretion is as ridiculous as giving a pig a gold nose-piercing (11:22). The sarcasm is evident; it is absurd, an utter waste. Follow the good; wise people, the righteous, long only for good for others. Seek that, not what will lead to anger and wrath (11:23). One very specific way to do this, following our theme of money and riches, is not just to be fair, but to be generous (11:24–5). Be the one who distributes wealth widely and generously (11:24) and bestows blessing (11:25). Be the one who sells grain, rather than hoarding it (11:26; it could imply those who sell reasonably, at a normal price, not trying to drive up the price in price gouging). This behaviour, in the interests of others, is what God rewards.

It makes sense that God will bless those who are generous with more money; after all, those are the people who have proved they can be trusted with it! Missionary biographies and the lives of many Christians tell of the surprising provision that comes when sacrificial generosity is practised. It goes against our instincts; giving away our wealth hardly seems to be the way to be rewarded. It is certainly the way to emotional and relational reward, but even more than that, time after time we can see monetary reward itself coming from generosity (see 2 Corinthians 9:10–11).

One way in which this happens is through the attitudes of others: people love the generous. Seek the good, look for ways to do good (11:27), and people will like you (even though that's not your motivation for doing it); but seek harm, and you'll get it back. It's another one of the wisdom principles that is built into the way the world works. It may not happen in every individual instance, but it is a pattern that we can see working over and over. Don't trust in riches (11:28); the righteous flourish, as Psalm 1 has already told us.

The last three verses of this chapter sum up the principles we have seen, about the value of wisdom and its connection with money and other kinds of intangible wealth. Neglecting relationships, ruining a household, is not worth it (11:29). But the one who is wise saves lives (11:30), literally 'captures others' in the sense of making them safe. Righteousness, moral behaviour towards God and others, is like the tree of life – the image so familiar not just from Psalm 1, but from Genesis through to Revelation as a symbol of God's blessing and of eternal life. There could hardly be a greater commendation. And verse 31 brings us back to earth; even in this life, we will be rewarded, just as sin brings suffering. Godliness is of gain for this life and the next; we should not be surprised by this (1 Timothy 4:8).

Conclusion to Proverbs 10:31–11:31

We have seen in this section the worthlessness of money without morality (10:31–11:8); in contrast, the value of good relationships (11:9–13), the way in which valuing people above money helps community (11:14–27), and the summary that generosity and seeking the good of others is what is truly rewarding (11:28–31). Love God and love others. This is God's wisdom.

17

Be a Good Friend

PROVERBS 12

If relationships are what I should be working on, how do I do it? Chapter 12 of Proverbs teaches about relationships, or, more particularly, how to be a good part of a relationship. The wisdom here, as well as continuing to show us what good moral character is in general, shows us how to please God by being a good friend; this is God's ideal of friendship.[1]

Friendship is not something that gets a major focus these days, in our sexualised culture. Where it does, it seems the advice is all about how to lose friends – how to cancel the toxic friend, how to whittle down your friend list, how to make sure you carve out time for yourself. But friendship is a major value in the Bible, as Christians have realised at other times in church history. Christ, as well as being our Saviour and Lord, chooses to be our friend (John 15:15). Moreover, the values that make a good friend are those that underlie any kind of relationship. We have seen already in Proverbs how the riches of relationship are far more valuable than those provided by money. This is how to prosper in life, and it is also how to please God.

1. Godly friendships • Proverbs 12:1–14

We see a wisdom commendation starting this section (12:1), and a reminder of the stakes – life and immortality – finish it (12:28). The relationship advice starts in general principles (12:1–14) then moves to the specific (12:15–28). Each half ends with a proverb that sums up (12:14 and 28).

1 See Kidner, 'The friend', in *Proverbs*, 44–6.

12 Whoever loves discipline
loves knowledge,
but whoever hates correction
is stupid.

2 Good people obtain favour
from the LORD,
but he condemns those who
devise wicked schemes.

3 No one can be established
through wickedness,
but the righteous cannot be
uprooted.

4 A wife of noble character is her
husband's crown,
but a disgraceful wife is like
decay in his bones.

5 The plans of the righteous are
just,
but the advice of the wicked is
deceitful.

6 The words of the wicked lie in
wait for blood,
but the speech of the upright
rescues them.

7 The wicked are overthrown
and are no more,
but the house of the righteous
stands firm.

8 A person is praised according
to their prudence,
and one with a warped mind is
despised.

9 Better to be a nobody and yet
have a servant
than pretend to be somebody
and have no food.

10 The righteous care for the
needs of their animals,
but the kindest acts of the
wicked are cruel.

11 Those who work their land will
have abundant food,
but those who chase fantasies
have no sense.

12 The wicked desire the stronghold of evildoers,
but the root of the righteous
endures.

13 Evildoers are trapped by their
sinful talk,
and so the innocent escape
trouble.

14 From the fruit of their lips
people are filled with good
things,
and the work of their hands
brings them reward.

The chapter begins with the heart; what do you love, what do you hate? This is the motivation for everything you say and do. We have seen earlier the value of heeding reproof (3:11; 5:12; 6:23; 10:17; 13:18; 15:5, 10, 32) It is a characteristic of wisdom that we will listen even to those things that we don't want to hear. Ultimately, it is the word of God that will provide our correction: it is useful not just for teaching and training, but also for rebuking and correcting (2 Timothy 3:16). A favourite (and very wise) saying of one of my old colleagues was, 'Will you let God disagree with you?' Sadly, too many people now, and in the past few centuries, have not been willing to do so. Rather than let God correct our false ideas, people have been far too quick to insist that the parts of Scripture that don't suit us need to be rejected as not really in the text, or for some reason not to be applied to today, or reinterpreted so as to say something totally different. The tactics for avoiding God's correction are myriad. People will insist that Scripture cannot be saying what it says. God cannot disagree with them.

But wisdom means being willing to accept correction, and this operates in friendship on a human level as well as with God. We do not want to be those who are always seeking fault, but we do want to be the friend who will listen to the correction of those who love us. To do otherwise, as the text so ably translates, is stupid. Don't be stupid.

Verses 2–4 go on to apply wisdom to two very important relationships. First, and absolutely foremost, is our relationship with God. The good person looks for God's favour. It is the same word translated 'delight' or 'favour' in 11:1 and 20 (also 12:22); it is a powerful word, and describes what we all should be aiming for. The opposite of 'good people' here, the people that the Lord condemns, are the ones who 'devise wicked schemes' – who look to take advantage of others. Our relationships with others will necessarily intersect with our relationship with God. Seeking to please God will mean seeking to serve others; treating others badly reflects a similar contempt for God. And contempt for God is an intensely unstable way to live (12:3). It will not lead to security, whereas the righteous 'cannot be uprooted' – they will be like the planted tree (see 11:28; Psalm 1:3, Colossians 2:7).

The second major relationship considered here is marriage. It speaks of a 'wife of noble character', of whom we will hear more in chapter 31 (Proverbs 31:10 uses the same word, *chayil*). This word implies someone resourceful, energetic, someone who can take care of herself and others. It is also used of a man's strength (Psalm 18:32; Ecclesiastes 12:3), military might (Psalm 18:39; 110:3) and wealth (Job 20:18; Ezekiel 28:5) as well as competence (Genesis 47:6; Exodus 18:21, 25; 1 Chronicles 26:7, 30). It is what characterised Ruth (Ruth 3:11).

This wife is her husband's 'crown' (Proverbs 12:4). Consider that for a moment. A crown symbolises royalty, honour, wealth, everything that is most valued in the world. But it is not worldly riches nor status that best signifies those valuable things; it is having a noble wife. A husband blessed with a good wife should value her above all else. The apostle Paul agrees: the husband is to love his wife as himself, willing to lay down his life for her – not just to die for her, but to live for her a life of service (Ephesians 5:25–30). This instruction, both Old and New Testament, is given in what is often derided as a patriarchal culture; yet this woman is not considered a threat, but someone worth laying down one's life for. She is beyond price, for the wife who is not this, who is disgraceful, is like 'decay in his bones'. It is an awful image, one of gnawing, aching rot that undermines everything. A good marriage partner makes life worth living, and a bad one – whether husband or wife – can make death seem preferable.

We go on in the next few verses to see something about that noble character. The righteous, the kind of person with this sort of noble character, plans with fairness, plans justly (12:5). This is not the person who plans wickedly, gives wicked advice, scheming craftily as in verse 2. That kind of person is deceitful, not trustworthy. The words of such people 'lie in wait for blood' (12:6); they set up ambushes, they seek to attack others sneakily, the opposite of fairness or justice. Those who use their words to entrap, to catch others out, to humiliate or otherwise bring down, are awful. It is a dreadful use of the gift of speech, the fundamental tool of relationship. Words should be used as 12:6b describes: to rescue people from such traps. Whether in oratory and public proclamation or simply in conversation, whether online or offline, words that seek to help and protect others are intensely powerful.

Again, this is something that can stabilise or destabilise life (12:7). A wicked life is an unstable one. The untrustworthy person is likely to be betrayed; slanderous people set themselves up for slander, those who seek to dominate others will breed resentment and attempts to overthrow. The righteous, however, build stability in their relationships and in their world. And their words will breed similar words (12:8). Those who speak wisely will garner praise (see Matthew 7:28–9; John 7:46); those who reveal a warped mind will be despised. Character will out, and will be responded to. (Of course, we should still strive for wise words, even if they are not recognised; Ecclesiastes 9:15.) Wisdom will judge the words a person utters, and so see which character is truly noble. Do people speak the truth, fairly, in a way that builds others up? Or do they use words to entrap? The witty character who nonetheless uses humour cruelly at the expense of others is not going to be a true friend. Look for the one who uses words to heal, and deeds likewise.

For in deeds, too, character will be revealed, and verses 9–12 describe a few ways in which this happens. The quiet worker, the nobody, who nonetheless gets on with the job ('have a servant' could mean 'employ a worker') is better than the self-important person with nothing to eat (12:9). Deeds speak, and sometimes contradict pompous words. How we treat others of God's creatures, both animal and human, also reveals our character (12:10). People of cruel character will be cruel in how they act, but those of kind character will be kind to all. Even the mercy of the wicked is cruel; this is sarcastic, like the slaver who feeds his captives simply in order to get a better price for them.

There is not much in the Bible about how to treat animals, but what is there reflects God's care for these parts of his creation (Deuteronomy 11:15; Psalms 36:6; 104:14, 17; Jonah 4:11). It is not godly to be cruel to animals. We do not need charters of 'animal rights'; we simply need to love animals as part of God's ordered creation. It is not loving to animals to treat them as humans, and it is certainly not godly to treat them badly. God provides food for all his creatures, and so should we for those under our care.

Similarly, how we work the land will reflect character and will be rewarded appropriately (12:11). Work diligently for food; don't 'chase fantasies'. The agricultural metaphor can be extended to other work in a non-agricultural society. The point is to get on with the job and be satisfied with its good rewards, not to be foolish in chasing empty vision. 'Follow your dreams' is not always good advice; paying attention to the job in front of you may be far wiser. Don't desire plunder, even of the evil; that is what the wicked desire (12:12a). Rather, have the good heart, which is the way to enduring life (12b).

In summary of the principles laid out in this first half of the chapter, we have verses 13 and 14. Words and deeds, which reflect character, receive appropriate rewards. The sinful talk of an evil man is a trap; but the righteous person, who will have righteous words and deeds, will escape the trap (12:13). Good speech brings good, just as good deeds bring good (12:14). These are the things that will win God's favour (see 12:2). This is wisdom.

2. *Getting specific* • *Proverbs 12:15–28*

So far, the advice has been fairly general. What, exactly, are the good words and good deeds we should have? What is the way to be a good friend? The second half of the chapter gets more specific, with a particular focus on speech.[2]

15 The way of fools seems right to them,
but the wise listen to advice.

16 Fools show their annoyance at once,
but the prudent overlook an insult.

2 Overland (*Proverbs*, 249–50) even renders verses 16–23 within the context of a narrative. Two onlookers are responding to someone who says something possibly insulting. The first onlooker, a fool, immediately takes offence and bursts out angrily, whereas the second, who is discreet, instead tries to control the damage. The outburst of anger now goes to court with the two as witnesses (12:17); the discreet person defends his friend as moral, and applies words of healing, while the fool uses smear tactics. Ultimately, the words of the good friend last, while the lies fade. The two witnesses are rewarded in kind: the fool, driven by deceit, finds misery, while the wise person, who sought wholeness, finds God's reward.

17 An honest witness tells the
truth,
but a false witness tells lies.

18 The words of the reckless
pierce like swords,
but the tongue of the wise
brings healing.

19 Truthful lips endure for ever,
but a lying tongue lasts only a
moment.

20 Deceit is in the hearts of those
who plot evil,
but those who promote peace
have joy.

21 No harm overtakes the
righteous,
but the wicked have their fill of
trouble.

22 The LORD detests lying lips,
but he delights in people who
are trustworthy.

23 The prudent keep their knowledge to themselves,
but a fool's heart blurts out
folly.

24 Diligent hands will rule,
but laziness ends in forced
labour.

25 Anxiety weighs down the heart,
but a kind word cheers it up.

26 The righteous choose their
friends carefully,
but the way of the wicked
leads them astray.

27 The lazy do not roast[a] any
game,
but the diligent feed on the
riches of the hunt.

28 In the way of righteousness
there is life;
along that path is immortality.

a 27 The meaning of the Hebrew for this word is uncertain.

Even taken as individual sayings, these proverbs are certainly not random. A good friend stays faithful and offers good advice, even when times are tough. This theme is introduced by another reminder of the value of listening to advice (12:15). Unwavering commitment to one's own ideas, something that is almost universally admired in our culture, is not actually a wise way to proceed. Being true to yourself is not wise if you happen to be wrong. The good friend is the one who speaks up when your way is the wrong one; being prepared to listen, even against the counsel of one's own heart, is true wisdom.

There are various ways in which counsel can be wise, seen in the next few verses. Don't speak rashly, reacting in immediate haste to an insult (12:16). Be honest in your speech; don't tell lies, especially in court, whatever the temptation (12:17). Hold back on reckless words; they can do serious damage: 'pierce like swords' (12:18a). 'Words will never hurt me' is simply not true; they may not actually break bones, and we know 'pierce like swords' is a figure of speech, but they can certainly hurt.

We have a problem with words in western culture. On the one hand, words can be given far too much weight. Speech that does not affirm people's preferences or disagrees with their philosophy can be labelled 'violence' and prosecuted as strongly as actual, physical violence. This is too strong a reaction.[3] Physical violence against a person is a crime, and should be prosecuted; disagreement in words, especially if the words are not actually abusive but simply express an alternative point of view, should not be a crime. Yet let us not be naïve; cruel words can certainly hurt. It is right that the Bible so frequently advises control of speech. Words can pierce to the soul. Sometimes they need to, and good, critical advice should be listened to, but cruelty should never be part of our speech. Rather, use words to heal (12:18b). But be reassured; truth lasts, and lies do not (12:19). Even if we are slandered or wrongly accused of hate, or evil, such lies will not last. Being lied about hurts intensely in the moment, but even if people never realise the truth, God knows it.

The same themes are reinforced in the next four verses: the bad that results from evil and deception, the good that results from the peaceful (*shalom*) aims of the righteous (12:20, 21); the delight of the Lord in truth, and his hatred of lies (12:22) and the wisdom of thinking before speaking (12:23). Our words matter. They should be true, thoughtful, aimed at bringing good. These are the words that promote good relationships, and the wise person will listen to them.

---

3 See Jonathan Haidt and Greg Lukianoff, *The Coddling of the American Mind: How Good Intentions and Bad Ideas Are Setting Up a Generation for Failure* (New York: Penguin, 2018).

Verses 24–7 sum this up nicely, with a neat pericope (symmetric pattern). In verse 24 we have diligence opposed to laziness, echoed in verse 27 ('laziness' there can also mean 'deceit', following the theme of truth and lies). In between these two, anxiety can be turned to joy by good advice (12:25); this is the work of a good friend, who will not lead a friend astray (12:26). Older versions of the NIV have the footnote alternative reading for verse 26 as 'is a guide to his neighbour'. The good friend is investigating what is causing the anxiety, and will utter good words in response, as opposed to the wicked person who will just lead the anxious person further into the morass.

Anxiety is life-destroying. Sufferers of anxiety know how deathly chronic anxiety can be; I have frequently heard the testimony, which I would agree with, that physical pain, however intense, is far easier to bear. Yet good words of a friend genuinely help, particularly the good words that tell of God – in verse 25, they literally make the person rejoice. The longing of any anxious person is to have joy, truly the opposite of anxiety (even more than joy is the opposite of sadness). This is more than 'cheers it up'; the NIV translation tones down the effect of the contrast. Anxiety, which saps life, can be turned to joy, through the right words; over time, to be sure, but such words are powerful. They are life-giving (12:28).

Conclusion to Proverbs 12

Friendship thrives on kind words and wise advice. Our conclusion is verse 28: this is not just about the pleasure of having a good friend, for righteousness is crucial to life, even immortality (literally 'not death'). Be a good and righteous friend. It is likely the most important quality you can have.

18

Living Your Best Life

PROVERBS 13:1–15:6

Living your best life is the main goal of wisdom; this is how to have life to the full. Chapter 13 begins with a summary of the principles for a flourishing life.

1. Invest in life • Proverbs 13

Chapter 13 will conclude this intermediate section (chapters 10–13). In it we have seen discussed questions of gaining wealth, planning for the future, seeing the higher value of relationships, and what good relationships involve. The chapter will end with advice for continuing this focus on wise living for future generations.

First, in the wisdom summary that starts the section, be prepared to listen to advice, especially when it involves a rebuke (13:1). Second, have self-control (13:2–4). Third, act morally (13:5–6, 9). Fourth, understand the true value of money (13:8). The rest of the chapter gives further advice for achieving these, and so investing in life.

13 A wise son heeds his
father's instruction,
but a mocker does not respond
to rebukes.

2 From the fruit of their lips
people enjoy good things,
but the unfaithful have an
appetite for violence.

3 Those who guard their lips
preserve their lives,
but those who speak rashly
will come to ruin.

4 A sluggard's appetite is never
filled,
but the desires of the diligent
are fully satisfied.

5 The righteous hate what is
false,
but the wicked make them-
selves obnoxious
and bring shame on
themselves.

6 Righteousness guards the
person of integrity,
but wickedness overthrows the
sinner.

7 One person pretends to be
rich, yet has nothing;
another pretends to be poor,
yet has great wealth.

8 A person's riches may ransom
their life,
but the poor cannot respond
to threatening rebukes.

9 The light of the righteous
shines brightly,
but the lamp of the wicked is
snuffed out.

10 Where there is strife, there is
pride,
but wisdom is found in those
who take advice.

11 Dishonest money dwindles
away,
but whoever gathers money
little by little makes it
grow.

12 Hope deferred makes the heart
sick,
but a longing fulfilled is a tree
of life.

13 Whoever scorns instruction
will pay for it,
but whoever respects a
command is rewarded.

14 The teaching of the wise is a
fountain of life,
turning a person from the
snares of death.

15 Good judgment wins favour,
but the way of the unfaithful
leads to their destruction.[a]

16 All who are prudent act with[b]
knowledge,
but fools expose their folly.

17 A wicked messenger falls into
trouble,
but a trustworthy envoy brings
healing.

18 Whoever disregards discipline
comes to poverty and shame,
but whoever heeds correction
is honoured.

19 A longing fulfilled is sweet to
the soul,
but fools detest turning from
evil.

20 Walk with the wise and
become wise,
for a companion of fools
suffers harm.

21 Trouble pursues the sinner,
but the righteous are rewarded
with good things.

22 A good person leaves an inheritance for their children's
children,
but a sinner's wealth is stored
up for the righteous.

23 An unploughed field produces
food for the poor,
but injustice sweeps it away.

24 Whoever spares the rod hates
their children,
but the one who loves their
children is careful to discipline them.

25 The righteous eat to their
hearts' content,
but the stomach of the wicked
goes hungry.

a 15 Septuagint and Syriac; the meaning of the Hebrew for this phrase is uncertain.
b 16 Or *prudent protect themselves through*

Being prepared to listen to correction is a key part of wisdom (13:1). Only mockers pay no attention (to their cost: 30:17). That's how they become mockers – they have failed to learn. Rebukes can be hard to receive, and they are not always well motivated or true; in that case, wise judgment will develop a certain level of thick skin and remain unmoved by the malice of others. However, it is always worth considering rebuke, for sometimes it is just what wisdom needs, especially when it comes from a respected teacher (as the father here, passing on his wisdom, clearly is).

Our second principle involves controlling the appetites. Have an appetite for what is good – in this case, good teaching (13:2) and not violence. (Note: in verse 2a the fruit is not necessarily from the same people who benefit. This could be referring to the blessings we can give others, as in verse 14a.) Watch yourself, the import of guarding your lips (13:3) – the NIV has contrasted this with 'those who speak rashly', but speech is actually not mentioned – the person who comes to ruin is the one who 'opens wide his lips',[1] which could refer to appetite as well as speech. (It also parallels verse 2: those with an

1 Overland, *Proverbs*, 255.

appetite for violence are now coming to ruin, but those with right use of lips produce good things and preserve life.) This would make sense in the context of 13:4 which continues the theme of appetite, condemning the sluggard who will not be satisfied (13:4a), unlike the one with self-control, the diligent person who has (implicitly) right desire (13:4b). Right desire is as important as right action, for it flows from a right heart. The heart that is truly aligned to God's will can be absolutely satisfied.

Right morals are closely connected to right desires (13:5). Be the righteous person who hates falsity. The righteous person has already appeared in 1:3; 10:2, 3; the language is also used of the person thirsting for God in Psalm 42:1–2. This is the person whose desires are aligned with God's desires, and so hates what God hates – in this case, what is false, literally a false word. We should truly hate lying and deception. Don't be the wicked, who are 'obnoxious', actually a shameful stench, with overtones of social disgrace. For (13:6) righteousness is your protection, and wickedness is not; possibly, in context, protection against the falsehood that brings the shame of verse 5.

Finally, in recapitulation of earlier chapters, have a right attitude to wealth (13:7, 8). This particular attitude is in great need of controlling. Learn how to judge what truly constitutes riches (13:7); this verse is against pretension, as well as against those who can't recognise what real wealth is. True riches are those that can save a life; true poverty can't even respond to rebukes (13:8; 'threatening' is not necessary. This could be saying that a poor person is incapable of responding, but that poverty consists of not heeding rebuke; poverty flows from such an insolent attitude, see 13:18). In summary, true life flourishing will come from righteousness, the shining light symbolising life and joy. This is the person who has listened to rebuke and learned from it; the one who has diligence and self-control, and knows that these things are the true wealth. The wicked, who don't, will only find darkness (13:9).

Expanding on these principles, we come to the next few verses. People with wisdom will take advice, but the pride that resists advice accompanies strife (13:10). Put into practice the principles given above. Work, day by day, little by little, for your money, not seeking it dishonestly (13:11); this daily diligence is better than a vain dream that never comes true (13:12) which will only hurt, as opposed to a longing that can come true – again we have our 'tree of life' imagery, the symbol of life itself. (The ultimate longing, which will be overwhelmingly fulfilled, is for God himself; hungering and thirsting for him and his righteousness will lead to life for ever; Psalm 42:1; Matthew 5:6; Revelation 22:17.) Listen to instruction and respect commands (13:13); listen to wise teaching and so obtain the reward of this fulfilled life, not death (13:14 – read 13 and 14 in parallel). Live morally and wisely, with good judgment and faithfulness (13:15).[2] And avoid being the fool; rather, act on the teaching you have received, and be prudent (13:16; see also John 2:23–4; 2 Corinthians 2:11), like the trustworthy envoy, not the untrustworthy one (13:17). For – now combining the themes of wealth and listening to correction – poverty follows those who don't heed reproof, and honour follows those who do (13:18, reflecting verse 13). This is also a way to have the sweetness of fulfilled longing. It won't come to those who can't bring themselves to reject evil (13:19).

So, in conclusion walk with the wise, not the foolish (13:20)! In a time when some denominations are urging the ultimate value of 'walking together', it is important to recognise that Scripture has very definite instructions on whom we are to walk with. Not the fools, who reject God, but the wise, who will listen to reproof – who will let God disagree with them – and so obey him. Our companions, those we associate with, will affect us. The best life, the blessed life, comes from not walking with sinners, Psalm 1 tells us, and Proverbs reinforces this principle (1:10–19; 16:29; 22:24–5; 28:7; 29:3; 22:24; see also Ruth 1:16; 2 Kings 2:4; Psalm 1:1; 106:35; 119:63; 1 Corinthians 5:6–7; 2 Corinthians 6:14–18; Hebrews 10:25). Walk with sinners, and there will be trouble (13:21). It is the righteous who are rewarded. This is wisdom.

And what about future generations? Wisdom should not end with its current students. Look to pass on a good inheritance (13:22), which we have seen will not consist just of monetary wealth, but also of wise teaching. But it may also involve physical wealth, even the wealth of sinners whom, we have seen, may lose their wealth

2 See Waltke, *The Book of Proverbs*, I.548 note 29 for translation issues.

through their wickedness (13:11; see also 2:20–22). Poverty represents the ultimate dissatisfaction (13:23), for even what is there (possibly referring to the sabbatical year, Exodus 23:10–11; Leviticus 25:1–7) can be lost through injustice. Our world is capable of producing enough food for everyone, but corruption and waste mean that many still go hungry. It may be that the mention of injustice alludes to evil people not listening to reproof earlier (13:8).

So look to future generations, and teach them truly. Serve them by offering rebuke where necessary (13:24). The verse talks about corporal punishment, but in context of the wider teaching on discipline the point is reproof, which is how to gain righteousness and flourishing.[3] Loving parents will correct their children.[4] For satisfaction comes from righteousness, not wickedness (13:25) – the appetite that longs for the right things is the one that will be satisfied.

Overland identifies two 'most monumental' themes of Proverbs: that true wealth 'consists of rescuing others' and that 'poverty traces primarily to treating reproof with indifference'.[5] Do we understand this? Poverty is not a matter of how much money you have, but how much wisdom; and wisdom will never come without listening to teaching and accepting its correction. True wealth, on the other hand, will serve others, and so wisdom will multiply. Listen to wisdom and put it into practice, and shape your plans, desires and aspirations accordingly. Work diligently and honestly, for right goals, and so be satisfied.

2. The thriving community • Proverbs 14:1–27

So far, we have seen a great deal of advice to individuals, for their character, attitudes, behaviour and relationships. The next ten chapters of Proverbs (14–24) look at community.[6] This move to advice

3 See the comment on Proverbs 23:13–14.

4 Waltke adds that the Suffering Servant 'condescended to the painful school of discipline to "learn obedience" (Isaiah 50:5; Hebrews 5:8)'; Waltke, *The Book of Proverbs*, I.551. Children whose parents fear the Lord are the ones with a refuge (14:26). Failing to heed correction leads to death (15:10).

5 Overland, *Proverbs*, 268.

6 Following Overland's division.

for communities makes sense in the flow of the book. The advice given to individuals ended up focusing outwards: what individuals should do is think of others and what benefits relationships. The next logical step is to consider the communities built when such relationships are built.

We start the section with a play on *bayit*, house, meaning a material house or a household or ongoing family group; sometimes the advice broadens to wider society. We will see that wisdom and morality still go hand in hand, with the wise and foolish separated not just by the amount of intellectual ability or knowledge of facts, but also by character and moral actions. The character summary that often comes at the end of a unit shows that this portion of teaching ends in 15:6, and the mention of the house gives us what has been the main topic of this teaching.

14 The wise woman builds her house,
but with her own hands the foolish one tears hers down.

2 Whoever fears the LORD walks uprightly,
but those who despise him are devious in their ways.

3 A fool's mouth lashes out with pride,
but the lips of the wise protect them.

4 Where there are no oxen, the manger is empty,
but from the strength of an ox come abundant harvests.

5 An honest witness does not deceive,
but a false witness pours out lies.

6 The mocker seeks wisdom and finds none,
but knowledge comes easily to the discerning.

7 Stay away from a fool,
for you will not find knowledge on their lips.

8 The wisdom of the prudent is to give thought to their ways,
but the folly of fools is deception.

9 Fools mock at making amends for sin,
but goodwill is found among the upright.

10 Each heart knows its own
bitterness,
and no one else can share its
joy.

11 The house of the wicked will
be destroyed,
but the tent of the upright will
flourish.

12 There is a way that appears to
be right,
but in the end it leads to
death.

13 Even in laughter the heart may
ache,
and rejoicing may end in grief.

14 The faithless will be fully
repaid for their ways,
and the good rewarded for
theirs.

15 The simple believe anything,
but the prudent give thought
to their steps.

16 The wise fear the LORD and
shun evil,
but a fool is hotheaded and yet
feels secure.

17 A quick-tempered person does
foolish things,
and the one who devises evil
schemes is hated.

18 The simple inherit folly,
but the prudent are crowned
with knowledge.

19 Evildoers will bow down in the
presence of the good,
and the wicked at the gates of
the righteous.

20 The poor are shunned even by
their neighbours,
but the rich have many friends.

21 It is a sin to despise one's
neighbour,
but blessed is the one who is
kind to the needy.

22 Do not those who plot evil go
astray?
But those who plan what
is good find[a] love and
faithfulness.

23 All hard work brings a profit,
but mere talk leads only to
poverty.

24 The wealth of the wise is their
crown,
but the folly of fools yields folly.

25 A truthful witness saves lives,
but a false witness is deceitful.

26 Whoever fears the LORD has a
secure fortress,

and for their children it will be
a refuge.

27 The fear of the LORD is a
fountain of life,
turning a person from the
snares of death.

a 22 Or *show*

In 14:1 we welcome back our familiar character, the wise woman, although the expression is different; this is not a personification of wisdom so much as a description of what wise women do. They build. The opposite, the fool, is destructive. This could equally apply to a physical house or a household of people. This contrast between what builds (buildings, relationships, people) and what tears down will be seen at other points (14:11, 28, 32, 15:6). It is no accident that verse 2 takes us to fear of the Lord; this is central to the kind of constructive activity that builds, as opposed to the deviousness that tears down (14:2). Walking uprightly is walking according to the Lord's desire. It will lead to protective speech (14:3), not speech that hurts others. Verse 3 and 4 are continuing the idea of what builds up communities: the right kind of speech does so, as does the right kind of power and strength (14:4).

How do you obtain the kind of wisdom necessary for building a community? First you need honesty (14:5); you need to be able to rely on witnesses. You need those who wish for wisdom (14:6), and not fools (14:7). Verse 6 demonstrates that the mocker will not find wisdom even when it's there for the perceptive person to see; obtaining wisdom depends on the character of the one seeking it, not on the source. So we have completed a pattern:

Be the wise person who fears the Lord (1–2)
Wise not foolish speech (3)
  Build through strength (4)
Wise not foolish speech (5)
Be wise, not a mocker, and avoid fools (6–7)

We go on to see more about the kind of character that builds community, builds the houses referenced in 14:1. It requires prudence, the ability not to be deceived but to know the right way forward

(14:8). It requires morality, for that breeds goodwill; only a fool will despise such community-building activities as making amends (14:9). We must, of course, try not to sin in the first place, but 'if we claim to be without sin, we deceive ourselves' (1 John 1:8), and so we must be prepared to make amends when we do sin. That is how to restore relationships and build harmony.

Building also requires discretion in what is shared (14:10). Some things require self-restraint, for they will not build others up. The brief summary of 14:11 describes the consequences: the tent of the upright, the house or household of the wise and moral, will flourish; that of the wicked will perish.

The instruction about discretion goes on; the reason we must live this way is that we need to choose the right path, which is not always easy. It is important to see where a path is leading (14:12).[7] We need to understand what may underly surface appearances (14:13). Choose the right pathway (14:14), for ultimately, Proverbs teaches, there will be consequences for your choices. Don't accept just anyone's advice, but have prudence in making decisions about how to go forward (14:15). The best advice, of course, is to fear the Lord; don't do the opposite of this, letting decisions be guided by quick temper or anger, or remaining cool simply to devise evil (14:16–17). For decisions have ongoing consequences (14:18).

We have another little summary in verse 19: what is good and righteous is the best way to go, and determines whether in the end there will be honour. Ultimately, even the wicked will recognise the good (Philippians 2:10).

More specifically, what kind of morality benefits a community? It is true that people love the rich and hate the poor (14:20), but far better is being kind to the poor – the person who does so is the truly blessed one (14:21). When you despise others and plot evil against them you are going the wrong way; planning good is the way to find love and faithfulness (14:22). Building community is based on loving one's neighbour, which is what the person who fears the lord and shuns evil does.

7 It is foolishness that hinders right perception: 'The path leading to death is not actually straight but just perceived by the fool to be so.' Longman, *Proverbs*, 300.

So get on with the job (14:23). Hard work is good; more work, less talking. Seek the crown of wealth, in context the true wealth of kindness (14:24), as opposed to the reward of folly, which is just more folly. Be truthful. In that way serve others. And serve the Lord, for that is what brings a secure house, now and in the future, and abundant life (14:26–7).

3. The wise nation • Proverbs 14:28–15:6

We now turn to a wider context, even to a whole nation. There may be more people involved, but the principles of wisdom are still the same.

29 Whoever is patient has great
understanding,
but one who is quick-tempered
displays folly.

30 A heart at peace gives life to
the body,
but envy rots the bones.

31 Whoever oppresses the poor
shows contempt for their
Maker,
but whoever is kind to the
needy honours God.

32 When calamity comes, the
wicked are brought down,
but even in death the righteous
seek refuge in God.

33 Wisdom reposes in the heart of
the discerning
and even among fools she lets
herself be known.[b]

34 Righteousness exalts a nation,
but sin condemns any people.

35 A king delights in a wise servant,
but a shameful servant arouses
his fury.

15 A gentle answer turns away
wrath,
but a harsh word stirs up
anger.

2 The tongue of the wise adorns
knowledge,
but the mouth of the fool
gushes folly.

3 The eyes of the LORD are
everywhere,
keeping watch on the wicked
and the good.

4 The soothing tongue is a tree
of life,

but a perverse tongue crushes
the spirit.

5 A fool spurns a parent's
discipline,
but whoever heeds correction
shows prudence.

6 The house of the righteous
contains great treasure,
but the income of the wicked
brings ruin.

b 33 Hebrew; Septuagint and Syriac *discerning / but in the heart of fools she is not known*

Again, we have the pattern of first giving the conventional wisdom: most people judge a king's glory by how big his kingdom is (14:28; see also 14:20), and indeed, there is a truth in this (2 Thessalonians 1:10; Revelation 7:9–10). However, far more important is the king, or any other person, who is patient, who controls his temper (14:29), who does not envy, but seeks peace and so gives life and healing, not rottenness (14:30). This is the one who is kind, who does not oppress the poor (14:31), who honours God and seeks him (14:31–2). In conclusion: be the discerning person of wisdom, and even if you are a fool, take note (14:33), for righteousness is what exalts a nation (14:34), not numbers or power.

A new short subsection continues across the chapter boundary. Having addressed rulers (and anyone else who would be wise), now the sage gives advice to the ruled. The servant, too, should strive for wisdom (14:35); but even if fury arises, respond gently, do not escalate the rage (15:1; we see this in practice with Nabal, David and Abigail in 1 Samuel 25:10–13, 23–31). In this way, seek to speak wisdom, not folly (15:2). For the Lord will know (15:3). This is the theological basis for this teaching about wisdom. So be the life-giving source of words, not the one who destroys others (15:4).

As we conclude the advice given to communities, we are reminded of the right response to teaching: listen to teaching, in particular to reproof (15:5). Our concluding character summary, then, is to be the righteous person who builds up a house, for the wicked will only ruin it (15:6).

Conclusion to Proverbs 13:1–15:6

We started this section by talking about how to live your best life. This is a popular phrase, and there is a great deal of wrong advice out in the world about how to achieve it. Proverbs, however, is very clear that the best way to live – as individuals, in relationships and in communities – is to love God and listen to him. Then, and only then, we will know how to love others.

19

Right Minds

PROVERBS 15:7–17:3

We can make a division to a new section of Proverbs over the next two chapters, by seeing the theme of the inner person, *lev*, mind/heart.[1] It is, surprisingly, about joy; this is the aim of having inner wisdom.

1. The joyful heart • Proverbs 15:7–19

The Bible is overwhelmingly emphatic about joy, and the necessity of believers having it – something that is contrary to most popular conceptions of Christianity, and certainly absent from a lot of evangelical preaching, which is (rightly) suspicious of an emotional gospel that evacuates real doctrine. The joy of the Scriptures is not the opposite of rational activity, but the desired result of it. The way to achieve joy is for the mind to be properly developed in understanding God; in this section of Proverbs, by obtaining wisdom. First this involves inner discernment, proper analytical thinking so as to understand the motives behind actions and plans; and it also involves listening to wise counsel from others, even when painful. The most important counsel to listen to is that which comes from the Lord. The ability to do both these things is what will bring joy.

7 The lips of the wise spread
knowledge,
but the hearts of fools are not
upright.

8 The LORD detests the sacrifice
of the wicked,
but the prayer of the upright
pleases him.

1 Although Waltke (*The Book of Proverbs*, I.619). links verse 6 with verse 7 as a quatrain.

9 The LORD detests the way of
the wicked,
but he loves those who pursue
righteousness.

10 Stern discipline awaits anyone
who leaves the path;
the one who hates correction
will die.

11 Death and Destruction[a] lie
open before the LORD –
how much more do human
hearts!

12 Mockers resent correction,
so they avoid the wise.

13 A happy heart makes the face
cheerful,
but heartache crushes the spirit.

14 The discerning heart seeks
knowledge,
but the mouth of a fool feeds
on folly.

15 All the days of the oppressed
are wretched,
but the cheerful heart has a
continual feast.

16 Better a little with the fear of
the LORD
than great wealth with turmoil.

17 Better a dish of vegetables with
love
than a fattened calf with
hatred.

18 A hot-tempered person stirs up
conflict,
but the one who is patient
calms a quarrel.

19 The way of the sluggard is
blocked with thorns,
but the path of the upright is a
highway.

a 11 Hebrew *Abaddon*

We begin with a contrast between the lips of the wise and the mind/heart of the fool. The wise both discern and spread knowledge; they understand, and they share their understanding, giving wise counsel to others. The foolish do not (15:7, 14), because their hearts/minds are not right.

We have begun, then, with the theme of this section – the importance of the heart and mind – with this verse of wisdom-praise. And the first thing the wise will get right is their attitude to the Lord. The Lord will not accept the sacrifice of the wicked; this, Waltke says, is an oxymoron, an attempt to manipulate God by ritual, as opposed to the righteous seeking relationship in the way he specified (15:8; see also Exodus 32:7–8; 1 Samuel 15:22; Isaiah 1:10–17; Jeremiah 7:22–3; Hosea 6:6; Amos 5:21–5; Psalm 50:8–14; Matthew 23:23).[2] God knows the difference, for he has ultimate discernment (15:9a); this is our theological rationale. The wise will be moral and will listen to reprimand (9b–10).[3]

The same teaching is repeated and heightened in the next two verses; God knows the place of death itself, so he certainly knows all hearts (15:11), but the foolish will not listen to correction (15:12; see also John 3:20; Galatians 4:16).

And, we see in verse 13, it is not just knowledge (even knowledge of morality) that is desired, but also happiness. Heartache is rightfully acknowledged as self-destructive. The 'happy heart' could equally be translated 'joyful mind'; it is the same word as the 'discerning heart' of verse 14. The heart/mind state that is desired is both discerning and happy. This is the mind that keeps on seeking knowledge. The fool, on the other hand, keeps on seeking folly (15:14).

We go on to see more benefits of having this right kind of attitude. The good mind – translated 'cheerful heart' – is a continual feast, a picture of joy, even under oppression and wretchedness (15:15). For the cheerful heart does not depend on circumstances, but on the right attitude towards the Lord. This is a qualification of the teaching that righteousness brings prosperity; while it can do so, Proverbs also teaches that it may not always, but that contentment and joy in life does not depend upon prosperity in any case. Even relative poverty with a right approach to God (15:16) and neighbour (love, 15:17) is better than physical wealth with turmoil and hatred, disturbance of spirit and immorality. The attitude that tends to rage or laziness (15:18–19) is definitely the wrong kind of attitude. Instead, be calm (16:32; 19:11; Ecclesiastes 7:8–9), and do what is right.

2 Waltke, *The Book of Proverbs*, I.621.

3 The desperate consequences of failing to be corrected put into context the intensity of instruction to correct children.

2. *Finding joy in the right places • Proverbs 15:20–16:15*

What characterises this right path, the one that will result in joy? Joy is what almost all of us want, after all – does it matter where we find it?

20 A wise son brings joy to his
father,
but a foolish man despises his
mother.

21 Folly brings joy to one who has
no sense,
but whoever has understanding
keeps a straight course.

22 Plans fail for lack of counsel,
but with many advisors they
succeed.

23 A person finds joy in giving an
apt reply –
and how good is a timely
word!

24 The path of life leads upward
for the prudent
to keep them from going down
to the realm of the dead.

25 The LORD tears down the
house of the proud,
but he sets the widow's
boundary stones in place.

26 The LORD detests the thoughts
of the wicked,
but gracious words are pure in
his sight.

27 The greedy bring ruin to their
households,
but the one who hates bribes
will live.

28 The heart of the righteous
weighs its answers,
but the mouth of the wicked
gushes evil.

29 The LORD is far from the wicked,
but he hears the prayer of the
righteous.

30 Light in a messenger's eyes
brings joy to the heart,
and good news gives health to
the bones.

31 Whoever heeds life-giving
correction
will be at home among the
wise.

32 Those who disregard discipline
despise themselves,
but the one who heeds correction gains understanding.

33 Wisdom's instruction is to fear
the LORD,
and humility comes before
honour.

16 To humans belong the
plans of the heart,
but from the LORD comes the
proper answer of the tongue.

2 All a person's ways seem pure
to them,
but motives are weighed by the
LORD.

3 Commit to the LORD whatever
you do,
and he will establish your
plans.

4 The LORD works out everything
to its proper end –
even the wicked for a day of
disaster.

5 The LORD detests all the proud
of heart.
Be sure of this: they will not go
unpunished.

6 Through love and faithfulness
sin is atoned for;
through the fear of the LORD
evil is avoided.

7 When the LORD takes pleasure
in anyone's way,
he causes their enemies to
make peace with them.

8 Better a little with righteousness
than much gain with injustice.

9 In their hearts humans plan
their course,
but the LORD establishes their
steps.

10 The lips of a king speak as an
oracle,
and his mouth does not betray
justice.

11 Honest scales and balances
belong to the LORD;
all the weights in the bag are
of his making.

12 Kings detest wrongdoing,
for a throne is established
through righteousness.

13 Kings take pleasure in honest lips;
they value the one who speaks
what is right.

14 A king's wrath is a messenger
of death,
but the wise will appease it.

15 When a king's face brightens, it
means life;
his favour is like a rain cloud
in spring.

This next little subsection is introduced by praise of the wise son, who spreads joy, while the fool rejects the mother who is the source of wisdom (15:20; see also 10:1; 12:1; 13:1). That fool, that person who has no sense – lacks heart/mind (15:21a) – will take joy in folly; only a fool would do so. The wise person, however, the one with right understanding, will not be diverted by such a false path (15:21b). That person will listen to advisors and so their plans will come to fruition (15:22). In this context, the 'reply' of verse 23 can be taken as advice/counsel;[4] such words are truly joyful, benefiting others as well as the self, leading to life (15:24).

On the other hand, pride is destructive. It will bring the Lord's wrath, for the Lord despises the proud, who might even exploit a widow (15:25) – God cares for those who are weak (15:25; see also 22:28; Deuteronomy 19:14; 27:17; Hosea 5:10; Job 24:2). He wants 'gracious words' (15:26), the kinds of wise sayings of 15:23, which are not morally evil, not like the thoughts of the wicked, nor the kinds of greedy plans or bribery of verse 27.[5] The righteous heart/mind is key to having good words, right words (15:28), and that will determine God's response (15:29).

What is the 'light in the messenger's eyes' that brings such joy in verse 30? These are eyes that see clearly, that have discernment, that see things rightly and are bringing good news – that is what creates true joy and gives health to the whole person, symbolised by the bones. These eyes go along with the ears that hear 'life-giving correction' in verse 31, as opposed to the ones who 'disregard discipline' (15:32) and in doing so reject their own selves.

Proverbs 15:33–16:15 now take us through the connection between listening to good counsel and attitude to God. The height of wisdom is to fear the Lord, to have humility (15:33), which is better than any human's insight (16:1–2); so the best thing to do is commit all plans to the Lord, who is the one who works out all plans, and does so rightly, for he is sovereign (16:3–4). He will punish the proud, the 'wicked' of verse 4b, those who do not have the humility of 15:33 (1:5). Fear

4 Waltke, *The Book of Proverbs*, I.633.

5 Bribery will always exist in a fallen world, and in cultures where it is endemic God's people may have to be brave to take a stand against it. See Sudhakar Mondithoka, 'Bribery and corruption', in Swarup, 'Proverbs', 790–1.

the Lord in love and faithfulness, which will lead to atonement (see also 1 Samuel 15:22; Matthew 6:12, 14–15; Luke 7:47; James 2:8) and avoiding evil (16:6); it is the way to peace in God's providence (16:7). Don't chase after 'much gain' if it involves injustice, but be content with little (16:8; see also 1 Samuel 2:3–10; Psalm 37:16–17; Luke 1:51–3; 1 Timothy 4:8), for it is the Lord who is in control (16:9).[6]

This is what a king should do (16:10) – a wise king (14:35; 20:8, 26, 28; 22:11; 25:2–5; 29:4a) who will maintain justice, which is of God (16:11). Righteousness, not wrongdoing, is what will establish the king's throne (16:12), and honest speech (16:13). The king will back this up with action, punishing evil and sparing the wise (who will have acted righteously) (16:14) – that is how to get his favour (16:15). In other words, the wise king is acting justly, as God does.

3. The right guides • Proverbs 16:16–17:3

As well as looking for the right path, we need the right guides to lead us along it. We now have a section about wise instruction, wise advice.

16 How much better to get
wisdom than gold,
to get insight rather than silver!

17 The highway of the upright
avoids evil;
those who guard their ways
preserve their lives.

18 Pride goes before destruction,
a haughty spirit before a fall.

19 Better to be lowly in spirit
along with the oppressed
than to share plunder with the
proud.

6 John Calvin (1509–64) wrote that this verse affirms God's sovereignty but does not relieve us of responsibility for our actions, nor of the need to plan prudently. 'This means that we are not at all hindered by God's eternal decrees either from looking ahead for ourselves or from putting all our affairs in order, but always in submission to his will . . . It is very clear what our duty is: thus, if the Lord has committed to us the protection of our life, our duty is to protect it; if he offers helps, to use them; if he forewarns us of dangers, not to plunge headlong; if he makes remedies available, not to neglect them.' John Calvin, *Institutes of the Christian Religion*, I.XVII. 4; John T. McNeill (ed.), Ford Lewis Battles (trans.) (Philadelphia: Westminster Press, 1960), 216.

20 Whoever gives heed to instruction prospers,[a]
and blessed is the one who trusts in the LORD.

21 The wise in heart are called discerning,
and gracious words promote instruction.[b]

22 Prudence is a fountain of life to the prudent,
but folly brings punishment to fools.

23 The hearts of the wise make their mouths prudent,
and their lips promote instruction.[c]

24 Gracious words are a honeycomb,
sweet to the soul and healing to the bones.

25 There is a way that appears to be right,
but in the end it leads to death.

26 The appetite of labourers works for them;
their hunger drives them on.

27 A scoundrel plots evil,
and on their lips it is like a scorching fire.

28 A perverse person stirs up conflict,
and a gossip separates close friends.

29 A violent person entices their neighbour
and leads them down a path that is not good.

30 Whoever winks with their eye is plotting perversity;
whoever purses their lips is bent on evil.

31 Grey hair is a crown of splendour;
it is attained in the way of righteousness.

32 Better a patient person than a warrior,
one with self-control than one who takes a city.

33 The lot is cast into the lap,
but its every decision is from the LORD.

17 Better a dry crust with peace and quiet
than a house full of feasting, with strife.

2 A prudent servant will rule over a disgraceful son,
and will share the inheritance as one of the family.

3 The crucible for silver and the
furnace for gold,
but the LORD tests the heart.

a 20 Or *whoever speaks prudently finds what is good*
b 21 Or *words make a person persuasive*
c 23 Or *prudent / and make their lips persuasive*

First, praise of wisdom starts the section in verse 16 (see also 3:13, 14; 8:10). We then set the baseline with the establishment of moral good as the important guide, the 'highway' that leads to life (16:17). One keeps to the road by having humility of spirit, not pride (16:18) even if it comes with poverty (16:19) – a timely warning in these days when pride is so celebrated. Good instruction matters, especially taking instruction from God (16:20); for wisdom and wise instruction, which lead to discernment and prudence, bring rewards and fullness of life (16:21–2). This wise instruction comes from the hearts of the wise, another reason to train the heart (16:23), for these words are not just attractive, but also bring healing (16:24). Clear discernment is crucial, to see past appearances (16:25). The wrong way to go is to be guided by appetite. It may be a motivation to get work done (16:26), but if you let evil impulses guide you, disaster can come to the community; 'scorching' others (16:27), creating conflict and division (16:28) and bringing others to evil (16:29–30). If you follow the way of righteousness, however, look at the rewards: long life, long enough to attain grey hair – a mark of splendour, no less! (16:31; see also Genesis 15:15; 25:8; Psalm 92:14).[7] For restraining oneself (16:32, 17:1), trusting God (16:33; 17:3) and prudence (17:2) are the way to reward. This depends upon God's will; it is not an automatic formula, but a working out of God's sovereignty, as 16:33 makes clear.

Conclusion to 15:7–17:3

In all these ways, the inner character, mind/heart, is to be cultivated. Listening to wise counsel and giving it; restraining appetites and exercising self-control; following the way of righteousness, even if

7 This is a welcome counter to the fear that old age just brings unattractiveness and uselessness, and that the only real remedy is increased access to euthanasia.

it is hard; and, ultimately, trusting the Lord. This is the way to bring harmony among neighbours and personal satisfaction, indeed, joy. It is *better* to live this way, even if other circumstances of life appear poorer. The wise person will develop the discernment to see this, to see past appearances to what is truly valuable. *Tov-lev*, goodness of mind, translated 'a cheerful heart' in 15:15, is that which, because of its righteousness, is able to discern a situation truly, and rejoice even under oppression, for fear of the Lord makes all the difference.

20

Contrasting Bad and Good

PROVERBS 17:4 19:9

So far, the teaching has mostly been for the wise student to avoid foolishness. Worse than the foolishness is evil, and there is evil in the world. The wise person above all follows the good, protects the good and takes all precautions to recognise and avoid evil. We are moving into sayings that teach of the necessity of moral goodness even more emphatically. The text seems quite disparate in its sayings, but context guides interpretation, and so themes can be identified. The placing of sayings is not accidental or random.[1]

We have nineteen sayings in praise of wisdom, which introduce specific wisdom advice. Several specifically concern speech, an important theme in the whole of Proverbs. There are three specific contrasts intertwined in this section: evil/good, riches/poverty and community/aloneness. The three work together: evil people use wealth to deceive and destroy community, but the good value people and justice. Overwhelmingly, the importance of serving others comes through.

1. Shun evil • Proverbs 17:4–26

Some of the sayings here seem to be deliberately obscure, to force the reader to think. By this stage, someone who has started at the beginning of Proverbs could now be considered an advanced student, if not quite yet a black belt (to use a martial arts analogy); but the

1 See Overland for some of the intertwined patterns. For instance, six times in this section sayings are presented in threes. Two of these have two verses on a topic, with a third in contrast. The other four have two statements about wisdom, followed by wise advice.

puzzles are becoming harder, and the student is forced to work more, with fewer textual signposts for meaning. This can be considered part of the teaching strategy of the book.

4 A wicked person listens to
deceitful lips;
a liar pays attention to a
destructive tongue.

5 Whoever mocks the poor
shows contempt for their
Maker;
whoever gloats over disaster
will not go unpunished.

6 Children's children are a crown
to the aged,
and parents are the pride of
their children.

7 Eloquent lips are unsuited to a
godless fool –
how much worse lying lips to a
ruler!

8 A bribe is seen as a charm by
the one who gives it;
they think success will come at
every turn.

9 Whoever would foster love
covers over an offence,
but whoever repeats the matter
separates close friends.

10 A rebuke impresses a
discerning person
more than a hundred lashes a
fool.

11 Evildoers foster rebellion
against God;
the messenger of death will be
sent against them.

12 Better to meet a bear robbed of
her cubs
than a fool bent on folly.

13 Evil will never leave the house
of one who pays back evil for
good.

14 Starting a quarrel is like
breaching a dam;
so drop the matter before a
dispute breaks out.

15 Acquitting the guilty and
condemning the innocent –
the LORD detests them both.

16 Why should fools have money
in hand to buy wisdom,
when they are not able to
understand it?

17 A friend loves at all times,
and a brother is born for a
time of adversity.

18 One who has no sense shakes
hands in pledge
and puts up security for a
neighbour.

19 Whoever loves a quarrel loves
sin;
whoever builds a high gate
invites destruction.

20 One whose heart is corrupt
does not prosper;
one whose tongue is perverse
falls into trouble.

21 To have a fool for a child
brings grief;
there is no joy for the parent of
a godless fool.

22 A cheerful heart is good
medicine,
but a crushed spirit dries up
the bones.

23 The wicked accept bribes in
secret
to pervert the course of
justice.

24 A discerning person keeps
wisdom in view,
but a fool's eyes wander to the
ends of the earth.

25 A foolish son brings grief to his
father
and bitterness to the mother
who bore him.

26 If imposing a fine on the innocent is not good,
surely to flog honest officials is
not right.

First, in 17:4–15, we find out some of the characteristics of evil people; twice we have two sayings about evil followed by a good contrast. Evil people are false and destructive, and mock others, enjoying their suffering (17:4–5). They are not like those who value family and delight in them (17:6). This is followed by a second triad. An evil person – the 'godless fool' (17:7; also in Deuteronomy 32:6; 2 Samuel 13:13; Job 2:9–10; Psalm 14:1; 39:8; 74:22; Isaiah 32:6–7; Jeremiah 17:11) gives false flattery and bribes (17:7–8). The alternative in verse 9 is generosity and forgiveness to friends, not gossip. The fool will not listen to the kind of rebuke that will benefit the wise (17:10). If strife is what evil people want, strife is what they will get, and it will end in suffering (17:11). Avoid folly (17:12), but evil is even worse: evil brings more evil (17:13). So avoid it from the start (17:14) – as long as that does not mean not caring about justice, for God hates that (17:15).

But evil is wily, and we need to be on the lookout. We go on to see more of the connections between folly and evil. Folly breeds more folly (17:16); imagine thinking you could buy wisdom! Wisdom, in contrast, cares for friends and family (17:17). Anyone who has benefited from the love of friends during times of trial knows the deep truth of this proverb. But the fool might misjudge a friend and guarantee a loan too hastily (17:18). Love is not always good, if you love the wrong things (17:19 – the 'high gate' probably refers to pride), and a corrupt heart without wisdom will lead to misuse of the tongue and evil (17:20). Even the good of family can be twisted by folly. Foolish children give parents grief and no joy (17:21), but the joyful heart brings healing – which tells us something about the importance of joy (see also 14:30; 15:13, 30; 16:24; 18:14). The evil person, in context the godless fool of a child, will take bribes to overturn justice. But wisdom comes from being focused, not being distracted by foolish dreams (17:24). This kind of stupidity is what makes for a stupid son who disappoints both parents (17:25, harking back to 21). So don't persecute the innocent (17:26, escalating from verse 23).

2. Speak no evil • Proverbs 17:27–18:12

We proceed to discover more about what the evil do in 17:27–18:22. First, we focus on what characterises their speech in 17:27–18:12.

27 The one who has knowledge
uses words with restraint,
and whoever has under-
standing is even-tempered.

28 Even fools are thought wise if
they keep silent,
and discerning if they hold
their tongues.

18 An unfriendly person
pursues selfish ends
and against all sound judgment starts quarrels.

2 Fools find no pleasure in
understanding
but delight in airing their own
opinions.

3 When wickedness comes, so
does contempt,
and with shame comes
reproach.

4 The words of the mouth are
deep waters,
but the fountain of wisdom is a
rushing stream.

5 It is not good to be partial to
the wicked
and so deprive the innocent of
justice.

6 The lips of fools bring them strife,
and their mouths invite a
beating.

7 The mouths of fools are their
undoing,
and their lips are a snare to
their very lives.

8 The words of a gossip are like
choice morsels;
they go down to the inmost
parts.

9 One who is slack in his work
is brother to one who destroys.

10 The name of the LORD is a
fortified tower;
the righteous run to it and are
safe.

11 The wealth of the rich is their
fortified city;
they imagine it a wall too high
to scale.

12 Before a downfall the heart is
haughty,
but humility comes before
honour.

Wisdom would advise us to be restrained in speech and not say too much – even a fool can appear wise by following this strategy (17:27–28). But the evil person – the unsociable, unfriendly person – uses speech for litigation, and not community (18:1).

This theme continues. The fool by nature will have no restraint, exposing his own folly (18:2); even worse, the evil person expresses contempt and reproach (18:3). Words can be unfathomable, unless they are wise; then they are generous and beneficial (18:4). The opposite is when an evil person gets away with injustice (18:5). Again, the fool only reveals his stupidity with what he says (18:6–7, perhaps reflecting on verse 2), but even worse, the evil person speaks gossip that hurts others (18:8; see also 16:28; 17:9; 26:20, 22) and breeds destruction, just as much as laziness will (18:9). To escape this, the good person will seek the Lord (18:10). This is in contrast to the delusion that wealth will give protection (18:11). It will not (18:12).

3. Wise justice • Proverbs 18:13–22

We have had some examples of the wicked distortion of justice and of administering justice (such as 18:2), and we now have some examples of what the wise will do.

13 To answer before listening –
that is folly and shame.

14 The human spirit can endure
in times of illness,
but a crushed spirit who can
bear?

15 The heart of the discerning
acquires knowledge,
for the ears of the wise seek it
out.

16 A gift opens the way
and ushers the giver into the
presence of the great.

17 In a lawsuit the first to speak
seems right,
until someone comes forward
and cross-examines.

18 Casting the lot settles disputes
and keeps strong opponents
apart.

19 A brother wronged is more
unyielding than a fortified
city;
disputes are like the barred
gates of a citadel.

20 From the fruit of their mouth a
person's stomach is filled;
with the harvest of their lips
they are satisfied.

21 The tongue has the power of
life and death,
and those who love it will eat
its fruit.

22 He who finds a wife finds what
is good
and receives favour from the
LORD.

The wise path is not to rush to judgment (18:13), for that brings crushing defeat; and a destroyed spirit is, indeed, worse than any physical suffering (18:14). Instead, the wise will search for the truth (18:15) and not use wealth to gain favour, perhaps buying the right to speak first (18:16–17a). The right way is to follow due process in justice (18:17b), and perhaps even using a lot – a way of discovering the Lord's will (see 16:33; 1 Samuel 14:40–42) – which can resolve conflict (18:18). For injustice is wrong, hard to resolve and hurts people (18:19).

4. Crucial contrasts • Proverbs 18:23–19:9

We are coming to the conclusion of this section (17:4–19:9).[2] The contrasts come thick and fast as we see the wrong and right ways to live.

23 The poor plead for mercy,
but the rich answer harshly.

24 One who has unreliable friends
soon comes to ruin,
but there is a friend who sticks
closer than a brother.

19 Better the poor whose way
of life is blameless
than a fool whose lips are
perverse.

2 Desire without knowledge is
not good –
how much more will hasty feet
miss the way!

3 A person's own folly leads to
their ruin,
yet their heart rages against
the LORD.

4 Wealth attracts many friends,
but even the closest friend of the
poor person deserts them.

5 A false witness will not go
unpunished,
and whoever pours out lies will
not go free.

6 Many curry favour with a ruler,
and everyone is the friend of
one who gives gifts.

7 The poor are shunned by all
their relatives –
how much more do their
friends avoid them!

2 Waltke (*The Book of Proverbs*, II.87) starts a new section 'health and wisdom in the court and in the home' at 18:22–19:23.

Though the poor pursue them
with pleading,
they are nowhere to be found.[a]

8 The one who gets wisdom
loves life;
the one who cherishes understanding will soon prosper.

9 A false witness will not go
unpunished,
and whoever pours out lies will
perish.

a 7 The meaning of the Hebrew for this sentence is uncertain.

Wise speech is rewarding (18:20), even ultimately (18:21). Relationships are good, in contrast with the loner of 18:1 (18:22). If you don't have relationships, the isolation that poverty brings can be destructive when the rich refuse to help (18:23); the solution is to have good friends (18:24). Either way, it is better for the poor person to stay righteous (19:1), as it is for anyone, and not to be misled by appetites (19:2). For the opposite – folly – only leads astray (19:3). Trusting wealth is no solution: friends bought by wealth are not true friends (19:4, 6), with a warning against perjury in the middle (19:5), which will be punished (19:9). Wisdom and righteousness are still the answer (19:8), despite poverty or even betrayal (19:7). Acquire wisdom and avoid evil.

Conclusion to Proverbs 17:4–19:9

It is worth spending time in this section, pondering over the sayings and seeing how the themes emerge. It is impossible within the limits of this commentary to do justice to the material for contemplation here. This literature is meant to be read slowly and meditatively. Its lessons are not quick slogans, but words to chew on (18:20, 21). They are meant to form character; this is not just about what you do, but who you are.

In particular, there are pertinent lessons about wealth and injustice. It has always been true that the rich use their wealth to subvert justice. Even in the best of cases, litigation is expensive, and the court system – however much honest officers of the court may try to do their jobs well – takes time and money that the poor often just do not have. When wealth is also used in bribes or intimidation, to subvert witnesses or gain favour, it seems that the poor will always be denied justice.

The wealth of the poor, however, lies in relationships and integrity. Good friends who are loved rightly and treated well are better than any riches with loneliness and isolation. Evil will tend to destroy friendship and community, for it is very hard for the evil to trust; their own inclinations are to deceive and betray for profit, so they will always suspect others of doing so, too. This destroys relationships and ultimately is even worse than folly. It will bring God's disapproval and eventual failure.

So the wise will look to value people and to treat them rightly, to put relationships ahead of profit. That is the way to have justice in community. But even if the wealthy appear to triumph, as they buy friends and reputation, integrity is still ultimately far more valuable. The poor and oppressed can take comfort that the Lord will see their actions, and those of the evildoers. Justice will not ever, ultimately, be lost.

21

Use Your Power Wisely

PROVERBS 19:10–20:4

While there are themes that continue between sections, the sections themselves are marked by subtle changes in emphasis, as well as structural features such as word patterns. For instance, Overland points out that the previous section mentioned evil/wickedness frequently, while the present section mentions it only once. In this new section, the emphasis moves to focus on money and power, and their implications. Both topics are introduced in 19:10. Proverbs 20:2–4 likewise sum up the connections between power, relationships and laziness. Proverbs 19:10 and 20:4 both use the negative *lo*, creating boundaries to the section, as well as ending two portions within it (19:24 and 20:4. The roaring of a lion also appears in three verses from the start and finish, showing the wrong use of power. In this way, we can see a development of the text, and a way of reading individual sayings within their immediate context; these are not just random proverbs carelessly listed together.

1. Having and using riches • Proverbs 19:10–17

The world would tell us that money and power are the most important things that we can have. They enable us to have choice, autonomy and self-determination, which are absolutely dominant values for many people. Yet wealth and power are only relative goods, Proverbs would teach us, and not everyone should have them.

10 It is not fitting for a fool to live
in luxury –
how much worse for a slave to
rule over princes!

11 A person's wisdom yields
patience;
it is to one's glory to overlook
an offence.

12 A king's rage is like the roar of
a lion,
but his favour is like dew on
the grass.

13 A foolish child is a father's ruin,
and a quarrelsome wife is like
the constant dripping of a
leaky roof.

14 Houses and wealth are inherited from parents,
but a prudent wife is from the
LORD.

15 Laziness brings on deep sleep,
and the shiftless go hungry.

16 Whoever keeps command-
ments keeps their life,
but whoever shows contempt
for their ways will die.

17 Whoever is kind to the poor
lends to the LORD,
and he will reward them for
what they have done.

We see the themes of wealth and power introduced in 19:10. Foolish people should not have them; it's 'not fitting', the NIV has it, not attractive; it's like an unqualified person being given authority. If you are going to have power, have it with wisdom, which includes restraining anger in patience (19:11), not giving way to it (19:12).

Within the family, wealth is all very well, but good family relationships are better (19:13–14); indeed, lack of peace in the home can destroy all pleasure. Also bringing the good life are hard work and listening to instruction (19:15–16), as opposed to laziness and ignoring good advice, both of which we have seen are characteristic of foolish sons (6:6–11; 10:1, 4–5; 24:30–34). The right attitude towards riches and relationships is what matters and is what the Lord will reward (19:17).

2. Instructing children in this wisdom • Proverbs 19:18–20:1

This, then, is what sensible parents will teach their children. Proverbs often switches between direct instruction to students and instruction to the teachers.

18 Discipline your children, for in
that there is hope;
do not be a willing party to
their death.

19 A hot-tempered person must
pay the penalty;
rescue them, and you will have
to do it again.

20 Listen to advice and accept
discipline,
and at the end you will be
counted among the wise.

21 Many are the plans in a
person's heart,
but it is the LORD's purpose
that prevails.

22 What a person desires is
unfailing love;[b]
better to be poor than a liar.

23 The fear of the LORD leads to
life;
then one rests content,
untouched by trouble.

24 A sluggard buries his hand in
the dish;
he will not even bring it back
to his mouth!

25 Flog a mocker, and the simple
will learn prudence;
rebuke the discerning, and
they will gain knowledge.

26 Whoever robs their father and
drives out their mother
is a child who brings shame
and disgrace.

27 Stop listening to instruction,
my son,
and you will stray from the
words of knowledge.

28 A corrupt witness mocks at
justice,
and the mouth of the wicked
gulps down evil.

29 Penalties are prepared for
mockers,
and beatings for the backs of
fools.

20 Wine is a mocker and beer
a brawler;
whoever is led astray by them
is not wise.

b 22 Or *Greed is a person's shame*

Wise parents will instruct their children (19:18); part of this is instructing them to control anger and allowing them to feel its consequences, for if you don't you will be forever paying (19:19).

So how can parents instruct their children? 19:20–24 gives some specific instructions. First, it involves listening; that in itself is a skill that needs to be learned (19:20). Especially, listen to the Lord, for his plans are the ones that prevail (19:21; see also 16:1–9). What will such a listening person learn? That faithful love is central, the way to ultimate satisfaction, rather than lying for gain (19:22), and the concept of humble, faithful love leads naturally to the fear of the Lord (19:23), where true contentment lies. The opposite is laziness, an attitude of giving into desire, which is the very thing that does not satisfy (19:24) – in this case, the person is too lazy even to eat what is in front of him.

Instead, evil mocking needs to be punished, and such correction needs to be appropriately serious (19:25) although 'flog' is probably too strong a translation. (The discerning will respond to a simple rebuke.) For evil children only bring shame and disgrace (19:26); this is the basis of the strong warning of 19:27.[1] If you mock justice you will accept evil, and there will be penalty (19:28–9). It's as bad as being drunk; the person who mocks and scoffs is similarly a fool (20:1).

3. Learn to control your anger • Proverbs 20:2–4

It is important for everyone, but especially for the powerful, to learn how to control themselves. To wrap up this section, we go back to the problem of uncontrolled anger.

2 A king's wrath strikes terror
like the roar of a lion;
those who anger him forfeit
their lives.

3 It is to one's honour to avoid
strife,
but every fool is quick to
quarrel.

4 Sluggards do not plough in
season;
so at harvest time they look
but find nothing.

1 Waltke points out that here Solomon is constructing his own gibbet (*The Book of Proverbs*, I.36) – if only he had listened to his own advice!

It is very dangerous for the powerful not to be able to control their anger (20:2). Don't be the fool who cannot control temper; instead be the one who avoids it (20:3), and don't be the lazy person with no self-control, for that will not bring success (20:4).

Conclusion to Proverbs 19:10–20:4

I can remember being in a car with a friend and her small daughter as two men started a scuffle on the footpath. One of the men stalked off and, in his rage, slammed his fist on the car, frightening all of us in the car. My friend chose this teaching moment: 'That's what happens,' she said, 'if you don't ever learn to control your anger.' Rage is powerful, and part of the breakdown in intergenerational teaching these days appears to be the lack of instruction in self-control to children. If it is not learned young, it is very difficult to learn later, even with the blessing of salvation in later life. An inability to control powerful emotions such as anger leads to serial suffering both for the angry individual and for everyone around him or her. Self-control is one of the most crucial life skills for success, and for good relationships; it is the key to faithfulness and the ability to keep promises, as well as to the kind of diligent work that is the backbone of prudent life. Parents who teach their children self-control are doing them a great favour.

22

Wisdom for a Lifetime

PROVERBS 20:5–21:4

Whether a child (20:11), a youth or old (20:29), wisdom is what should shape a life. Here we get a sense of the span of a life, and what will make it meaningful and successful.

1. The meaning of life • Proverbs 20:5–23

What is the thing we should be pursuing with all this attainment of wisdom? What is the true goal of life? What are the deep waters that we should be drawing out (20:5)? In this very important section we discuss what people of understanding will discover about life as they move from childhood to old age. The section finishes with a summary of two contrasting ways, the right and the wrong one.

5 The purposes of a person's
heart are deep waters,
but one who has insight draws
them out.

6 Many claim to have unfailing
love,
but a faithful person who can
find?

7 The righteous lead blameless
lives;
blessed are their children after
them.

8 When a king sits on his throne
to judge,
he winnows out all evil with
his eyes.

9 Who can say, 'I have kept my
heart pure;
I am clean and without
sin'?

10 Differing weights and differing
measures –
the LORD detests them both.

11 Even small children are known
by their actions,
so is their conduct really pure
and upright?

12 Ears that hear and eyes that see –
the LORD has made them both.

13 Do not love sleep or you will
grow poor;
stay awake and you will have
food to spare.

14 'It's no good, it's no good!' says
the buyer –
then goes off and boasts about
the purchase.

15 Gold there is, and rubies in
abundance,
but lips that speak knowledge
are a rare jewel.

16 Take the garment of one
who puts up security for a
stranger;
hold it in pledge if it is done
for an outsider.

17 Food gained by fraud tastes
sweet,
but one ends up with a mouth
full of gravel.

18 Plans are established by
seeking advice;
so if you wage war, obtain
guidance.

19 A gossip betrays a confidence;
so avoid anyone who talks too
much.

20 If someone curses their father
or mother,
their lamp will be snuffed out
in pitch darkness.

21 An inheritance claimed too
soon
will not be blessed at the end.

22 Do not say, 'I'll pay you back
for this wrong!'
Wait for the LORD, and he will
avenge you.

23 The LORD detests differing
weights,
and dishonest scales do not
please him.

After the encouragement to seek deep understanding in verse 5, we have what might be considered a topic sentence: the important thing that is so hard to find is unfailing love, despite the fact that many claim it (20:6).[1] How is it, then, to be found? Through righteousness and blameless lives (20:7 – note that this is the way to bless children, not through expensive holidays and education), through the exercise of justice and destruction of evil (20:8; precisely what a king should do, Psalm 72:1–2; 122:5), and through inner purity (20:9). To do this requires being scrupulously fair in business, as we are reminded again how much the Lord hates people who cheat (20:10). From childhood it means acting with purity (20:11). Note the pattern of justice (verses 8 and 10) alternated with human sin (9 and 11). In the face of such sinfulness, wisdom is teaching us to value purity and justice. The Lord has given us our bodies for that purpose (20:12); we see elsewhere in Proverbs what we should be doing with eyes and ears (see 2:2; 4:21; 17:24; 23:9; 24:32). The actions that a child should learn, as well as everyone else, involve not being lazy (20:13), and again being honest in business dealings with others (20:14).

It also involves understanding a right attitude to wealth. Good advice is the true wealth (20:15, as opposed to the marketplace lying of verse 14), which may mean trying to prevent a person entering a bad deal (20:16), or at least avoiding it yourself, because the consequences are severe (losing your very garment). Continuing the marketplace setting, we see unfaithful dealing is not worth it (20:17). So listen to good advice, in war or otherwise (20:18), but don't partner with gossips, who are not faithful (20:19), and avoid those who reject their parents and their blessings, failing to honour them (20:20–21; see also Deuteronomy 5:16; Ephesians 6:1–3). Don't seek revenge – that is for the Lord (20:22; see Deuteronomy 32:35, 43; 2 Samuel 3:39; Psalms 27:14; 37:34; 39:7; 62:5; Matthew 5:38–9; Luke 18:7–8; 1 Peter 2:23; 4:19; Romans 12:17–21; 1 Thessalonians 5:15; Hebrews 10:30) – or practise injustice (20:23; in context, this might be understood as 'even if you have been cheated in the marketplace yourself').

---

1 I like Overland's reading, but Waltke reads verses 5 and 6 differently, seeing 5a as negative ('deep waters' meaning inaccessible and potentially dangerous), in parallel with 6a; the contrast is in the two b verses, the person who is genuine and faithful. Either way, the point is to commend faithful love. Overland, *Proverbs*, 420; Waltke, *The Book of Proverbs*, II.131–2.

2. What to seek • Proverbs 20:24–21:4

The key to training oneself in righteousness is not just knowing what not to do, but also knowing how to focus on the positive. Proverbs teaches us both.

24 A person's steps are directed
by the LORD.
How then can anyone understand their own way?

25 It is a trap to dedicate something rashly
and only later to consider
one's vows.

26 A wise king winnows out the
wicked;
he drives the threshing wheel
over them.

27 The human spirit is[a] the lamp
of the LORD
that sheds light on one's
inmost being.

28 Love and faithfulness keep a
king safe;
through love his throne is
made secure.

29 The glory of young men is their
strength,
grey hair the splendour of the
old.

30 Blows and wounds scrub away
evil,
and beatings purge the inmost
being.

21 In the LORD's hand the
king's heart is a stream of
water
that he channels towards all
who please him.

2 A person may think their own
ways are right,
but the LORD weighs the heart.

3 To do what is right and just
is more acceptable to the
LORD than sacrifice.

4 Haughty eyes and a proud
heart –
the unploughed field of the
wicked – produce sin.

---

a 27 Or *A person's words are*

Instead of the dishonesty, vengefulness and injustice that have just been disussed, seek the right things, which will now be detailed in 20:24–8.

Instead of vengeance, understand the Lord's sovereignty and follow him, for you don't know everything (20:24). This means being faithful to the Lord, considering one's vows carefully (20:25) and rejecting evil (20:26) in favour of faithful love (20:28), understanding that the Lord will see this (20:27).

How can this kind of purity continue through life? This is a lesson for young and old (20:29) – make every effort to be pure (20:30). For the Lord is sovereign (21:1), so follow him, not your own ideas (21:2). In summary: do what is right and just (21:3), without pride (21:4).

Conclusion to Proverbs 20:5–21:4

It is hard to learn that God's ways are the right ways, for the essence of sin is to exalt ourselves. Augustine (AD 354–430) rightly diagnosed that pride is precisely our problem, not something to be celebrated.[2] Martin Luther (1483–1546) described this essential pride as 'turning in on ourselves' – looking inwards for fulfilment and meaning, instead of to God.[3] But such pride is not just wrong, bringing God's displeasure; it is also profoundly unsatisfying. Looking outwards to God in obedience means faithful love to others, inner purity and outward acting in justice and righteousness. That is the humble heart that listens to good advice and puts it into practice, treating others fairly. It is how we want to be treated, but we must first act that way ourselves. This is wisdom, the way to true human flourishing.

2 Augustine, *City of God*, XII.6.

3 Martin Luther, *Lectures on Romans*, L.515–516.

23

Way to Go

PROVERBS 21:5–22:16

Power and wealth continue to be themes in this section. They are not bad in themselves, but there are right and wrong ways to attain them, and right and wrong ways to think about them. There is also some advice, which has been seen occasionally in the last few chapters, about passing on wisdom to others.

1. Planning your path • Proverbs 21:5–10

The section opens with its topic word: 'plans'. This idea, of the strategy that takes you to your goal, is repeated in five usages of the word for the path you take: in 21:8 ('way'), 21:16 ('path'), 21:29 ('ways'); 22:5 ('paths') and 22:6 ('way'). The route you take to a goal matters as much as the goal itself. If it is not pursued with integrity and righteousness, it will displease God and may well lead to disaster.

5 The plans of the diligent lead to profit
as surely as haste leads to poverty.

6 A fortune made by a lying tongue
is a fleeting vapour and a deadly snare.[a]

7 The violence of the wicked will drag them away,
for they refuse to do what is right.

8 The way of the guilty is devious,
but the conduct of the innocent is upright.

9 Better to live on a corner of the roof
than share a house with a quarrelsome wife.

10 The wicked crave evil;
their neighbours get no mercy
from them.

a6 Some Hebrew manuscripts, Septuagint and Vulgate; most Hebrew manuscripts *vapour for those who seek death*

We see this advice immediately in verse 5. Being diligent is what leads to success, not haste; we should rightly be wary of 'get rich quick' strategies. We then see two ways to fail: by lying (21:6) or violence (21:7). What matters is character, being innocent rather than guilty (21:8; see also Isaiah 53:6; Titus 1:15). We then see two relationship failures that come from the wrong character: being contentious in marriage and unmerciful to one's neighbour (21:9–10). Selfishness will destroy relationships; men and women both can testify to this.

2. *Not that way!* • *Proverbs 21:11–21*

Verses 11–21 dig deeper into these wrong ways to proceed in the pursuit of wealth and power. We begin with a wisdom statement in verse 11. First, wealth (21:11–21).

11 When a mocker is punished,
the simple gain wisdom;
by paying attention to the wise
they get knowledge.

12 The Righteous One[b] takes
note of the house of the
wicked
and brings the wicked to ruin.

13 Whoever shuts their ears to the
cry of the poor
will also cry out and not be
answered.

14 A gift given in secret soothes
anger,
and a bribe concealed in the
cloak pacifies great wrath.

15 When justice is done, it brings
joy to the righteous
but terror to evildoers.

16 Whoever strays from the path
of prudence
comes to rest in the company
of the dead.

17 Whoever loves pleasure will
become poor;
whoever loves wine and olive
oil will never be rich.

18 The wicked become a ransom
for the righteous,
and the unfaithful for the
upright.

19 Better to live in a desert
than with a quarrelsome and
nagging wife.

20 The wise store up choice food
and olive oil,
but fools gulp theirs down.

21 Whoever pursues righteousness and love
finds life, prosperity[c] and
honour.

b 12 Or *The righteous person*
c 21 Or *righteousness*

We are reminded that wisdom is what we want, and it comes through listening to instruction and correction (21:11). So what will the wise person learn? That wickedness leads to ruin (21:12) – whether 'the Righteous One' refers to the righteous person or to God himself, the outcome is the same.

One way that wickedness hurts is seen in verse 13: if you fail to care for others, you will not be cared for (21:13). Verse 14 could be seen as isolated advice about the effect of bribes, but in context it would be better to see the anger being pacified as the result of wrong behaviour. If you follow the wrong strategies condemned in previous verses, you will make people angry, and you will have the added penalty of having to bribe them to avoid the consequences.[1] For only the righteous can love justice; it's the last thing that evildoers want (21:15). In climax, if you take the wrong way, you'll meet death (21:16).

Another incorrect strategy is that loving the wrong things will not lead to wealth (21:17). Good gifts are to be received gratefully and enjoyed, but they are *gifts*, not to be pursued above all else (Psalm 45:7; 2 Timothy 3:4). Wickedness costs (21:18), and being selfish and contentious in relationships is destructive (21:19).

Summing up this teaching: worldly wealth will come through wisdom (21:20; oil is a symbol of wealth and luxury), but even better are the intangible rewards of wisdom (21:21).

1 Or this could be a further indictment of the wrongdoer, who ignored the poor but will accept a bribe. However, reading this in parallel with verse 18 suggests that the one paying the cost is the wrongdoer.

3. True strength • Proverbs 21:22–30

We now turn to the pursuit of power. We are still digging deeper into the wrong ways to go.

22 One who is wise can go up
against the city of the mighty
and pull down the stronghold
in which they trust.

23 Those who guard their mouths
and their tongues
keep themselves from
calamity.

24 The proud and arrogant
person – 'Mocker' is his
name –
behaves with insolent fury.

25 The craving of a sluggard will
be the death of him,
because his hands refuse to
work.

26 All day long he craves for more,
but the righteous give without
sparing.

27 The sacrifice of the wicked is
detestable –
how much more so when
brought with evil intent!

28 A false witness will perish,
but a careful listener will testify
successfully.

29 The wicked put up a bold
front,
but the upright give thought to
their ways.

30 There is no wisdom, no insight,
no plan
that can succeed against the
LORD.

We start with a reminder again that wisdom is actually the most important thing, stronger than a city (21:22; see also Psalms 18:29; 144:1). But, in the context of power and military action, think first of guarding the tongue, itself a very powerful instrument (21:23; see also James 3:5–8). Don't be arrogant in pursuit of power (21:24), and don't think laziness will work (21:25); that kind of craving, using power for self-centredness (passively in the case of the sluggard, as opposed to the active arrogance of the mocker), wanting more without being prepared to work for it, is contrasted with the generosity of the righteous (21:26). Trying to gain through attempts to manipulate God with sacrifices won't work either (21:27; see also 2 Samuel 15:7–13; 1 Kings 21:9–12; Matthew 23:23) – God will not be fooled. Neither will using words falsely (21:28). The Bible is consistently against false witness, combining the sins of lying and injustice (Exodus 23:1; Deuteronomy 19:18–19).

In conclusion, righteousness, not a show of power, is the way to go forward (21:29). For in the end it is the Lord who determines success (21:30; see also Deuteronomy 32:30; Job 5:13; Psalm 33:10–11; Isaiah 8:10; 14:27; 46:10; Acts 2:23; 4:27–8; 1 Corinthians 1:18–25; 3:19).

4. True value • Proverbs 21:31–22:16

Overall, even if worldly wealth and power can be gained through wisdom and used well (in generosity and mercy), in the end God will show up their fleeting value.

31 The horse is made ready for
the day of battle,
but victory rests with the LORD.

22 A good name is more
desirable than great riches;
to be esteemed is better than
silver or gold.

2 Rich and poor have this in
common:
The LORD is the Maker of
them all.

3 The prudent see danger and
take refuge,
but the simple keep going and
pay the penalty.

4 Humility is the fear of the LORD;
its wages are riches and
honour and life.

5 In the paths of the wicked are
snares and pitfalls,
but those who would preserve
their life stay far from
them.

6 Start children off on the way
they should go,
and even when they are old
they will not turn from it.

7 The rich rule over the poor,
and the borrower is slave to
the lender.

8 Whoever sows injustice reaps
calamity,
and the rod they wield in fury
will be broken.

9 The generous will themselves
be blessed,
for they share their food with
the poor.

10 Drive out the mocker, and out
goes strife;
quarrels and insults are
ended.

11 One who loves a pure heart
and who speaks with grace
will have the king for a friend.

12 The eyes of the LORD keep
watch over knowledge,
but he frustrates the words of
the unfaithful.

13 The sluggard says, 'There's a
lion outside!
I'll be killed in the public square!'

14 The mouth of an adulterous
woman is a deep pit;
a man who is under the
LORD's wrath falls into it.

15 Folly is bound up in the heart
of a child,
but the rod of discipline will
drive it far away.

16 One who oppresses the poor to
increase his wealth
and one who gives gifts to the
rich – both come to poverty.

Human power, signified by a battle horse, is not what determines the outcome; God's will is what does it (21:31; see also Deuteronomy 17:16; Isaiah 31:1; Hosea 1:7; Zechariah 9:10). Wealth is not as valuable as righteousness (22:1; see also Ecclesiastes 7:1). Rich and poor are alike before the Lord (22:2; see also Ecclesiastes 7:2; 8:8); prudent people recognise their powerlessness and avoid danger, which the simple do not (22:3; see also Isaiah 26:11). For the most important strategy of all is to honour the Lord, the way to real riches (22:4; see also 1 Kings 3:12–14) and to avoid evil – that is the way to avoid the traps of life (22:5).

So train children in this kind of wisdom, for it will last (22:6). Teach them about true wealth: it does bring power (22:7) (even though the proverb incites us to wonder about this, especially since becoming 'slave' to a lender, possibly through being charged interest, is forbidden in law, Exodus 22:25; Leviticus 25:36–7; Deuteronomy

23:19), but it is not worth it if gained with injustice (22:8). Instead, be generous (22:9; see also Deuteronomy 15:10; Nehemiah 5:16–18; Job 31:17; Psalm 34:10; Isaiah 32:8; 58:7; Matthew 25:31–46; Luke 14:13; 2 Corinthians 9:6; 1 Timothy 6:17–18,) and don't put up with mockers (22:10; see also 2 Peter 3:3). Rather, value gracious speech, which is a better way to power (22:11). The guarantee for this advice is that God will see and act (22:12; see also Psalm 146:9).

We have two more ways to avoid in 22:13, 14 – the lazy person who gives absurd excuses for not working (22:13), and the sexually immoral (22:14), before our conclusion in verses 15 and 16. Youth should be trained (22:15), and what they need to learn is that abusive power and wealth is not worth pursuing (22:16).

Conclusion to Proverbs 21:5–22:16

Once again, the very terseness of these Proverbs creates the opportunity for considerable wondering, questioning and pondering. There is no space for us to do this properly here, so make sure you take time to stop and think. For the implications are profound.

We saw in the previous section that the most valuable attribute to seek is faithful love, the love that values others. We see in this section the problems that come from pursuing wealth and power greedily instead of valuing others, a deep diagnosis of our fallen world. That is not the way of wisdom; it will displease God and it will not ultimately lead to reward. Using the power selfishly in indulging laziness, or in words to manipulate others, is not right and will bring problems. Instead, value righteousness and seek God's approval. True power and wealth, the kind that is valuable, works through self-control and humility before God, generosity towards others and valuing relationships. Love God and neighbour – that is wisdom.

24

The (Probably) Thirty Wise Sayings

PROVERBS 22:17–24:34

We now close the section that began in Proverbs 10, with a collection of sayings 'of the wise'. This seems to be addressed to young people, perhaps about to start their careers as courtiers (22:22, 29; 23:1, 21),[1] who need to be honest and just (22:21; 24:23–6), who enjoy privileges (22:22–3) and have wealth (22:26–7) and new temptations (23:1–8, 29–35). They are given advice about their attitudes to the Lord and their moral integrity. There are similarities with *The Instruction of Amenemope*, the Egyptian wisdom writings, so it is likely that the Israelite wisdom writer studied Egyptian wisdom.[2]

The NIV has translated 22:20, 'Have I not written thirty sayings for you', as is traditional, and most commentators take them as being thirty sayings (there are parallels with the thirty sayings of *The Instruction of Amenemope*).[3] However, there is disagreement as to how exactly to count them (for example, is 24:10–12 one saying or two? Is 22:17–21 a saying or a prologue?), and an alternative reading of 22:20 is possible.[4]

These sayings, whether strictly thirty or not, have an introduction (22:17–21), then three sections that give the content of the wisdom teaching (22:22–23:11; 23:12–24:22; 24:23–34). Interspersed are encouragements to keep listening because of the value of wisdom.

1 Overland, *Proverbs*, 458.

2 Overland, *Proverbs*, 459–60; Waltke, *The Book of Proverbs*, II.217.

3 Only 22:16–23:11 depends on Amenemope; other sayings are similar to the Aramaic *Ahiqar*. Waltke, *The Book of Proverbs*, II.217; see also J. A. Emerton, 'The Teaching of Amenemope and Proverbs XXII 17–XXIV 22: Reflections of a Long-Standing Problem', *Vetus Testamentum* 51 (2001): 431–65.

4 Overland (*Proverbs*, 461) has, 'Have I not written for you, for some time, concerning counsels and knowledge?'

The section is framed by the two exhortations to trust in the Lord (22:19) and to fear the Lord (24:21).

1. *Introducing the thirty sayings • Proverbs 22:17–21*

In the pattern we have seen frequently so far, the section starts with the value of learning wisdom.

Thirty sayings of the wise

Saying 1

17 Pay attention and turn your ear
to the sayings of the wise;
apply your heart to what I teach,
18 for it is pleasing when you
keep them in your heart
and have all of them ready on
your lips.
19 So that your trust may be in
the LORD,
I teach you today, even you.
20 Have I not written thirty
sayings for you,
sayings of counsel and
knowledge,
21 teaching you to be honest and
to speak the truth,
so that you bring back truthful
reports
to those you serve?

We start in 22:17–21 with encouragement to learn wisdom; two quatrains around a centre (22:19). Those who would be wise, and wish to teach wisdom to others ('have all of them ready on your lips'), should pay attention. The student needs to listen and absorb this teaching (22:17), because wisdom is good in itself (22:18; note: 'keep them in your heart' – actually 'in your belly' – probably means memorise them), and it teaches a right attitude towards the Lord, of trusting him (22:19). That is why the sage teaches that the point is to have a relationship with the Lord daily. This is not merely repetition of another culture's wisdom; this is inspired teaching put in its right context, of knowing the Lord. Such knowledge will also bring integrity and make one a good servant (22:20–21); it is what a king would want to be teaching his court.

2. Don't move your moral boundaries! • Proverbs 22:22–23:11

The content of the wisdom teaching in these sayings of the wise begins with advice about living rightly.

Saying 2

22 Do not exploit the poor
because they are poor
and do not crush the needy in court,
23 for the LORD will take up their case
and will exact life for life.

Saying 3

24 Do not make friends with a hot-tempered person,
do not associate with one easily angered,
25 or you may learn their ways
and get yourself ensnared.

Saying 4

26 Do not be one who shakes hands in pledge
or puts up security for debts;
27 if you lack the means to pay,
your very bed will be snatched from under you.

Saying 5

28 Do not move an ancient boundary stone
set up by your ancestors.

Saying 6

29 Do you see someone skilled in their work?
They will serve before kings;
they will not serve before officials of low rank.

Saying 7

23 When you sit to dine with a ruler,
note well what[a] is before you,
2 and put a knife to your throat
if you are given to gluttony.
3 Do not crave his delicacies,
for that food is deceptive.

Saying 8

4 Do not wear yourself out to get rich;
do not trust your own cleverness.
5 Cast but a glance at riches, and they are gone,
for they will surely sprout wings
and fly off to the sky like an eagle.

Saying 9

6 Do not eat the food of a stingy host,

do not crave his delicacies;
7 for he is the kind of person
who is always thinking about
the cost.[b]
'Eat and drink,' he says to you,
but his heart is not with you.
8 You will vomit up the little you
have eaten
and will have wasted your
compliments.

Saying 10
9 Do not speak to fools,
for they will scorn your
prudent words.

Saying 11
10 Do not move an ancient
boundary stone
or encroach on the fields of the
fatherless,
11 for their Defender is strong;
he will take up their case
against you.

a 1 Or *who*
b 7 Or *for as he thinks within himself, / so he is; or for as he puts on a feast, / so he is*

Students should beware abuse of legal power, as the Lord cares for the vulnerable, a frequent Old Testament theme (22:22–3; see also Job 24:2; Exodus 22:21–22, 25–6; 23:1–9; Leviticus 19:13; Deuteronomy 27:25; Ezekiel 18:7–18 Micah 2:1–11; 3; 6:9–16; 7:1–6; and others), and beware those who would respond in anger (22:24), for such behaviour is catching (22:25). Those things should *not* be learned. The students should also learn wise stewardship of resources and beware losing protections against economic exploitation (22:26–7); the Hebrew is not just 'do not be one who shakes hands', but actually 'do not be among those' (22:26) – don't share that identity. Again, it is important to be aware of whom you are allowing to influence you. In all these, you should not be moving the boundaries that are there for people's protection, and would especially protect the poor (22:28; see also 15:25; 23:10; Isaiah 5:8; Hosea 5:10 – the reference to boundary markers alludes to the ideas of law and tradition). Instead, copy the skilled and faithful servant who is rewarded with high office (22:29).

In chapter 23, we begin advice about situations fraught with temptation to break moral boundaries. Don't be tempted by a king's delicacies, which are deceptive, and if you are tempted, take drastic action (23:1–3; see also Matthew 5:29–30); and don't be tempted by riches, which can take all your efforts and energy and are not worth it (23:4–5; see also Ecclesiastes 5:8–12; 1 Timothy 6:6–10; James 3:13–16). Don't be fooled by generosity that is not really generosity; it's disgusting, and like poison (23:6–8). And don't bother teaching fools (23:9). In all these ways, boundaries both physical and metaphorical ('stones' is not actually mentioned in verse 10) are meant to protect the vulnerable, so don't try to change them; they are of the Lord (23:10–11; see also Job 6:27; 22:9; 24:3, 9; 29:12; 31:16–17, 21–3).

3. Teachers and learners • Proverbs 23:12–24:22

Our teaching on wisdom now includes some advice for you becoming a teacher of wisdom yourself.

Saying 12

12 Apply your heart to instruction
and your ears to words of knowledge.

Saying 13

13 Do not withhold discipline from a child;
if you punish them with the rod, they will not die.
14 Punish them with the rod
and save them from death.

Saying 14

15 My son, if your heart is wise,
then my heart will be glad indeed;
16 my inmost being will rejoice
when your lips speak what is right.

Saying 15

17 Do not let your heart envy sinners,
but always be zealous for the fear of the LORD.
18 There is surely a future hope for you,
and your hope will not be cut off.

Saying 16

19 Listen, my son, and be wise,
and set your heart on the right path:
20 do not join those who drink too much wine
or gorge themselves on meat,
21 for drunkards and gluttons become poor,
and drowsiness clothes them in rags.

Saying 17

22 Listen to your father, who gave
you life,
and do not despise your
mother when she is old.
23 Buy the truth and do not sell it –
wisdom, instruction and
insight as well.
24 The father of a righteous child
has great joy;
a man who fathers a wise son
rejoices in him.
25 May your father and mother
rejoice;
may she who gave you birth be
joyful!

Saying 18

26 My son, give me your heart
and let your eyes delight in my
ways,
27 for an adulterous woman is a
deep pit,
and a wayward wife is a
narrow well.
28 Like a bandit she lies in wait
and multiplies the unfaithful
among men.

Saying 19

29 Who has woe? Who has
sorrow?
Who has strife? Who has
complaints?
Who has needless bruises?
Who has bloodshot eyes?
30 Those who linger over wine,
who go to sample bowls of
mixed wine.
31 Do not gaze at wine when it is
red,
when it sparkles in the cup,
when it goes down smoothly!
32 In the end it bites like a snake
and poisons like a viper.
33 Your eyes will see strange sights,
and your mind will imagine
confusing things.
34 You will be like one sleeping
on the high seas,
lying on top of the rigging.
35 'They hit me,' you will say, 'but
I'm not hurt!
They beat me, but I don't feel
it!
When will I wake up
so I can find another drink?'

Saying 20

24 Do not envy the wicked,
do not desire their
company;
2 for their hearts plot violence,
and their lips talk about
making trouble.

Saying 21

3 By wisdom a house is built,
and through understanding it
is established;
4 through knowledge its rooms
are filled
with rare and beautiful
treasures.

Saying 22

5 The wise prevail through great power,
and those who have knowledge muster their strength.
6 Surely you need guidance to wage war,
and victory is won through many advisors.

Saying 23

7 Wisdom is too high for fools;
in the assembly at the gate they must not open their mouths.

Saying 24

8 Whoever plots evil
will be known as a schemer.
9 The schemes of folly are sin,
and people detest a mocker.

Saying 25

10 If you falter in a time of trouble,
how small is your strength!
11 Rescue those being led away to death;
hold back those staggering towards slaughter.
12 If you say, 'But we knew nothing about this,'
does not he who weighs the heart perceive it?
Does not he who guards your life know it?
Will he not repay everyone according to what they have done?

Saying 26

13 Eat honey, my son, for it is good;
honey from the comb is sweet to your taste.
14 Know also that wisdom is like honey for you:
if you find it, there is a future hope for you,
and your hope will not be cut off.

Saying 27

15 Do not lurk like a thief near the house of the righteous,
do not plunder their dwelling-place;
16 for though the righteous fall seven times, they rise again,
but the wicked stumble when calamity strikes.

Saying 28

17 Do not gloat when your enemy falls;
when they stumble, do not let your heart rejoice,
18 or the LORD will see and disapprove
and turn his wrath away from them.

Saying 29

19 Do not fret because of evildoers

or be envious of the wicked,
20 for the evildoer has no future
hope,
and the lamp of the wicked
will be snuffed out.

Saying 30
21 Fear the LORD and the king,
my son,
and do not join with rebellious
officials,
22 for those two will send sudden
destruction on them,
and who knows what calami-
ties they can bring?

If you are going to be a teacher, start by learning (23:12); in this way you can model the kind of discipline that you should also exercise with your students, for reproof is part of learning how to live (23:13–14).[5] There is great joy in teaching, especially when the student listens, as all good teachers know (23:15–16). What should you teach? That there are right things to long for. It can be tempting to envy sinners, especially if they seem to have things you don't, and the antidote is to remember what will ultimately gain the greatest reward (23:17–18; see also Revelation 21:27). Don't long for drunkenness and gluttony, partying and indulgence; that's actually the way to poverty (23:19–21). Instead, listen to wisdom; desire it, and listen to your teachers, for truth is invaluable (23:22–3). That's the way to bring joy to your parents (23:24–5; see also Luke 2:52).

If what you crave is the party lifestyle, 22:26–35 gives ample warning against it. It's deceptive, it's tempting, but it's poison. Adulterous sex just won't be satisfying (a 'narrow well', 23:27) and will be destructive (23:28).

5 It is uncomfortable in the modern (western) climate to read about physical chastisement and correction. What appears to be recommended here may be condemned in some philosophies and laws, not just a matter of differing parenting techniques. It is worth remembering that such a move is a very recent, and local, innovation in the liberal West. Nonetheless, there is no need to read these verses as recommending violence against children. The emphasis is correction, not its means. The necessity of correcting wrong paths, and the importance of being able to heed such correction, is a very strong theme in Proverbs. On our own, we will go astray; it is the duty of a good teacher to correct such wrong directions, and a mark of a wise person that such correction is listened to. See Daniel J. Treier, *Proverbs and Ecclesiastes* (Grand Rapids: Brazos Press, 2011), 111.

Saying 19 is a vivid description of drunkenness, which is just going to lead to discomfort and hangovers (23:29–30). The language is masterful and evocative. Drink is tempting when it is first presented, and how pleasant it is to drink and keep drinking (23:31), but the results are not such fun – illness, swaying, altered vision, dull reflexes (23:32–5a). But what do we do when it's over? Look for another drink! (23:35b). It's destructive, and it keeps poor company: people with violent hearts, not hearts of wisdom (24:1–2). Once again, watch the company you keep.

The alternative, however, is wonderful. Wisdom is practical; it establishes security and treasure, wealth and beauty (24:3–4). It brings power and strength (24:5),[6] it helps win wars; verse 6 has a sense of rescuing others, not just fighting on one's own behalf. It's not within the reach of fools (24:7). The opposite of wisdom, folly and mocking, is the way of evil and social failure (24:8–9). (Think for a moment about the sorts of mockers that people detest.) Lacking wisdom brings cowardice that fails to rescue others, and God will know it (24:10–12). So go to wisdom; that's the thing to eat and indulge in (24:13). That's a hunger worth satisfying.

With 24:15 we begin advice about what longings not to indulge. Don't lurk like a thief (24:15; we have seen examples of such lurkers before, in 1:11, 18; 7:12; 12:6). Such evil will only bring calamity (24:16; note the recognition that the righteous also suffer, just not ultimately). Don't give in to revenge or gloating over enemies; that's not godly. This is a wrong joy (24:17). The Lord might even temporarily let evil people get away with their evil, in response. This sounds horrific to us, that the Lord might, for a time, *not* punish evil because of us, but it does emphasise how bad our seeking revenge or gloating over enemies is (24:18). Resist such wrong temptations to worry over evildoers or to envy them (24:19; see also Psalm 37:1, 7, 8). Just don't waste thought or emotional energy on them at all. What enables us to do that is the knowledge that there's no future in it (24:20). Instead, fear the Lord and obey your superiors (24:21–2; the 'two' are most logically the Lord and the king, as the NIV implies).

6 The Hebrew is difficult, but the effect is praise of wisdom and knowledge. See Waltke, *The Book of Proverbs*, II.272.

4. Further sayings • Proverbs 24:23–34

The further sayings of the wise continue with advice for those who would learn wisdom. The sayings here, following the pattern of 24:3–22, cover justice at court and a right approach to work. This section recaps the teaching of 6:10–11.

Further sayings of the wise

23 These also are sayings of the wise:
To show partiality in judging is not good:
24 whoever says to the guilty, 'You are innocent,'
will be cursed by peoples and denounced by nations.
25 But it will go well with those who convict the guilty,
and rich blessing will come on them.

26 An honest answer
is like a kiss on the lips.

27 Put your outdoor work in order
and get your fields ready;
after that, build your house.

28 Do not testify against your neighbour without cause –
would you use your lips to mislead?
29 Do not say, 'I'll do to them as they have done to me;
I'll pay them back for what they did.'

30 I went past the field of a sluggard,
past the vineyard of someone who has no sense;
31 thorns had come up everywhere,
the ground was covered with weeds,
and the stone wall was in ruins.
32 I applied my heart to what I observed
and learned a lesson from what I saw:
33 a little sleep, a little slumber,
a little folding of the hands to rest –
34 and poverty will come on you like a thief
and scarcity like an armed man.

Justice is the first concern (24:23). Be righteous in court, not ignoring guilt (24:24–5). Be honest, do your work and count the cost wisely (24:26–7). Act rightly to your neighbour, without dishonesty or revenge (24:28–9); instead, in a short vignette, we are taught to avoid indolence and to work hard to stay responsibly solvent (24:30–34). In the centre of this vignette, we see that the sage observed the world, paid attention and learned; that in itself is a teaching to us, which will help us interpret the world (24:32).

Conclusion to Proverbs 22:17–24:34

There have been a few important repetitions in this section of sayings of the wise; references to Yahweh, and to ear, mind and knowledge (these three together only appear elsewhere once, 18:15). The command to listen occurs three times, and truth three times. It is important to listen to wisdom, to speak wisdom (truth), for this is the way of the Lord. In doing one's work, and in teaching others, wisdom – which comes from God – must be one's guide. There is the assumption that whatever work one does, the wisdom one has acquired to live well will be taught to others. The learner will become the teacher.

What the learner primarily learns in this section is not to change ancient boundaries, not just physical (which have to do with justice and honesty), but moral boundaries in general. Do not take what belongs to another; do not try to change the rules so as to hurt others; do not try to avoid the basic rules of earning one's wealth through diligent, hard, honest work. God will be watching, and will punish those who hurt the innocent.

When teaching wisdom, too, we must not shift the boundaries – not deviate from what is tried and true teaching. We must therefore be willing to be corrected when we deviate, and to correct others when they do. This is loving. Teaching must be based on truth (22:20–21; 23:16) and on fearing God (23:17; 24:21–2). This is what allows one to avoid the temptation of earthly appetites (23:19–20, 26–8, 29–35), which bring poverty (23:21).

Truth matters, for the true, moral life is what brings joy (23:24–5). So avoid those who are evil (24:1–2). The wise life brings security

(24:3–4) and rescue of others (24:5–6, 10–12). Proverbs 24:23–4 sums up the section, again emphasising the importance of boundaries and diligent, honest work, being observant (24:33–4). Pay attention to what works, and so learn wisdom. This will help both ourselves and others.

PART THREE

PROVERBS 25–9

25

ROYAL WISDOM

Our assumed student is now employed in the royal court, and we have here kingly advice on how to conduct oneself successfully. In four sections, rulers and courtiers are taught about wise leaders, those who bring glory to their courts but who can also learn from the humble and honest workers. These are known as the second Solomonic collection.

Chapters 25–7 have almost no reference to God, containing direct teaching to the listener illustrated by metaphors. Chapters 28–9 are more theological.

26

Wise Government

PROVERBS 25–7

The advice here is relevant for all leaders, whatever the political system. Democracy is preferred in the West, but it is still a human system with flaws. Other cultures may differ: as an African commentator observes, 'In traditional African society, authority is community based and derived from the community and its ancestors.'[1]

1. In the king's presence • Proverbs 25:1–12

The reference to King Hezekiah's men could reflect a wish on Hezekiah's part to reform the nation under God. In any case, it was a good thing to do.

More proverbs of Solomon

25 These are more proverbs of Solomon, compiled by the men of Hezekiah king of Judah:

2 It is the glory of God to conceal
a matter;
to search out a matter is the
glory of kings.
3 As the heavens are high and
the earth is deep,
so the hearts of kings are
unsearchable.
4 Remove the dross from the silver,
and a silversmith can produce
a vessel;
5 remove wicked officials from
the king's presence,
and his throne will be
established through
righteousness.

6 Do not exalt yourself in the
king's presence,
and do not claim a place
among his great men;

1 Yusufu Tiraki, 'Democracy', in Habtu, 'Proverbs', 812.

7 it is better for him to say to
you, 'Come up here,'
than for him to humiliate you
before his nobles.

What you have seen with your
eyes
8 do not bring[a] hastily to court,
for what will you do in the end
if your neighbour puts you to
shame?

9 If you take your neighbour to
court,
do not betray another's
confidence,
10 or the one who hears it may
shame you
and the charge against you will
stand.

11 Like apples[b] of gold in settings
of silver
is a ruling rightly given.
12 Like an earring of gold or an
ornament of fine gold
is the rebuke of a wise judge to
a listening ear.

a 7,8 Or *nobles / on whom you had set your eyes. / 8Do not go*
b 11 Or *possibly apricots*

Both kings and courtiers are addressed in this first section, with the proverbs collected by King Hezekiah's men (25:1). We remember that we have just heard advice to those about to take up leadership positions; now we see how to proceed once in post. What will ensure a court that reflects God's splendour? God's glory, and a king's, consists in wisdom; this is the matter (or saying) that is hard to find but should be sought (25:2). For a king is meant to be wise and knowledgeable, as far beyond ordinary people as heaven is beyond earth – an impressive responsibility! Our leaders should take note (25:3).

Verses 2–3 have set our context of the royal court, ruling under God; verses 4–5 set up the major theme, the contrast between righteousness and wickedness. Rulers are meant to ensure justice; that is like (and as important as) purifying silver (25:4–5), and the way to establish a throne through righteousness (see 2 Samuel 7).

In turn, courtiers should restrain themselves, not exalt themselves, if they want to gain honour (25:6–7b; see also 1 Samuel 15:17; 18:18; 1 Kings 1:5, 30; Matthew 18:1–4; Luke 14:8–11; John 13:1–15; 3 John 9, 10). Similarly, restraint should be practiced in litigation (7c–10).

Don't rush to court, and don't divulge confidences in an effort to win. Overall, if rulers want the glory of gold and silver, they should speak wisdom appropriately (25:11; see also Job 6:25; Ecclesiastes 12:10; Isaiah 40:1–4; 50:4; Luke 14:15; Ephesians 5:14; 1 Timothy 6:13; 2 Timothy 2:15), and take correction well – let the attentiveness of your ear match the fine jewellery you might be wearing in it (25:12).

The advice for rulers, then, is that for all walks of life, wisdom, coming from ardent seeking of it and a willingness to be taught and corrected, is the true wealth. If a king or his court wants the court to be truly glorious, they will seek God's wisdom and reflect it in their justice, their self-control, and their words. This is certainly what Solomon's early heritage reflected, even if he forgot his own advice later in life. This is what leaders should be concentrating on; magnificence comes from humility and listening to God, not gathering of jewels and self-importance.

In an age where political leaders are increasingly known for their corruption and lies, reflecting self-interest and self-aggrandisement, this picture of what rulers should be doing is increasingly attractive.

One Anglican collect (prayer) asks this for leaders:

Almighty Father,
whose will is to restore all things
in your beloved Son, the King of all:
govern the hearts and minds of those in authority,
and bring the families of the nations,
divided and torn apart by the ravages of sin,
to be subject to his just and gentle rule;
who is alive and reigns with you,
in the unity of the Holy Spirit,
one God, now and for ever.[2]

The best we can pray for our leaders is for them to be subject to the Lord. That is what will bring them to govern with justice.

---

2 Collect for the third Sunday before Advent, *Common Worship: Daily Prayer* (London: Church House Publishing, 2005), 444.

2. Being the best servant • Proverbs 25:13–28

Now we turn to more advice for those who would serve a king. Moderation is key to their attitude: neither greedy nor foolishly generous. This is taught through understanding various types of people, in seven relationships, and the best way to treat them. The wise servant will act with self-control and integrity.

13 Like a snow-cooled drink at
harvest time
is a trustworthy messenger to
the one who sends him;
he refreshes the spirit of his
master.
14 Like clouds and wind without
rain
is one who boasts of gifts never
given.

15 Through patience a ruler can
be persuaded,
and a gentle tongue can break
a bone.

16 If you find honey, eat just
enough –
too much of it, and you will
vomit.
17 Seldom set foot in your
neighbour's house –
too much of you, and they will
hate you.

18 Like a club or a sword or a
sharp arrow
is one who gives false
testimony against a
neighbour.
19 Like a broken tooth or a lame
foot
is reliance on the unfaithful in
a time of trouble.
20 Like one who takes away a
garment on a cold day,
or like vinegar poured on a
wound,
is one who sings songs to a
heavy heart.

21 If your enemy is hungry, give
him food to eat;
if he is thirsty, give him water
to drink.
22 In doing this, you will heap
burning coals on his head,
and the LORD will reward you.

23 Like a north wind that brings
unexpected rain
is a sly tongue – which
provokes a horrified look.

24 Better to live on a corner of the
roof

than share a house with a
quarrelsome wife.

25 Like cold water to a weary soul
is good news from a distant
land.
26 Like a muddied spring or a
polluted well
are the righteous who give way
to the wicked.

27 It is not good to eat too much
honey,
nor is it honourable to search
out matters that are too
deep.

28 Like a city whose walls are
broken through
is a person who lacks
self-control.

The best kind of messenger is a trustworthy one (25:13; see also 13:17; 26:6; 1 Corinthians 16:17–18; Philippians 2:25–30; 1 Thessalonians 3:1–7), not someone who promotes himself falsely. We have all met people like that – full of self-puffery, with no substance (25:14; see also Jude 12). The patient, self-controlled subordinate is the one who eventually wins over his boss (25:15) – see Paul's example in 1 Corinthians 9:2–22 (see also Galatians 5:22–4; 2 Timothy 2:24–6).[3] Self-control is also recommended in regard to food (even the sweetest food) and sociability (25:16–17).[4] The wise servant is one who acts with integrity and insight towards others, neither acting dishonestly (25:18; see also Exodus 20:16; Deuteronomy 5:20) nor trusting unwisely (25:19; see also 14:22; 17:17; 19:22; 20:6) – both things are compared to something extremely painful.

The next proverb (25:20) warns against false solicitousness. One who 'takes away a garment on a cold day' might seem to be generous, helping a person remove his coat, but it's actually not a generous act. Neither is giving a gift of vinegar, if it's being poured on a wound and causing pain.[5] This is describing a neighbour who is only pretending to be generous, or at best is being incredibly insensitive; don't be that neighbour.

---

3 Waltke suggests that 'breaking a bone' refers to overcoming deep resistance to an idea (*The Book of Proverbs*, II.325).

4 Note how 16–27 mark out this subsection about self-control, bounded by the idea of control in eating honey.

5 The traditional interpretation for this word *neter* was natron, carbonate of soda; vinegar poured on soda will just make it bubble away and so is useless.

Neither should you be the neighbour who seeks revenge (25:21–2; see also Leviticus 19:17–18; Proverbs 17:13; 20:22; 24:17–18; Matthew 5:43–4). Self-control should be exercised here, too, as is taken up in Romans 12:17–21. This is such an important principle. It is sadly largely absent from modern popular stories, where revenge upon the evil enemy is a key theme of films and action literature. Instead, self-control which acts in generosity and forgiveness to an enemy is the truly noble, and wise, action; and it does not forgo justice, as Romans 12:19 reminds us. In verses 23 and 24, similar self-control in regard to close relationships is advised; do not give into self-centredness that would erupt in bitterness and contention (see also Acts 8:20–23; Ephesians 4:31).

We sum up this teaching with a positive and negative example, and then a reminder of the principles. Proverbs 25:25 reminds us of the positive example of 25:13: how to be refreshing. The opposite in verse 26 is to muddy one's moral waters. The principle: don't be greedy, but self-controlled (25:27–8).[6]

3. Take care • Proverbs 26:1–27:4

Having seen the need to control oneself, avoiding greed and revenge, we now turn to some people to beware of.[7]

26 Like snow in summer or
rain in harvest,
honour is not fitting for a fool.
2 Like a fluttering sparrow or a
darting swallow,
an undeserved curse does not
come to rest.
3 A whip for the horse, a bridle
for the donkey,
and a rod for the backs of fools!
4 Do not answer a fool according
to his folly,
or you yourself will be just like
him.
5 Answer a fool according to his
folly,
or he will be wise in his own
eyes.

6 The suggestion of 27b is that one is trying to increase one's own glory by the search.

7 Overland sums this up in the theme of avoiding over-generosity.

6 Sending a message by the
hands of a fool
is like cutting off one's feet or
drinking poison.
7 Like the useless legs of one
who is lame
is a proverb in the mouth of a
fool.
8 Like tying a stone in a sling
is the giving of honour to a
fool.
9 Like a thorn-bush in a drunkard's hand
is a proverb in the mouth of a
fool.
10 Like an archer who wounds at
random
is one who hires a fool or any
passer-by.
11 As a dog returns to its vomit,
so fools repeat their folly.
12 Do you see a person wise in
their own eyes?
There is more hope for a fool
than for them.

13 A sluggard says, 'There's a lion
in the road,
a fierce lion roaming the
streets!'
14 As a door turns on its hinges,
so a sluggard turns on his
bed.
15 A sluggard buries his hand in
the dish;
he is too lazy to bring it back
to his mouth.
16 A sluggard is wiser in his own
eyes
than seven people who answer
discreetly.

17 Like one who grabs a stray dog
by the ears
is someone who rushes into a
quarrel not their own.

18 Like a maniac shooting
flaming arrows of death
19 is one who deceives their
neighbour
and says, 'I was only joking!'

20 Without wood a fire goes
out;
without gossip a quarrel dies
down.
21 As charcoal to embers and as
wood to fire,
so is a quarrelsome person for
kindling strife.
22 The words of a gossip are like
choice morsels;
they go down to the inmost
parts.

23 Like a coating of silver dross
on earthenware
are fervent[a] lips with an evil
heart.
24 Enemies disguise themselves
with their lips,
but in their hearts they
harbour deceit.

25 Though their speech is
charming, do not believe
them,
for seven abominations fill
their hearts.
26 Their malice may be concealed
by deception,
but their wickedness will be
exposed in the assembly.
27 Whoever digs a pit will fall into
it;
if someone rolls a stone, it will
roll back on them.
28 A lying tongue hates those it
hurts,
and a flattering mouth works
ruin.

27 Do not boast about
tomorrow,
for you do not know what a day
may bring.

2 Let someone else praise you,
and not your own mouth;
an outsider, and not your own
lips.

3 Stone is heavy and sand a
burden,
but a fool's provocation is
heavier than both.

4 Anger is cruel and fury
overwhelming,
but who can stand before
jealousy?

---

a 23 Hebrew; Septuagint *smooth*

First, how to respond to the stupid (26:1–2; note that in 26:1–12 the word *kesil* (or the plural *kesilim*), fool, is in every verse except verse 2). Fools do not always present themselves as foolish; in this section, fools are able to quote proverbs, get a job and even be given honour, although it appears doing so turns out badly. One might need to exercise discernment to recognise them – this is important, for being overly generous to fools is not wise; we have seen that a fool will not listen to wisdom and will lead others astray (26:1; see also 19:10; 1 Kings 12:1–20). One might think of the 'honour' given to some extremely foolish celebrities.

But also, do not make baseless curses (26:2; see also Psalm 109:28), and remember that stupid people only understand the strongest of communication (26:3) – not necessarily a command for corporal punishment! But it is hard to communicate with fools (26:4–5) who are likely to respond badly. Fools also make bad messengers because they do not understand (26:6–7). So, as we saw in 26:1, don't give too much glory to the stupid, those who refuse wisdom (26:8). For again, they handle wisdom badly (26:9), they make bad employees (26:10), they don't learn (26:11) – but a know-it-all is even worse than a fool (26:12). The moral of these twelve verses: avoid the fool. Don't let your generosity be carried away by giving them too much credit.

Also (26:13–16) avoid the lazy. They are all talk without doing anything (26:13; see also 22:13); they just aimlessly waver back and forth (26:14). They don't bother completing their own actions (26:15), and think themselves far wiser than they are (26:16).

Another kind of person to avoid is the meddler, the difficult neighbour; the descriptions escalate in severity (26:17–28). They are not the same as the fools; indeed, they may have a great deal of social acumen, but this hides evil motives. They poke their noses into other people's business and so create painful havoc (26:17); they are deceptive and cause mayhem but try to laugh it off (26:18–19). Remove them and quarrels will sort themselves out (26:20; see also 22:10), because they just love to create trouble (26:21). As in 18:8, they create trouble through gossip, which is insidious (26:22; see also 2 Corinthians 12:20; Galatians 5:9), with attractive but deceptive speech (26:23; see also 2 Samuel 15:1–9; Psalm 62:4; Jeremiah 9:8). Their true motivation is evil (26:24–6), but they will ultimately fail (26:27; see also Daniel 6:24; Job 5:13). In summary, this kind of trouble-making, deceptive evil is destructive, so stay away from it (26:28).

There is a summary in 27:1–4. Don't boast: wisdom will involve knowing one's own limits. Don't be presumptuous, or full of your own praise (27:1–2). Be aware of the strength of your emotions (27:3–4). Avoid the fool who is likely to provoke you.

4. *Accepting correction* • *Proverbs 27:5–22*

We have seen how important the ability to accept reproof is; in the next few verses we can see various angles on accepting reproof, and the importance of close relationships in which it can happen. We start with a comparison; rebuke is better than hiding love; indeed, it can be a form of love (27:5). A friend who gives such reproof, even if it hurts, is a good one; and an enemy only gives false praise (27:6). The one who has a proper appetite will accept even such bitter things (27:7); don't wander away from such relationships, which are indeed the kinds of relationships in which people might be willing to give a loving rebuke (27:8). For such friends and their counsel are valuable (27:9), and these relationships are worth keeping close (27:10). The person nearby, even if not as closely related as one's own family, is hugely valuable.

Within these relationships, remember wisdom, which will bring joy to those close to you (27:11). This wisdom will lead you to take notice of danger (or warnings of it) (27:12). Such perception might be urgently needed (27:13). Make sure any advice, even good and wise, is fitting and well timed; even a blessing is not well received if it's at the wrong time (27:14)! Don't be quarrelsome – that's annoying and gets out of hand (27:15–16; this certainly applies whether you are male or female). But giving reproof within mutual relationships where you are prepared to help each other is right (27:17 – or, if this is read negatively, it could be describing the way in which hostility can compound). Within a master–servant relationship, help and loyalty are (metaphorically) fruitful (27:18). In summary, then, be the kind of person with a right heart, which might be reflected to oneself and others (27:19).

In a recap of what was said earlier about greed and self-control, being unsatisfiable is like Death and Destruction (27:20) – a timely warning for our consumerist society. A desire for praise can be similarly unsatisfiable, so have a right attitude to praise (27:21). But the fool, the kind of person who will reject all this advice, cannot be helped (27:22; see also 12:15; 17:10, 16; 18:2; 26:11).[8]

This advice has been to courtiers, but it also reflects how wise courtiers will act in their other relationships. They are to have right motives and to treasure the wise friends who can give and take advice. They are to act rightly in marriage, for that relationship can go terribly wrong if either partner is not self-controlled. They are to refrain from greed and similarly from foolish praise. They are to

8 See Overland for the overlapping patterns in 26:1–8 and 4–12, then 27:5–10c. Overland, 531–533.

avoid fools and not get too caught up with them. In all these ways, wisdom will lead to the court where he serves gaining glory. Towards superiors, towards friends, towards enemies and in marriage, self-control and conduct with integrity lead to praise. Shrewdness in being able to treat the foolish or lazy properly, without being caught up in their foolishness, is part of treating other people well. Learning all this wisdom will be hard, so a right attitude to correction is essential; only the humility that will accept this has the chance of attaining right wisdom towards other people.

5. *Homegrown wisdom* • *Proverbs 27:23–7*

This chapter ends with a few verses of down-to-earth rural wisdom that the rich and powerful should pay heed to. Those who work in royal courts can still learn from the more humble (and Israelite nobles may well have owned flocks themselves).

23 Be sure you know the condition of your flocks,
give careful attention to your herds;
24 for riches do not endure for ever,
and a crown is not secure for all generations.
25 When the hay is removed and new growth appears
and the grass from the hills is gathered in,
26 the lambs will provide you with clothing,
and the goats with the price of a field.
27 You will have plenty of goats' milk to feed your family
and to nourish your female servants.

Know your flock (27:23): from kings to business leaders to church leaders, the command is essential. If you want to lead well, know those you are leading. Pay attention to them. Know them thoroughly; the verb is doubled for emphasis. If you are a church leader, make sure your church is not so big that you cannot know your flock. The bigger the audience and the less well known they are by the preacher, the more general and necessarily less focused the application must be. Do people need rebuke just now, or encouragement? If you don't know your people, you can't know what they need. God's word can still be powerful, but as a model of church leadership, it is lacking.

Why is the leader told to know the flock? Because such leadership will not last without paying attention. Even crowns can be lost (27:24). So pay attention; look after your assets, whether they be grass (27:25) or any other kind of resource. Look after your assets, and they will repay you (27:26–7). The emphasis of verses 25–7 is not causality, but the wisdom of treating the created order – meant to give life – well. Assets can come and go, so look after them.

Conclusion to Proverbs 25–7

Where should our attention be? We have seen the poor outcomes when we are inwardly focused in anger or bitterness or greed. Instead, we should look outwards, paying attention to whatever is under our care. Kingship, like farming, requires paying attention and knowing what is going on.

27

Godly Leaders

PROVERBS 28–9

In this final lecture to kings, we wrap up the advice for good leadership, for leaders who want a land that is thriving, bountiful, peaceful and living with justice. This is a fallen world, and things will go wrong; how should leaders do right, and resist the wicked who would oppose them or hurt their people? Through learning what is taught here: through heeding instruction (28:4) and so learning to hate wrongdoing (28:16) and walk in wisdom (28:26), and not listen to lies (29:12) – in short, learning to trust in the Lord (29:25).

1. Take power with care • Proverbs 28

We start with a picture of what happens when things go wrong, then move to the necessity of the king and other leaders to exercise justice and right reproof. It will be a struggle, and tiring; good judgment must prevail regardless. Greed and lawlessness are opposed to generosity and integrity. Community at all levels will benefit when morality wins out.

28 The wicked flee though no one pursues,
but the righteous are as bold as a lion.

2 When a country is rebellious, it has many rulers,
but a ruler with discernment and knowledge maintains order.

3 A ruler[a] who oppresses the poor
is like driving rain that leaves no crops.

4 Those who forsake instruction praise the wicked,
but those who heed it resist them.

5 Evildoers do not understand
what is right,
but those who seek the LORD
understand it fully.

6 Better the poor whose way of
life is blameless
than the rich whose ways are
perverse.

7 A discerning son heeds
instruction,
but a companion of gluttons
disgraces his father.

8 Whoever increases wealth by
taking interest or profit from
the poor
amasses it for another, who
will be kind to the poor.

9 If anyone turns a deaf ear to
my instruction,
even their prayers are
detestable.

10 Whoever leads the upright
along an evil path
will fall into their own trap,
but the blameless will receive a
good inheritance.

11 The rich are wise in their own
eyes;
one who is poor and
discerning sees how
deluded they are.

12 When the righteous triumph,
there is great elation;
but when the wicked rise
to power, people go into
hiding.

13 Whoever conceals their sins
does not prosper,
but the one who confesses
and renounces them finds
mercy.

14 Blessed is the one who always
trembles before God,
but whoever hardens their
heart falls into trouble.

15 Like a roaring lion or a
charging bear
is a wicked ruler over a helpless people.

16 A tyrannical ruler practises
extortion,
but one who hates ill-gotten
gain will enjoy a long reign.

17 Anyone tormented by the guilt
of murder
will seek refuge in the grave;
let no one hold them back.

18 The one whose way of life is
blameless is kept safe,
but the one whose ways are
perverse will fall into the pit.[b]

19 Those who work their land will
have abundant food,
but those who chase fantasies
will have their fill of poverty.

20 A faithful person will be richly
blessed,
but one eager to get rich will
not go unpunished.

21 To show partiality is not good –
yet a person will do wrong for
a piece of bread.

22 The stingy are eager to get rich
and are unaware that poverty
awaits them.

23 Whoever rebukes a person will
in the end gain favour
rather than one who has a flattering tongue.

24 Whoever robs their father or
mother
and says, 'It's not wrong,'
is partner to one who destroys.

25 The greedy stir up conflict,
but those who trust in the
LORD will prosper.

26 Those who trust in themselves
are fools,
but those who walk in wisdom
are kept safe.

27 Those who give to the poor
will lack nothing,
but those who close their
eyes to them receive many
curses.

28 When the wicked rise to power,
people go into hiding;
but when the wicked perish,
the righteous thrive.

a 3 Or *A poor person*
b 18 Syriac (see Septuagint); Hebrew *into one*

A contrast between the wicked and the righteous begins the section. Proverbs 28:1a has a singular subject (the wicked person) but a plural verb, 'they flee'. Waltke regards this as 'elegant variation', followed by 1b which has a singular verb with a plural subject.[1] The verse then reads as a comment on the paranoia of the wicked who flee even when not pursued, as contrasted with the confidence of the righteous who fear God and so do not fear people. Overland, however, translates 28:1, 'They had fled since no one was pursuing

1 Waltke, *The Book of Proverbs*, II.395 note 1.

the guilty person,'[2] a picture of the chaos that ensues when the guilty are not punished, even if the chaos is not total.

In any case, in verse 2 we see an unruly country beset with a top-heavy leadership, contrasted with one where order is maintained (28:2). Rulers should not oppress the poor; the NIV footnote to 28:3 points out that this ruler is himself poor, and that is probably why he oppresses others, in his greed to become rich. For greed is destructive. Those who reject instruction (28:4) – *torah*, which could be the sage's teaching (which is inspired by God) or God's law – admire the guilty; those who respect God fight them. It is the basic attitude that makes the difference, and this is expanded in verse 5: whether you seek the Lord or not determines whether you actually understand right and wrong (see also 1:7; 2:1–4, 9). This basic attitude of blamelessness towards God and his law is what really matters (28:6) – and it may cost you. It may leave you poor.

We continue with more teaching against greed. Again, it comes from one's basic attitude towards God, the 'discerning son' being the son who has listened to the teaching about righteousness, as opposed to the son who associates with those who squander it (28:7). Greed is pointless; you can amass money immorally, only to find that it goes to the very people you despised (28:8; see also 13:22). It's not worth ignoring spiritual instruction in that way, for it leads to spiritual hopelessness (28:9). It will not ultimately bring success, in the way that righteousness will (28:10). Instead, cultivate humility and discernment; they are worth more than having than wealth (28:11). Real flourishing comes from leaders who live by righteousness, not wickedness (28:12), and not trying to hide one's guilt (28:13). Fear of the Lord – that's what matters (28:14; see also Psalm 1; Proverbs 3:13). That's the way to blessing. The opposite just leads to trouble.

So, rulers: don't give into vicious wickedness, as an abusive leader (28:15; see also Daniel 7:1–8; Luke 22:25). That's senseless; instead, hate that kind of wickedness and greed, and enjoy long life (28:16). Guilt will pursue you to the grave (28:17), so keep yourself blameless (28:18). The cure for greed, and the way to true abundance, are faithful integrity and contentment. Work your land diligently, and

2 Overland, *Proverbs*, 552.

get rid of foolish fantasies (28:19). Be faithful, not greedy (28:20). Don't show partiality; bribes are not mentioned, but the parallelism between the two halves suggests that this is the topic here, a further condemnation of greed (28:21; see also 1 Samuel 2:12–16). In fact, greed may not even work (28:22).

Instead, be a good friend (28:23) – being prepared to rebuke when it is needed is the picture of faithfulness, as opposed to the one who flatters and lies, possibly for gain. Greed ruins relationships (28:24) and communities (28:25a). Trust the Lord (not yourself): that's the way to true prosperity and security (28:25b–6), as is generosity (28:27). Wickedness will destroy community, but justice creates it (28:28; see also 2 Chronicles 29–30; Esther 8:17).

2. Don't be greedy • Proverbs 29

This teaching against greed and wicked rule continues in chapter 29.

29 Whoever remains stiff-
necked after many rebukes
will suddenly be destroyed –
without remedy.

2 When the righteous thrive, the
people rejoice;
when the wicked rule, the
people groan.

3 A man who loves wisdom
brings joy to his father,
but a companion of prostitutes
squanders his wealth.

4 By justice a king gives a
country stability,
but those who are greedy for[a]
bribes tear it down.

5 Those who flatter their
neighbours
are spreading nets for their feet.

6 Evildoers are snared by their
own sin,
but the righteous shout for joy
and are glad.

7 The righteous care about
justice for the poor,
but the wicked have no such
concern.

8 Mockers stir up a city,
but the wise turn away anger.

9 If a wise person goes to court
with a fool,

the fool rages and scoffs, and
there is no peace.

10 The bloodthirsty hate a person
of integrity
and seek to kill the upright.

11 Fools give full vent to their
rage,
but the wise bring calm in the
end.

12 If a ruler listens to lies,
all his officials become wicked.

13 The poor and the oppressor
have this in common:
the LORD gives sight to the
eyes of both.

14 If a king judges the poor with
fairness,
his throne will be established
for ever.

15 A rod and a reprimand impart
wisdom,
but a child left undisciplined
disgraces its mother.

16 When the wicked thrive, so
does sin,
but the righteous will see their
downfall.

17 Discipline your children, and
they will give you peace;
they will bring you the delights
you desire.

18 Where there is no revelation,
people cast off restraint;
but blessed is the one who
heeds wisdom's instruction.

19 Servants cannot be corrected
by mere words;
though they understand, they
will not respond.

20 Do you see someone who
speaks in haste?
There is more hope for a fool
than for them.

21 A servant pampered from
youth
will turn out to be insolent.

22 An angry person stirs up conflict,
and a hot-tempered person
commits many sins.

23 Pride brings a person low,
but the lowly in spirit gain
honour.

24 The accomplices of thieves are
their own enemies;
they are put under oath and
dare not testify.

25 Fear of man will prove to be a
snare,

but whoever trusts in the LORD
is kept safe.

26 Many seek an audience with a
ruler,
but it is from the LORD that
one gets justice.

27 The righteous detest the
dishonest;
the wicked detest the upright.

a 4 Or *who give*

Pay attention when you are rebuked, or suffer destruction (29:1). Rebuke has been a prominent theme in Proverbs, and we should never disregard how important it is to be prepared to give correction where needed, and, even more importantly, to accept it with a right spirit and so benefit from it, and so grow in righteousness. In the context of ruling a country, the multiplication of righteousness brings a happy populace (see also Isaiah 9:3), but corrupt leaders hurt the people, as can be seen in multiple examples throughout history (29:2).

It's the same on the small scale, and indeed all countries are built up out of households; so, in this context too, love wisdom, and don't give into greedy appetites (29:3). Similarly, a king should follow justice, not greed (29:4). Don't deceive (in context, possibly flattery in the interests of greed), for wickedness is a snare (29:5–6a; Job 18:7–10), while joy comes from righteousness (29:6b).[3] Also, the wise king will beware greed in others. The good king will care about the poor, that they receive justice (29:7); and the wise king will be against the kind of inflammatory mockery that creates dissent (29:8; see also Isaiah 28:14; James 3:17). The wise ruler will also be against foolish litigiousness (29:9), while the violent will just want to oppose the righteous (29:10). The wise king is thus self-controlled and does not give into violent emotion (29:11). For the good king values truth and integrity (29:12); in contrast, oppressors, just as much as the poor, are at the mercy of God (29:13). The king is to rule fairly – that is the way to security and secure rule (29:14).

3 The theme of joy in Proverbs is a healthy rejection of the idea that morality involves being a killjoy, or is a matter of gritted-teeth endurance. It is the opposite of what is considered 'puritanical' – and indeed the Puritans themselves were people who greatly emphasised joy.

At any level, a leader should be prepared to teach wisdom and act fairly. Correction is sometimes necessary (29:15), for sin unchecked will just multiply (29:16a), even if God deals with it in the end (29:16b). So be prepared to discipline where necessary; the emphasis is not on the strength of reproof, but on the fact that you are willing to give it (29:17 – the rewards are for both child and parent, seen in this verse and 15a). God gives such instruction, which is truly a blessing, and without it people will just run wild (29:18; see also Isaiah 8:16; Lamentations 2:9; Hosea 4:6; Amos 8:11, 12; Romans 10:13–17), and sometimes human words are not enough (29:19). Nonetheless, even human words can be powerful, so must not be used unwisely: the person who is too quick with their words can be worse than a fool (29:20).

To sum up, if you are not prepared to rebuke, it leads those under your care to disaster (29:21). People who do not learn self-control create trouble far beyond themselves (29:22). The secret is humility, not self-seeking pride (29:23). This attitude of humble self-knowledge and self-control is what true correction is meant to teach.

The conclusion to the teaching of these two chapters is in verses 24–7. Greed, here symbolised by thieves, and injustice are both evils (29:24; see also Leviticus 5:1). So trust the Lord instead of fearing man (29:25): that is the true source of justice (29:26). Our final comparison is between the righteous and the wicked. They are not the same, and they are opposed; you must choose one or the other (29:27).

Conclusion to Proverbs 28–9

Greed is destructive. The New Testament teaches extensively on this, for 'godliness with contentment is great gain' (1 Timothy 6:6). If we could be content, and teach people to be content, how many pastoral problems would just disappear?! The way to such contentment is work, and serving others in generosity. Be satisfied with what you have and enjoy it, and spread that joy by treating others fairly, respecting God's law. For those under your care, be prepared to teach, and that will mean, at times, correction. That is the sign of a good friend and a good parent. Good and evil are opposed; don't think that any evil path, however tempting, is worth it.

PART FOUR

PROVERBS 30–31

28

The Advice of a King . . .

PROVERBS 30

We are coming to the conclusion of the book of Proverbs, and we will find that awe of God is the way to end in wisdom, just as the fear of God begins it. We began with the teaching of a wise father; we will end with the teaching of a wise mother. Throughout the course of the book, we have covered people from the lowest ranks of society to the highest, in all stages of life. We have been gifted with all the tools we need for the art of living well.

Before we reach the climax of Proverbs – the industriously wise woman of chapter 31 – we are presented with the sayings of Agur. These are not just a random appendix attached to the teaching of Solomon, but in fact sum up and conclude the wisdom teaching. This is the final word of a wise teacher who is approaching death (30:7). This is the keynote talk, the ultimate in wisdom.

Sayings of Agur

30 The sayings of Agur son of Jakeh – an inspired utterance.

This man's utterance to Ithiel:
'I am weary, God,
but I can prevail.[a]
2 Surely I am only a brute, not a man;
I do not have human understanding.
3 I have not learned wisdom,
nor have I attained to the knowledge of the Holy One.
4 Who has gone up to heaven and come down?
Whose hands have gathered up the wind?
Who has wrapped up the waters in a cloak?
Who has established all the ends of the earth?
What is his name, and what is the name of his son?
Surely you know!

5 'Every word of God is flawless;

he is a shield to those who
take refuge in him.
6 Do not add to his words,
or he will rebuke you and
prove you a liar.

7 'Two things I ask of you, LORD;
do not refuse me before I die:
8 keep falsehood and lies far
from me;
give me neither poverty nor
riches,
but give me only my daily bread.
9 Otherwise, I may have too
much and disown you
and say, "Who is the LORD?"
Or I may become poor and
steal,
and so dishonour the name of
my God.

10 'Do not slander a servant to
their master,
or they will curse you, and you
will pay for it.

11 'There are those who curse
their fathers
and do not bless their mothers;
12 those who are pure in their
own eyes
and yet are not cleansed of
their filth;
13 those whose eyes are ever so
haughty,
whose glances are so
disdainful;
14 those whose teeth are swords
and whose jaws are set with
knives
to devour the poor from the earth
and the needy from among the
human race.

15 'The leech has two daughters.
"Give! Give!" they cry.

'There are three things that are
never satisfied,
four that never say, "Enough!":
16 the grave, the barren womb,
land, which is never satisfied
with water,
and fire, which never says,
"Enough!"

17 'The eye that mocks a father,
that scorns an aged mother,
will be pecked out by the
ravens of the valley,
will be eaten by the vultures.

18 'There are three things that are
too amazing for me,
four that I do not understand:
19 the way of an eagle in the sky,
the way of a snake on a rock,
the way of a ship on the high
seas,
and the way of a man with a
young woman.

20 'This is the way of an adulterous woman:

she eats and wipes her mouth
and says, "I've done nothing
wrong."

21 'Under three things the earth
trembles,
under four it cannot bear up:
22 a servant who becomes king,
a godless fool who gets plenty
to eat,
23 a contemptible woman who
gets married,
and a servant who displaces
her mistress.

24 'Four things on earth are small,
yet they are extremely wise:
25 ants are creatures of little
strength,
yet they store up their food in
the summer;
26 hyraxes are creatures of little
power,
yet they make their home in
the crags;
27 locusts have no king,
yet they advance together in
ranks;
28 a lizard can be caught with the
hand,
yet it is found in kings' palaces.

29 'There are three things that are
stately in their stride,
four that move with stately
bearing:
30 a lion, mighty among beasts,
who retreats before nothing;
31 a strutting cock, a he-goat,
and a king secure against
revolt.[b]

32 'If you play the fool and exalt
yourself,
or if you plan evil,
clap your hand over your
mouth!
33 For as churning cream
produces butter,
and as twisting the nose
produces blood,
so stirring up anger produces
strife.'

a 1 With a different word division of the Hebrew; Masoretic Text *utterance to Ithiel, / to Ithiel and Ukal:*
b 31 The meaning of the Hebrew for this phrase is uncertain.

Who is Agur? Apart from this text he is unknown. He might even not be an Israelite! But he has a right attitude to the Israelite God. *Agur* means 'I am in awe' (see Psalms 22:23 and 33:8), and what he teaches is this kind of awe towards God. His sayings are 'an inspired utterance' (30:1) in the NIV; an oracle, a pronouncement (*massa*).

Alternatively, Agur might be 'of Massa', a people in North Arabia.[1] It could even be that both are meant; it could be a play on words, showing that even those outside God's people can recognise the wisdom of a right attitude towards God. Either way, *neum* (utterance) in 1b suggests that this Scripture is inspired by God. In outline:

Introduction, 30:1–9: Agur's confession and declaration that these sayings are inspired, and his plea for truthfulness and humility.

Main teaching, 30:10–31: here are seven sayings in two sections. First is a single-line proverb about the moral order, followed by three sayings; then in verse 17 another proverb about keeping the moral order, and in verses 18–31 four sayings. The idea that there is a moral order that should be kept is very strong, and it works both ways: those in (rightful) authority are to be obeyed, and they are to treat those under them well. So abusing a slave (30:10) will bring punishment, as will rejecting parents (30:17). The chapter concludes with a warning in verses 32–3.

We can detect a few details about Agur. The NIV renders verse 1b a declaration – more literally, it is, 'I have grown weary, but will prevail.'[2] In the context of verse 7, someone near death, verse 1b could be a statement of Agur's time of life; or it could refer to the weightiness of his teaching. He is humble, recognising his own ignorance (30:2; see also Job 25:4–6; Psalm 73:22). He says he has no wisdom – on his own, he cannot understand reality, for the only way to true wisdom is through knowing God. Does he have knowledge of the Lord? Contrary to the NIV, Overland suggests that the negative of the first half of verse 3 should not be continued to the second half, and Waltke also tempers the negative.[3] At the very least, Agur recognises that wisdom is tied up with knowledge of the Lord.

For proper awe of the Lord is what follows. The series of questions in verse 4 challenges the audience to answer, 'Only God' (see also Job 28:12–28; 38–9). 'Surely you know!' is not sarcastic so much as affirming that Israel, God's son, knows God and so knows the answer – ultimate knowledge comes from relationship, not human cleverness. The New

1 Commentators go different ways. See Overland, *Proverbs*, 591; Waltke, *The Book of Proverbs*, II.454.

2 The NIV footnote recognises that it could alternatively give the names of those to whom he is speaking; see Waltke, *The Book of Proverbs*, II.455–6.

3 Overland, *Proverbs*, 586, 593; Waltke, *The Book of Proverbs*, II.456.

Testament reveals that the Son who is the fulfilment of Israel is Jesus Christ (Luke 1:29–33).

Verse 5 adapts 2 Samuel 22:31 (also Psalm 18:30). God's word is flawless, and so he is the place to take refuge. His word cannot be added to; that is to lie (30:6; see also Revelation 22:18). For at least two centuries now, people have tried to add to God's word by arguing that Scripture projects a 'trajectory': that is, we need not just be content with what Scripture teaches, but we can legitimately extrapolate to what it might have developed into later – towards broader understandings of the nature of salvation, the uniqueness of Christ, human identity and so on. Verse 6 provides a timely warning to those who would do so.

In recognition of this, Agur asks two things of God, the final things he wants before he dies. This, then, is worth listening to (30:7). What does he want so urgently? To avoid lies, and to be content with what he has (30:8; see also Exodus 16:18). The two are connected: he will be protected from the temptation to tell lies owing to fear of poverty or greed for more, if God provides just what is sufficient. He does not want too much – that could lead to greed and arrogance; nor too little, which could tempt stealing. Either one would be against the Lord (30:9; see also Deuteronomy 8:12–14).

Agur goes on to teach wisdom in seven sayings that uphold community by teaching against pride and greed. He may think he is ignorant, but he has certainly learned wisdom as regards human nature. Beware slander in relationships, which can bring retribution (30:10); and beware the wicked and greedy (30:11–14). They are the ones who do not respect parents (30:11; see also Exodus 20:12; 21:17; Deuteronomy 5:16; 27:16; Proverbs 20:20; Romans 1:28–30), who excuse and exalt themselves (30:12; see also Matthew 6:22–3; 23:25–7; Luke 16:15; 18:9–14; John 8:44; 9:40–41; Revelation 3:17–18). They are contemptuous and arrogant (30:13; see also Psalm 131:1; Esther 5:11; Isaiah 16:6; Jeremiah 48:29; Ezekiel 28:2; Daniel 11:36; Acts 12:21–3; 2 Thessalonians 2:4). They are cruel and violent and abuse the weak (30:14; see also Job 29:17; Psalms 14:4; 57:4; Micah 3:1–4). They are illustrated by greedy leech-children, those who are never satisfied (30:15a), like the natural forces that cannot be assuaged (30:15a–16: these are illustrations, not condemnations of 'barren' wombs, which merely (and truly) represent a longing that cannot be assuaged; see Genesis 30:1; 1 Samuel 1; Luke 1:5–25).

The second half of the chapter describes the importance of maintaining moral order. The kind of contempt that rejects parents, which overturns the moral order, will be punished (30:17). The depth of evil is beyond understanding, like these four natural things that are amazing and hard to understand, in a glorious celebration of creation and human love (30:18–19).

Unrepentant wickedness is similarly incomprehensible, in the opposite way (30:20). It's as bad as these things that illustrate unbearable or wrong situations, overturning what should be (30:21): a usurper, vice being rewarded (30:22), the opposite of a prudent wife – someone who cannot keep herself moral, who is yet given charge of a home (30:23a; see also 12:4; 18:22; 31:10), and another usurper (30:23b).

What is the solution? Look to the small things that can yet be great, working in harmony with natural order (30:24–8). Tiny ants who can provide for themselves, hyraxes (about the size of a rabbit) who can nonetheless make secure homes, locusts that have great power when working together, and *semamit*, either lizards or spiders, lowly things who can nonetheless live in great honour (as in Christ we, miraculously, can: Ephesians 2:6; Colossians 3:1). These small creatures can be as strong as these powerful things (30:29–31): lions, cocks, goats, who are all formidable in their own way, and secure kings. They are 'stately', worthy of honour.

In conclusion, don't be arrogant, greedy or wicked (30:32); don't be the person who embodies any of the wrong traits that go against our place in creation, so graphically illustrated. The consequences will be dire (30:33).

Conclusion to Proverbs 30

Agur teaches us that the key to wisdom is knowing the Lord. He uses creation itself to teach us to know our createdness. Humans will by their fallen nature be greedy and discontent; but this will not bring satisfaction in life, and it will bring divine retribution. Resist it. Greed is insatiable; but small, humble things can be like true greatness. Follow the road of humility and contentment. Anything else will end in disaster.

29

. . . and a Queen

PROVERBS 31

Feminism has largely failed the Western world, completing the death knell of the sexual revolution. The assertions that the destruction of traditional teaching on marriage and faithfulness would lead to a new era of freedom, love and fulfilment have abjectly, and tragically, been shown to be utterly false. Instead, there is an increasing avalanche of recognition of abuse and devastation. It was always bound to be so. Women looked at the sexual freedom of sinful men and longed to have that 'freedom' for themselves. In a competition of who can be most sinful, however, women will usually come off the worse – not through having a less inherently sinful nature (Romans 3:23), but through lack of physical strength and aggression. The tragic results are becoming clear. Sexual licence leads to sexual abuse of women – and incidentally fails men as well, as suicide rates and tales of life dissatisfaction testify. Humans always needed teaching about the value of faithfulness and the security of marriage; now, more than ever.

The answer is not patriarchal misogyny. More-traditional societies are equally capable of failing in a different direction, by seeing marriage as an excuse to dominate women within the home, through violence, belittling or emotional abuse. That is equally wrong; and again, it is the physically weaker woman and her children who will suffer the consequences.

Whether society contains the abusive sexual license of the West or the abusive traditional structures of some majority world cultures, we need the teaching of Proverbs 31.[1] The wise mother instructs

1 See Beulah Herbert, 'The Bible and Gender', for ways in which biblical teaching has challenged Asian attitudes to women – the problems of widow burning (sati), issues that arise with bride price and dowry, for instance. In Swarup, 'Proverbs', 803–5.

her son about the value to be placed on the wife who is honoured for her abilities and strength, which she in turn uses faithfully to the benefit of her family and the wider community. True wisdom understands that strength is given to be used on behalf of others. This is important for any culture to know, and any culture that fails to honour women and to protect their right to exercise their strength in God-honouring safety is failing, to its own detriment.

1. Listen to your mother • Proverbs 31:1–9

It is telling that this book of wisdom teaching ends with the king's words about what his mother taught him, which is praise of a strong wife. The exhortations to listen to one's mother's wise teaching throughout the book of Proverbs are here exemplified and celebrated.

31 The sayings of King Lemuel – an inspired utterance his mother taught him.

2 Listen, my son! Listen, son of my womb!
Listen, my son, the answer to my prayers!
3 Do not spend your strength[a] on women,
your vigour on those who ruin kings.

4 It is not for kings, Lemuel –
it is not for kings to drink wine,
not for rulers to crave beer,
5 lest they drink and forget what has been decreed,
and deprive all the oppressed of their rights.
6 Let beer be for those who are perishing,
wine for those who are in anguish!
7 Let them drink and forget their poverty
and remember their misery no more.

8 Speak up for those who cannot speak for themselves,
for the rights of all who are destitute.
9 Speak up and judge fairly;
defend the rights of the poor and needy.

a 3 Or *wealth*

Again, we start with a word play; this is an oracle, *massa*, but it could also refer to Lemuel's origin in Massa (31:1; apart from this inscription, Lemuel is unknown). Lemuel's mother taught him about relationships and wise use of resources, and this is oppositeed at the end of Proverbs as the final teaching that a wise king should know if he is to rule well. Proverbs began with the teaching of a father to his son; it ends with a mother teaching her son. The wise king should listen.

What does the mother have to teach her son, this royal ruler? (31:1–2). Don't give into your appetites, whether for women (31:3; see also Deuteronomy 17:17; 2 Samuel 12:9–10; 1 Kings 11:11; Esther 2:10–14) – a warning both David and Solomon should have heeded – or substances (31:4; see also 1 Kings 16:9; 20:16; Esther 1:10–11; Ecclesiastes 10:16; Isaiah 5:22–3; 28:7; 56:12; Hosea 7:5; Micah 2:11; Mark 6:21–8; 1 Timothy 3:3; Titus 1:7). That's the way to injustice and oppression (31:5; see also Psalm 72:1–4, 12–14; Jeremiah 22:16). There are good uses of alcohol – you may give it to those who are dying, or in misery, as alleviation of pain (31:6–7).[2] Similarly, use your power to help the oppressed by speaking up for them and defending them, the opposite of forgetting them in verse 5 (31:8–9; see also Psalm 72:12–14; Jeremiah 22:15–19). As Micah reminds us all, this is what the Lord requires: 'To act justly and to love mercy and to walk humbly with your God' (Micah 6:8).

2. The best wife • Proverbs 31:10–31

As we reach the end of Proverbs, we are inspired by an image of wisdom itself, brought to life in a loving, virtuous woman. This is the answer to the teaching that Lemuel's mother gave at the start of the chapter. If not the disastrous women of verse 3, whom should Lemuel marry?

In a heartwarming tribute to both women and marriage, Proverbs ends with an acrostic poem that pictures the wise, industrious, caring

2 Although Waltke thinks this is sarcastic, used 'to debunk the value of liquor'; Waltke, *The Book of Proverbs*, I:40.

and altogether admirable wife.[3] It is similar in structure to heroic poetry which tells of a hero's great deeds.[4] Notice that this lecture is addressed to men, not women. It is not primarily setting up an example for women to follow; women who love the Lord will already know the way to wisdom. It is instruction to a young man as to what is truly valuable in a woman. This is the kind of woman who will be the queen who can help him to rule wisely and justly; we can extend this to the woman who will be the appropriate helper for the man in rule of the earth (Genesis 2:18). This is the truly wise woman, the embodiment of the wisdom teaching so far, who leads to success and prosperity within creation.[5]

Epilogue: the wife of noble character

10 [b]A wife of noble character who can find?
She is worth far more than rubies.
11 Her husband has full confidence in her
and lacks nothing of value.
12 She brings him good, not harm,
all the days of her life.
13 She selects wool and flax
and works with eager hands.
14 She is like the merchant ships,
bringing her food from afar.
15 She gets up while it is still night;
she provides food for her family
and portions for her female servants.
16 She considers a field and buys it;
out of her earnings she plants a vineyard.
17 She sets about her work vigorously;
her arms are strong for her tasks.
18 She sees that her trading is profitable,
and her lamp does not go out at night.
19 In her hand she holds the distaff
and grasps the spindle with her fingers.
20 She opens her arms to the poor
and extends her hands to the needy.
21 When it snows, she has no fear for her household;

3 In this case the first letters are in the order of the Hebrew alphabet.
4 Waltke, *The Book of Proverbs*, II.516.
5 See Clifford, *Proverbs*, 274.

for all of them are clothed in
scarlet.
22 She makes coverings for her
bed;
she is clothed in fine linen and
purple.
23 Her husband is respected at
the city gate,
where he takes his seat among
the elders of the land.
24 She makes linen garments and
sells them,
and supplies the merchants
with sashes.
25 She is clothed with strength
and dignity;
she can laugh at the days to
come.
26 She speaks with wisdom,
and faithful instruction is on
her tongue.
27 She watches over the affairs of
her household
and does not eat the bread of
idleness.
28 Her children arise and call her
blessed;
her husband also, and he
praises her:
29 'Many women do noble things,
but you surpass them all.'
30 Charm is deceptive, and
beauty is fleeting;
but a woman who fears the
LORD is to be praised.
31 Honour her for all that her
hands have done,
and let her works bring her
praise at the city gate.

b 10 Verses 10-31 are an acrostic poem, the verses of which begin with the successive letters of the Hebrew alphabet.

This woman is ideal, and perhaps rare (31:10a), but she is also real; a practical, talented woman who follows God.

She is worth pursuing, for such a woman is better than riches (31:10b). The husband will be amply rewarded as she is trustworthy. In fact, his trust is quite remarkable, as this is a phrase elsewhere used of trust in God; it is high praise (31:11) and deserved, for she brings great good (31:12). How does she do so? She invests in the home and family, with industry and resourcing (31:13–14) – the very things that a wise person should do. She does this work with 'eager hands', joyously (31:13), creating a feast like Solomon's (see 1 Kings 4:21–3). She remains busy in service to others (31:15) and in shrewd, hard work (31:16–17). Such working is rewarded (31:18). She has diligent hands (31:19), hands that are generous beyond her family with the results of her labours (31:20; see also Job 29:12–17; Acts 9:39). She provides security and protection (31:21). She is rightly recognised and benefits from her labours, wearing costly purple (31:22) even though she serves others first. This brings wider benefits for the household and her husband, as well as the community generally (31:23–4). Not only is her rich clothing physical, but it is also strength and dignity (31:25); she is joyful even about the unknowns of the future. This woman goes beyond providing physical goods to others. She also teaches wisely (31:26) and nourishes others physically and morally (31:27).

In conclusion, this is the woman who is universally recognised as wonderful (31:28). Her husband, in particular, will see her value (31:29), for – and this is the key to the whole of Proverbs – she reveres the Lord (31:30; see also 2 Corinthians 4:18). That is the way to true reward (31:31).

Conclusion to Proverbs 31

All can benefit from this example. Young men looking for wives, and husbands who need to know how to value a wife. Parents looking to raise wise children, both girls and boys. Those who will never marry, who can learn what wisdom in practice looks like. It is not an oppressive teaching to make wives feel unworthy – this woman is an embodiment of many virtues, after all – but a celebration of what female strength can be capable of: full of love, practical ability and shrewd intellect. Neither is it a standard for evil husbands to use to belittle struggling wives, but an encouragement to value and so promote opportunities for female flourishing. Ultimately, all people should learn from this picture of wisdom. This is the woman we must revere and emulate. She truly embodies what God would have us learn.

The book of Proverbs has taught us wisdom: love the Lord your God, and love others as yourself. This is the teaching to kings, and it is perfectly exemplified in the eternal King, Jesus, who laid down his life for others, in obedience to his Father. Through him, we will find the essence of wisdom, and the fulfilment of everything Proverbs teaches.